By Pen
&
By Spade

By Pen
&
By Spade

An Anthology of Garden Writing
from
HORTUS

Edited by David Wheeler

SUMMIT BOOKS
New York

Summit Books
Simon & Schuster Building
Rockefeller Center
1230 Avenue of the Americas
New York, New York 10020

Previously published in Great Britain
by Alan Sutton Publishing

SUMMIT BOOKS and colophon are trademarks
of Simon & Schuster Inc.

Manufactured in Great Britain

Library of Congress Cataloging in Publication Data
applied for

ISBN 0-671-74274-4

Typeset by Gloucester Typesetting Services and Ronset
in Monotype (hot metal) Van Dijck (203).
Printed in Great Britain by
The Bath Press, Avon.

This book is dedicated by
David Wheeler
to the memory of
Roger Machell, publisher,
1908–1984
mentor and friend

Foreword

SIR ROY STRONG

HORTUS arrived by stealth. My earliest awareness of it came from that great encourager Rosemary Verey who gave me a copy and said that we must all support it, and that David Wheeler was a good thing. She was, as usual, right. It certainly didn't resemble any gardening journal that I knew. There were no articles telling me what to do with my growbag tomatoes, or how to make a plant container from an old wellington boot. There were no colour plates. Instead its chaste cover bore a wood engraving. On a first glance its format seemed rather old-fashioned, with an earnest between-the-wars look. The paper was soft cream in colour and I was conscious of its tactile qualities as my fingers glided over its surface. No sign of the use of a fashionable high-tech typeface, and one's period observation was confirmed in a subsequent remodelled issue in which we were told that the type was Van Dijck, such as was used in the old botanical books but as recut for the Monotype system in 1937. The layout also evoked those between-the-wars private presses, and the wood engravings were by artists still part of this century's response to the rediscovery of Samuel Palmer. Even the photographs had the haunting quality of a stage set as seen through a gauze curtain. The atmosphere it exuded was above all considered and gentle.

So different was it that the indications were that this could be a transitory aberration, for it deliberately swam against every tide. The fact that it is in its fourth year and has become an international publication of repute tells us not only about the editor's remarkable perception and tenacity, but also that his statement was indeed the right one made at the right time. I think that the reason for this is a very simple one, HORTUS fills an important niche in current garden literature as the *thinking* gardener's journal. But it couldn't occupy that role without drawing on a peculiarly British phenomenon, a vigorous garden writing tradition that is utterly unique. Like our landscape, our gardens are embedded in our literary heritage. Many of our greatest writers and poets have embraced the garden as within the orbit of their pen: Francis Bacon, Andrew Marvell, Alexander Pope or Horace Walpole are all significant figures for the garden. Equally, we have garden writers who can stand as literary figures of some substance: John Gerard, John Parkinson, Sir Thomas Hanmer, Gertrude Jekyll or Vita Sackville-West are all a pleasure to read as literature, irrespective of their horticultural content. HORTUS draws on that fact.

Travelling around Europe and the United States I always make a point of going into bookshops to look under gardening. The amount of shelf space allocated to the subject varies wildly from country to country. One shelf in Italy, a hefty section on the east coast of America. Whatever the extent, I am always struck by the fact that most of the books are either translations from the English or actually in that language. To me this signals that our garden writers are not accorded the recognition which they deserve, nor – which is equally true – do we salute what must be a Renaissance in garden writing.

In this volume, which is an anthology from the first year of HORTUS, there is a lively spread of generations from Dame Sylvia Crowe, resilient in her nineties, through the middle generation, which includes Beth Chatto, Penelope Hobhouse and Rosemary Verey, to the younger new wave of Stephen Lacey and Stephen Haw. Although the majority of the authors are British, there are contributions from around the globe from places as far away as New Zealand.

I think that I would categorise these pieces less as articles than as essays – a rather forgotten literary genre, economic in terms of length, demanding in terms of prose style and elegance. What is important is the catholicity of their subject matter. The gardens of Flaubert, of 'Darling Daisy' Countess of Warwick, of Henry James and E. F. Benson join those of Cedric Morris and Iris Origo. We visit China, New England and the Azores. Plant hunting and green flowers stand side by side with the weird world of Ronald Firbank. And yet we are still strolling within the bounds of the garden, something which is too easily forgotten. HORTUS moves from its historic place within the pattern of civilisation as a meeting ground of many worlds, those of history, science, literature, the art of design, botany, geography, architecture, poetry, painting, sculpture and the graphic arts. It is the garden as an attribute of the cultured and educated person which emerges from these pages, someone who rises above its brute practicalities to embrace its greatest role as a supreme vehicle for the expression of man's intellect and imagination over the centuries.

ROY STRONG

Editor's Introduction

This volume brings to light again some of the treasured articles from the early issues of HORTUS.

I am often asked why in 1987 I decided to publish privately a horticultural or gardening journal. My answer is simple if not obvious: it was because as a jobbing gardener in my late thirties recently exiled from city life and the worlds of books and commerce, I felt starved of good garden reading.

I was naturally aware of the numerous periodicals which fought for my attention on newsagents' stands – all clamouring to tell me more than I ever wanted to know about mealy bugs and hanging baskets, and I subscribed to journals issued by a variety of horticultural organisations – most of whose specialist plant knowledge I found useful, but not exactly thrilling to read. I saw, too, the array of garden books rolling ceaselessly off the nation's printing presses, each containing a high proportion of beguiling photographs but mostly, it seemed, at the expense of text of any length or quality. Some of my needs and desires were catered for by libraries, public and private; some books I borrowed from friends. But where were the exploratory, deep-delving and literary publications which this country is so good at encouraging to spring up around all manner of subjects? Surely gardening, with its diverse and penetrating veins of curiosity and interest, should be a topic well endowed with small-circulation titles expounding every aspect? I searched, I enquired, I followed up false leads, but I found nothing which approximated to my ideal.

Having rarely in my life ever paused to test the temperature of the water, I threw myself, headlong, into producing just the sort of journal or magazine (call it what you like) that *I* would like to read: essentially well written and not, I hope, devoid of humour, well-produced yet affordable, and free from technical jargon, how-to advice, and second-hand offerings pilfered from other people's minds. Given these few guidelines I formulated my one editorial policy: NO EDITORIAL POLICY. The pages of HORTUS would be open to anyone who had something worthwhile, interesting or new to say and who could express it well. I would try to commission the very best of articles (which are by no means always written by the 'celebrity' writers), and I would concentrate on the human element as much as on the plant world: who were and are the garden makers, plant finders and growers; what was happening beyond British shores; what have the great novelists said about gardens and what have they allowed to happen in them? These themes would cross and recross like the paths in an intricate but accessible and well made pleasance. Henry James one minute, Chinese gardens the next; outrageous goings-on in Firbank novels juxtaposed to breezy wanderings in search of plants in the Azores; an East Anglian painter's garden following first-hand recollections of William Robinson at Gravetye; gardens for youngsters, gardens for oldies; gardens in high, and sometimes downright low, society; conservation; herbs, cistuses, gentians, hellebores and roses, green flowers and scented flowers; British gardens, Italian gardens, American gardens, Antipodean gardens; winter flowers, summer flowers, autumn flowers, spring flowers, even plants *without* flowers; and books – glimpses of authors and intelligent reviews of their work: this, so to speak, was my shopping list, and quickly my basket became laden.

I sought no financial backing, believing naïvely that my venture would be an instant and glorious success, and the better for not being modified by well-meaning partners or hungry backers. I would come home from whatever garden I had been working in and spend the evening putting into action the many ideas I had dreamt up that day. I knew very few people in the so-called 'gardening world' and no one in horticultural publishing. I did my sums crudely, knowing no other way of doing them, reckoned I wouldn't lose my shirt entirely (as it turned out, I barely paid the bills in the first year, and there have been subsequent anxious moments), then set about writing what I hoped were polite and enthusiastic letters to the dozen or so people whose writing I admired and who I thought would have, in an ideal world, the sort of things to say that *I* wanted to read.

I was amazed by the response. Generous, sometimes affectionate, above all positive letters came back in reply from each member of my chosen galaxy of writers – with one striking exception (from whom I still receive no reply to letters).

Articles from all these 'great gardening names' appeared in the first issues of HORTUS, and I must here thank each of them, including those unrepresented in this anthology, not only for their eager and immediate support, but for their immensely valuable goodwill and constructive ideas. Among the familiar names you will find new ones who I believe should be welcomed equally. In addition I wish to thank three other people for their behind-the-scenes help: Liz Robinson, John Commander and Simon Dorrell.

Early issues of HORTUS have become collectors' items: recently I heard of them changing hands in New York for $50 apiece. The journal is well received in Britain and America, and also in Australia and New Zealand, where a fresh awareness of gardening and garden writing seems to have emerged.

By large-circulation magazine standards I still sell in quantities other publishers would recognise only as returns, but the subscription list grows steadily longer and people in over thirty countries now receive HORTUS.

During its first four years of life the pages of HORTUS have been embellished by some fine drawings and wood-engravings – two styles of illustration which complement the hot metal typography, the specially made paper and careful production practices.

So whether you have bought BY PEN & BY SPADE for yourself, or whether a friend or relative has given it to you, I hope you will enjoy its rich variety. And remember, HORTUS is published quarterly, providing over five hundred pages a year of what has been described as 'some of the best garden writing you could find anywhere'. Subscription details can be found at the end of the book. Happy reading.

DAVID WHEELER, *Editor*
The Neuadd, Rhayader
October, 1990

Drawing of THE NEUADD *by Simon Dorrell*

Contents

Scent Gardening

STEPHEN LACEY

Of all the ingredients we employ in the creation of a garden, scent is probably the most potent and the least understood. Its effects can be either direct and immediate, drowning our senses in a surge of sugary vapour, or they can be subtle and delayed, slowly wafting into our consciousness, stirring our emotions and colouring our thoughts. Sometimes a scent will linger in the air for days, filtering through open windows and engulfing armchairs and dinner tables; at other times a fragrance will evaporate almost the moment it arrives, leaving only a tantalising taste in the nostrils. Plants themselves play tricks with their scents, exuding perfume one day and not the next, chemically altering their fragrance from sweetness to putrefaction, and even, in one notorious case (that of the musk plant, *Mimulus moschatus*), abandoning their scent altogether.

Faced with all this uncertainty and unpredictability, gardeners tend to shy away from any attempt to manage scent in the garden in any coherent way. Fragrance becomes very much an afterthought, an addition to a carefully composed planting scheme. Only after deciding that your border should consist of silver foliage and yellow flowers, for example, and after organising a pleasing arrangement of tiered heights and contrasting leaf forms, will you stop for a moment to consider whether you have incorporated any items to please your nose. To a large extent this sort of approach to planting is inevitable. This visual impact is after all crucial. But I wonder whether you have ever thought of attempting the process in reverse in one or two parts of the garden, and taken up the challenge of allowing scent to dictate the entire composition.

The best place to construct a scented scheme is somewhere sunny and sheltered, ideally against a warm wall where the air is still and where heat is radiated on cool evenings, somewhere you are inclined to sit and ruminate, where you will be most receptive to a fragrant siege. A seat is a most important component for, apart from encouraging relaxation, it enables you to enjoy many different scents simultaneously. Not only can you position aromatic foliage around your feet, scented perennials at your elbow and fragrant shrubs near your nose, but you can construct the seat out of scent as well by making a raised bed of chamomile and prostrate thymes and giving it arms and a back rest.

The next stage is to decide on a theme. Do you want, perhaps, an assortment of fruity scents, a blend of apple and plum, orange and pineapple, lemon and banana? Or an Indian bouquet of herbs and incense and hot spices? Or a pot pourri of rose petals with the perfume of violet and honey sharpened with mint or musk? Your choice of theme is obviously governed by the scents available in the plant world, but you will be surprised how many distinct fragrances you discover once you begin noting them down for future reference. Some readers may like to know that even the smell of bubblegum is available through the slightly tender but beautiful climber, *Trachelospermum asiaticum*.

Often a particular scented plant will be the inspiration for the entire scheme, but where the theme comes first you will probably need to use your notebook to jog your memory. In the above examples we could use, for our basket of fruit, the leaves of *Rosa eglanteria* (apple), *R. soulieana* (banana), *Lippia citriodora* (lemon), and *Ruta graveolens* (orange) and the flowers of *Iris graminea* (plum) and *Cytisus battandieri* (pineapple); for our Indian bouquet, a host of herbs including sage, rosemary, fennel and marjoram, curry-scented *Helichrysum angustifolium*, *Rosa primula* for incense, and viburnums and pinks for clove; and for our old-fashioned pot pourri, the flowers of rugosa, alba, bourbon, and hybrid musk roses blended with honeysuckle and the leaves of peppermint and *Pelargonium tomentosum*.

The visual appearance of your scented scheme is the next matter to consider. If all your ingredients are wild and wispy, untidy in foliage and dreary after flowering, then you have to introduce some strong architectural forms as a counterbalance. Box is ideal, especially when clipped into cones, for its leaves are scented of summer; meat-scented *Iris foetidissima* is also valuable as is the silver foliage of artemisias, and, if you are desperate, you can always turn to the resinous leaves of conifers. Where there is an interestingly leafed variant of a scented plant that you want to include, it may be wise to plump for that instead of the ordinary variety – the golden and variegated forms of *Philadelphus coronarius*, the variegated forms of applemint, thyme and lemon balm, and maybe the new golden form of *Choisya ternata* called 'Sundance' (though I have been told the leaf colour is at the expense of flowers) would be examples.

The most rewarding approach to gardening with scent is to pursue a strong visual theme in conjunction with your fragrant theme. Colour is the obvious visual medium to choose because it has a clear relationship with scent. While it is not true to say that similarly coloured flowers have similar scents, scientists have demonstrated that flowers in certain colour ranges are more likely to be scented than others: white, cream, pink and pale yellow are fruitful areas of the spectrum for scented flowers while purple, blue, gold, and red are relatively poorly endowed.

It is particularly amusing to devise schemes in which the colours and scents present are so well matched that they unite to give you one really potent sensuous encounter; the teaming up of lemon flowers and citrus scents, for instance, or sumptuous wine crimsons with rich French perfumes. Many flowers have exactly the fragrance that their appearance suggests – think of *Cosmos atrosanguineus* with its dark velvety blood red petals and its mysterious scent of hot bitter chocolate, or *Buddleia* × *weyeriana* with its soft orange yellow balls of flower and its warm fragrance of honey, or *Salvia discolor* with its hooded blooms of blackish purple and its sticky scent of blackcurrant. The most fabulous example is perhaps *Hedychium gardnerianum* whose curiously exotic heads of amber yellow and spiky orange are matched by an equally strange perfume, a mixture (unless my nose deceives me) of cloves and mothballs.

'Fairest of the Earth's Children'

SYLVIA CROWE

William Robinson shares with Gertrude Jekyll the credit for giving birth to a trend in gardens which has spread across the world.

The early tradition of formal gardens used plants as the infill of architectural designs, almost as if they were colour pigments, while the English landscape tradition, stemming from Kent to Lancelot Brown, practically banished flowers, relying solely on trees, grass, land form and water to create their compositions. In reaction, the Victorians paid tribute to the beauty of flowering plants but often failed to use them to the best advantage. The great influx of plants from all over the world, brought in by such explorers as Farrer, caused an *embarras de richesse* which took some time to digest.

Gertrude Jekyll and William Robinson, through their writings and example, showed the way to use this treasure selectively and to the best advantage, while at the same time reviving interest in the old plants which, in the nineteenth century, had been relegated to the cottage garden.

We are fortunate that the garden at Gravetye, in Sussex, which was Robinson's old home, still retains the character which he imparted to it. I am able to vouch for this continuity, for I first visited the garden during the First World War. At this time William Robinson was a pioneer in allowing the public to view his garden. There was nothing then so demeaning as an entrance fee, you went to the front door and the butler presented you with the visitor's book to sign, and the garden was yours. My second visit was during the 1920s and on this occasion I was privileged to meet William Robinson. He was then an old man in a wheel chair and he had caused the main flower border to be raised on a low retaining wall so that he could more easily see the plants and pull the occasional weed, from his wheel chair. But, despite his age, he gave short shrift to a gardener who looked sceptical as Robinson planned future improvements, saying 'You think I won't live to see it, just you wait.' My most recent visit was a few years ago, when I was delighted to find the garden much as I first remember it, and in charge was a very sympathetic head gardener.

One of the most striking features of the layout is the blend of formal and informal, giving a sense of unity despite the fact that the garden

The formal garden at Gravetye Manor in summer

contains so many diverse features. This unity is helped by the con-
figuration of the site and by the distinctive character of the grey stone
of which both mansion and garden walls are built. The ground slopes
away to a chain of lakes lying at the bottom of the valley, bounded on
the far side by wooded hills which provide a satisfying background,
and give a sense of contentment while linking the garden into the
composition of a typical Sussex landscape; small-scale, quiet, peaceful
and liveable. The formal element of the garden stretches out from the
side of the house, with a substantial wall to back the flower border.
The formal paved terrace is now an invaluable adjunct to the hotel,
providing a place for visitors to sit and sip.

The two features which impressed me most on my early visits were
the flowery meadows stretching down the slope from the terrace wall,
and the waterside of the lakes at the bottom of the valley. The meadow
garden has become a popular feature in many of today's gardens, but

William Robinson, 1838–1935

in the early years of the century it was a novelty. I remember well, on
my childhood visits, how enchanted I was by the miniature hayfield,
bejewelled with small tulip species, many kinds of anemones and many
other flowers not then usually seen in gardens. It was, however, an
intensification of the meadows of those happy days before the advent
of hygienic agriculture, which were a child's paradise rich in buttercups
and daisies, cowslips, orchids, milkweed and speedwell. The terrace
wall backing this meadow was festooned with swags of purple aubrietia.

I hope it still is. Down the hill by the waterside was a bold grouping of massed tritomas (*Kniphofia*) and pampas grass, an unlikely combination but remarkably effective. Other sections of the banks had lavish plantings of loosestrife (*Lythrum salicaria*) and trollius.

While it is a comparatively straightforward problem to conserve works of art such as pictures, sculptures and even buildings, it is immeasurably more difficult to perpetuate the nature of a garden, particularly one which relies on the composition of plants for its effect. The National Trust has discovered this and devotes much time and expertise to conserving the diverse characters of their many gardens. The problem is accentuated by change of use. In the case of the National Trust, the sheer number of visitors can destroy the spirit of a garden they have come to enjoy. At Gravetye the change of use to an hotel can more easily be accommodated, since the visitors may be considered as only an unusually large house party. But great care will be needed to ensure that the spirit which inspired the garden is respected, and all gimmicks eschewed.

Gravetye deserves respect as an historic milestone in the evolution of gardens, for it gives an example of how a plantsman's love of diversity can be contained within a unity of composition. It is the epitome of the English garden as it has evolved during the last century. Gravetye may be considered as a living illustration to Robinson's books. *The Wild Garden* was published in 1870 and is prophetic of a trend which is now in full swing. It starts with a lively polemic against carpet bedding and the over-use of exotic plants and continues with good advice on naturalisation and the creation of a garden of British wild flowers. The better known *English Flower Garden* was published in 1883. It is dogmatic and almost vitriolic against the misuse of plants, but it is rich in knowledge and good sense.

Perhaps Robinson's passion may be summed up in this quotation. 'Of all things made by man for his pleasure, a flower garden has least business to be ugly, barren or stereotyped, because in it we may have the fairest of the earth's children in a living, ever-changeful state, and not, as in other arts, mere representation of them.'

The Ephemeral and the Perennial

RONALD BLYTHE

There must be still, even at this late twentieth century hour, many a small or great garden which continues to breathe the principles and passions of the kind of managed profusion which became the hallmark of enlightened English gardening from William Robinson onwards. My garden certainly declares these free notions – shouts them, some might say. Its antecedents crop up everywhere, on the bookshelves, in the outhouses and, most of all, at the back of my mind. I have become much attached to this litter and find it highly eloquent. Of course, my garden and those like it can be provided with a fairly exact pedigree by tracing their roots to Robinson's masterpiece *The English Flower Garden* (1883) and then carrying their development along to the present via similar well-known influences, but this would be too easy. As with all familial spread, lesser known agencies have had a hand in these beautiful creations. So many notions, some of them in print, some let drop by word of mouth, some osmotic, have helped to make 'my garden', as I still guiltily describe it, for although I have seen it very nearly from the start, and now own it, it can only be John Nash's. It was this old artist friend who planted it just after the last war and who, as well as its maturity, left to me the hundred and one pointers to its conception, everything from a Six Hills Nursery catalogue to a pile of Sankey's garden-pots.

We came to our conclusion of what a garden should be in much the same way. As a boy in still rural Iver in Buckinghamshire before the First World War, he had observed how a group of elderly unmarried sisters down the road virtually ignored the grounds surrounding their house and continued to garden what had been their childhood patches, cramming them with 'treasures' which in the best gardening tradition had been begged, stolen or borrowed from where ever they happened to have 'discovered' them. John Nash's eyes were opened and he saw that what his father called 'the garden' was in fact a croquet lawn and nothing more. My first true garden also belonged to aged women, a mother and daughter. It was dense with what they called 'their bits', a ravishing cushion of flowers and scents threaded through with winding dirt paths just wide enough for them to shuffle along and pat and fluff things into place. They pronounced flowers, 'flors', which somebody said was Norfolk. The lesson which John Nash and I learned from these ladies was that a gardener accumulated delights.

It was Clarence Elliott, the owner of the Six Hills Nursery at Stevenage, who took John Nash into the horticultural scene proper during the twenties. 'I used to draw the plants he had collected on his expeditions to the Andes and the Falkland Islands and elsewhere, not excluding finds in English gardens, which he maintained were the best hunting-ground.' And it was John Nash and my old friend Stephen Garrett the Cambridge botanist who introduced me to the world of the plant hunters. Not that I was ever able in either sphere to do much more than listen and look. All the same, it was a green education which stretched back far before I was born and, as writers do, I have remained intrigued by having these direct links to the gardening past. Oddly central to such stay-at-home characters as John Nash was the Empire contribution to the shrubberies and flower-beds. Two of his close friends, and eventually mine, were Lord Cranbrook who, in 1932, had accompanied Frank Kingdon Ward on plant-hunting journeys in the Far East, and the painter Sir Cedric Morris, who every winter would desert Suffolk for the Mediterranean, returning home with precious shoots and seedlings concealed in his luggage.

But then the most untravelled gardener of their generation expected to have to keep some kind of pace with the plant-hunters. And in many respects garden imports were a two-way business, with works such as Mrs Earle's celebrated *Pot-Pourri from a Surrey Garden* (1897) inspiring the exiles of the Raj and A. E. P. Grierson's *The Evolution of the Mogul Gardens of the Plains of India* affecting the Home Counties. It was Grierson who had organised the floral background of the 1912 Durbar, just as it was Miss Jekyll who planned the gardens of Vice-Regal Lodge in New Delhi. It was much due to English gardeners born in India, like Eleanour Sinclair Rohde, for example, that a certain sensuousness invaded the gardening scene back home. Her *The Scented Garden*, *The Old World Pleasaunce* and *Gardens of Delight* introduced a languorous element disturbingly opposite to that created by carpet-bedding and ball-games. Nice, fat, battered old gardening books such as these lie around the house, every one a treat, and each a threat to that couple of hours' digging. Their inter-war equivalent were Marion Cran's *The Garden of Ignorance*, *The Garden of Experience* and

Garden of Good Hope. I suspect that John Nash and equals like Vita
Sackville-West and Margery Fish would have drawn the line at
Marion Cran, although at this distance her work fascinates because
it manages to convey the popular sentiment of her day. *The* popular
exponent of horticulture whom everybody read, the *cognoscenti* a
little sniffily, was Dean Hole. S. Reynolds Hole looked like Gregory
Peck and was Dean of Rochester. His *Book about Roses* became a best-
seller and he used the influence it gave him to launch devastating
attacks on the Victorian lawns-and-bedding-out gardeners who had
levelled the exquisitely mysterious gardens of his youth. Quoting
Pope,

> He wins all points who pleasingly confounds,
> Surprises, varies, and conceals the bounds,

the Dean laid about him with a will. He wrote other testy volumes
which I used to search for and give to John Nash. John's gardens, both
this last one in the Stour Valley and the previous one in Meadle, were
written about by friends like Robert Gathorne-Hardy, also discreetly
visited by plant-hunters and fellow artists.

Somebody arriving recently and seeing the tools said, 'Do you
collect old implements?' As these are in everyday use, I was momen-
tarily puzzled. Then I realised how ancient many of them are, not
least the roller, ladders and the right-angled fork for cleaning-out the

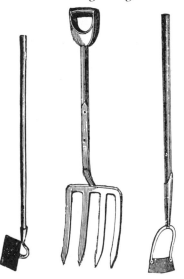

ditches. The most evocative artefact was the little greenhouse which once belonged to Eric Ravilious and which came to John after his death in a flying accident during the last war. It appears in Ravilious's woodcuts and always looked to me like one of those splendid Duncan Tucker glasshouses which cost £14 10s. in the thirties. Alas, alas, it rotted, bowed, swayed and collapsed the minute I saved its last few panes from splintering. It was empty of all plants save convolvulus and marestail, but interestingly full of such archaeological items as a fragment of Rippingille heater, lumps of crazy paving – that nuisance – pesticide tins called Katakiller, Eureka and Corry's White Fly Death, and masses of pale seed-packets from long ago springtimes; Ryders (St Albans), Dobbie (Edinburgh), Allwood Bros (Haywards Heath) and Thompson and Morgan (Ipswich). John would toil in this beloved building for hours on end, smoking like a trooper.

But to discover just how astonishingly garden methods, philosophy and economics have altered during a comparatively short time, as well as this litter and these gurus, I settle down to long, discursive hours with the journals of the time, the *Horticultural Advertiser*, Percy Cane's *Garden Design* and, best of all, *The Gardeners' Chronicle*, sixpence every Saturday during the thirties and as revealing a picture of the nation at this moment as can be found anywhere. It is, of course, the final era of the fully-staffed garden and there can be no proper understanding of modern gardening if these (very poorly) paid gardeners are not taken into account. While Ellen Willmott may have employed eighty-five of them and many a country house a dozen or more, countless modest gardens up and down the land were cared for by a man and a boy, and the demanding nature of today's toil was, for the middle classes, virtually unknown. In superior gardens young trainees were called journeymen and lived in a bothy. Their apprenticeship was long and severe but they could become highly influential authorities with a column in the magazines, such as Fred Streeter who worked at Petworth for Lord Leconfield and Mr Pateman, head gardener to Sir Charles Nall-Cain, who wrote regularly in *The Gardeners' Chronicle*. The Situations Vacant list made demands ranging from the tempting to the tyrannical and as the Situations Wanted list outbid it by ten to one, even ads such as the following would bring an avalanche of replies: 'Wanted, Good Gardener, aged about 40, one under kept. Protestant, abstainer, no family. Understand bees if possible. By letter only. Upper Norwood.' The reverse of this was the swelling number of employers, hit by the depression, politely trying to pass good gardeners on to others 'due to reduction'.

A factor quite forgotten now is that one was seldom alone in any sizeable garden; there were always men working – women too occasionally – 'Two Girl Gardeners wanted, age 18 to 25'. Both John Nash and Cedric Morris saw a good deal of 'girl gardeners' from the 1950s onwards. They included John's sister Barbara, who had a nursery near Princes Risborough, and Beth Chatto, who was Cedric's pupil and whose inspired garden at Elmstead Market contains some of his magic. Have feminists ever fully assessed the role of women in horticulture? It is a prodigious one. Lady Wolseley was aware of it half a century ago when she founded her college for women gardeners at Glynde, Sussex – just when Vita Sackville-West was planting Sissinghurst. And, proving that there is nothing new under the sun and *vide* Sir Roy Strong's recent recommendations, women with little gardens were, during these years, told to furnish as well as plant them so that they could be 'the Outdoor Living Room'.

An 'artist-plantsman', as John Nash liked to distinguish himself, tended to have nothing much to do with horticulture as public event, although his middle age coincided with the opening-up of private gardens by the hundreds to raise funds for hospitals and nurses, not to mention what sounds like the initiation of Interflora, when the Florists' Telegraph Delivery Service held a conference called 'Say it with Flowers'. He was far more likely to go to Stevenage or to the Physic Garden than to the Chelsea Flower Show. But he and Cedric, both possessing a wild sense of humour, might have enjoyed themselves at the 1932 Daily Mail Ideal Homes Exhibition at Olympia where there was a display entitled 'Gardens of the Novelists' in which garden scenes from Priestley's *The Good Companions* (*Erica carnea* planted in front of canvas moors), Galsworthy's *In Chancery* (flowering shrubs), Warwick Deeping's *Apples of Gold* (Mr John Klinkert's topiary) and Clemence Dane's *Author Unknown* (rocks and saxifrages) were on display. It was the golden age of the lending library. Carter's Tested Seeds' contribution to this entertainment was a reproduction of that 'charming little square plot . . . surrounded by yew hedges and intersected with paths of crazy pavement' from E. F. Benson's *Mapp and Lucia*, this 'being fed by a gushing waterfall'.

Re-hearing, as it were, these intellectual old friends in their richly planted gardens, I note a lot of laughter.

Gardening
for and by Children
WILL INGWERSEN

To my knowledge there is no gardening magazine or periodical that includes a page to encourage an interest in gardening directly to children. This is unfortunate as it is to the children of today that we look for the gardeners of tomorrow. All too often the only introduction that children are given to gardening is to be set to work at some monotonous task, such as weeding, or fetching and carrying. It is up to parents, and especially those who themselves have an interest and love for plants to imbue in their children some of their own enthusiasm.

Children quite often plead for a small garden of their own and, more often than not, even if the request is acceded to, they are given a totally useless odd corner, unsuitable in soil or aspect for even an experienced gardener to persuade plants to grow. Any child who displays a genuine interest in plants and would like to learn about them, should be provided with the best available facilities in which to develop this budding enthusiasm. Failures due to unsuitable sites and growing conditions will lead to discouragement.

There is a vacant place amongst the multitudes of gardening books
that roll off the press for one aimed directly at children, written in
simple terms that a child would understand and light enough to be
entertaining as well as instructive. I am sure that some such publication could give birth in a child's mind to what could become a
lifetime's interest in one of life's most rewarding pastimes and
would persuade the youthful reader that gardening is not just an
affair of boring chores.

A good way in which to encourage a budding interest in flowers is
to take children into the country and show them some of the wild
flowers. Tell them the names, preferably the common name to start
with and any story which may lay behind the name. Show them
Ladies bedstraw and explain that it used to be cut and dried and
used to stuff pillows. If you live within visiting distance of boggy
heathland areas, show them the sundew, a native insectivorous
plant and how it traps insects, which are digested to supply the
nitrogen lacking in the peaty soil it grows in. It is sensible always
to use the common names first, increasing interest will create the
desire to know its scientific, or botanical name, by which it is
internationally recognised.

Children are often impatient and it is essential that the first
plants they grow should be those which mature rapidly. It will
thrill them to sow seeds of, for example, Virginia stock, and to see
the rapid germination and how soon there will be flowers. Show them
too, that they can save seeds and sow them next year, knowing
that the results will be plants they have actually made themselves.

Provide them also with books in which there are plenty of pictures
of simple and easy plants which they can identify as ones that they
have in their own garden. It will also inspire them to spend some of
their pocket money on packets of seeds of kinds which have taken
their fancy. They can also be encouraged to buy plants from a local
garden centre or nursery.

With increasing experience and interest they will want to know
how to increase their own plants by cuttings or by division and they
can develop a portion of their gardens into a small 'nursery' area
and even perhaps have a small frame in which to put their initial
efforts at propagation.

Without becoming sloppily sentimental they will learn that plants
can become individuals, with their own personalities and can be

identified as friends who respond to sympathetic treatment. It may seem impractical and possibly ridiculous, but from my own experience I know that plants will respond. There was a rare plant which lingered unhappily in a part of my garden where it was seldom seen and infrequently visited. I moved it to a place near the house door and fussed over it whenever I passed by. To my surprise and delight it quickly responded to such personal attention and grew into an obviously contented plant.

Dare I suggest that an innovation which would delight me, and, I am sure, many other readers would be, if *Hortus* could devote a few pages in each issue to children. The children themselves could contribute short and simple stories of their successes and failures and parents too, might well like to contribute comments on their children's gardening interests.

A clear memory of my own is of the time, when I was six years old, visiting the potting shed on my father's nursery and discovering a discarded box of seedlings of *Gentiana verna* which I siezed and took to plant the seedlings in my own garden. Some months later I heard that the nursery had sold out of the gentian, and I was able to enter into business for the first time and sold them back to my father for a few pence each, a sum which was promptly expended on packets of seed.

Drawings by Charles Robinson for R. L. Stevenson's
A Child's Garden of Verses

Gardens in Fiction

Rye Humour

JOHN FRANCIS

One of the incidental pleasures of reading E. F. Benson's Mapp and
Lucia novels is in the way someone is always doing a little gardening.
Gardens play a part in many novels. What would Blandings Castle be
without the superb backdrop of its stately garden? Where would Lord
Emsworth potter, having gazed and gazed again at his beloved sow
The Empress of Blandings, unless among his roses? In the garden is
peace, of a kind. Within the castle disturbers of his lordly tranquillity
lurk, his deplorable sister and his equally distressing secretary, the
efficient Baxter. But the peace of Lord Emsworth's gardens is dis-
rupted. A hurled potted geranium has been known, shrewdly aimed,
to find its mark. In P. G. Wodehouse the garden is always possibly
about to turn into an arena. Not so in Benson.

Benson's gardens are essentially safe, even cosy places. Daisy
Quantock calls across her garden to Georgie Pillson in his as he is
rolling his lawn. What should she do about slugs, she wants to know.
The answer is good news indeed for slugs, for he advises her to pre-
tend she hasn't seen them. Gardening is a mysterious calling. Benson
understood this. Mrs Quantock has dismissed her gardener for smoking his pipe in the potting shed while on duty. She sets to work with
a will. She weeds with locust-blind enthusiasm. Not a weed, soon, is
in sight. On the other hand, the carefully planted out annuals are
quite gone, too. Satisfied that she has done a good job, Daisy gets in
a slight muddle and plants the phlox in the vegetable garden and
plants the broccoli close to the house. A true gardener, after a spell for
reflection in the shed, would not make such a mistake. Benson
cleverly tells us a great deal about Daisy Quantock obliquely. A
woman who can root prune a mulberry without consulting a gardening manual lacks subtlety.

Again in *Miss Mapp*, a dangerous but widely smiling woman is
smarting. Her new, rich neighbour Mrs Poppit has put up her glasses
and inspected Miss Mapp's roses, her 'friendship border'. Each rose,
you see, has been donated by a friend. Mrs Poppit detects a lack of
vigour and tells her so. She offers to send round a few vigorous bushes.

No lady of spirit could accept such an offer. Now, Mrs Poppit has suffered much from the hand of Miss Mapp. The offer of roses and the suggestion that she should plant some fuchsias are actually rather like a sniper's bullet. Not friendly. Miss Mapp tells Mrs Poppit, eyeing her brocaded silk costume, that fuchsias, unfortunately, remind her always of overdressed women. It is a telling, even deadly, metaphor. The physical appearance of poor Mrs Poppit is fixed forever in the reader's mind. But, of course, it only works if you have a clear picture of fuchsias in the first place.

A true gardener will find something to do in all seasons. He or she will only see the weather in terms of how it is affecting his or her plot – how is the mulberry faring in this gale? When, as in the carol, earth is hard as iron and water like a stone, the gardener will hug herself knowing that she planted fields of bulbs like mines which will detonate so pleasurably in due course, and if there is absolutely no chance of getting out there are always seedsman's catalogues and, I contend, the novels of Benson to evoke the high and gaudy pleasures of summer. If the frost has been remorseless and seems likely to be eternal, that is the time to look up the chapter where Mrs Poppit throws a card party in her garden. She cannot attend, and this is vital to the plot, as she is expected by King George and Queen Mary at the palace to receive her MBE. Read this chapter as the wind is howling wolfishly in the chimney, scolding the smoke so that it panics and is driven fleetingly into the room. You will read of jugs of lager beer with beads of moisture on their outer surface, of delicious redcurrant fool, fortified with matchless cunning by champagne and old brandy, and of the little wind that blows one of the cards into a bed of mignonette. What luxury to have to hand such a superb evocation of a perfect summer day in January.

Benson's Mapp and Lucia novels can provide also a little well-rotted compost to a gardener's ego. Diva Plaistow, fancy!, seems to have only the sketchiest idea of how to plant tulips. Luckily Georgie Pillson manfully asks her to pass the trowel. Diva, no fool, lards him with flattery ('What a neat hole!'). Then the kettle boils or something like that and Diva dives to her kitchen so Georgie, ever amiable, plants all her tulips for her. And makes an interesting, even a sensational discovery. Buried in the tulip bed he finds the silver head of Major Mapp-Flint's riding crop. Thus Diva's garden, like all the gardens in Tilling and Riseholme, pushes the action forward and fleshes out, by pointing up their foibles, Benson's delightful characters.

Unlike Georgie, Elizabeth Mapp is a callous, you could almost say brutal, gardener. Weeding while obsessed with a problem (how to meet, without seeming to pander to royalty, a train that might or might not contain the Prince of Wales) she pulls up a love-in-a-mist and fails to replant it. Reading this, the true gardener must surely wince. This is a signal encoded by Benson which the true gardener will not miss; it shows just how distracted his heroine is.

Even in winter Benson uses his characters' gardens. Eschewing her crowded card tables, Susan Poppit of fuchsia fame – Susan Poppit who is anxious to become Mrs Wyse – takes Algernon Wyse out into her garden in order to obtain his advice about her orchids. An odonto-glossum is giving rise to anxiety, that is the pretext. Even when play-ing cards, Miss Mapp is never less than lynx-eyed. She too rises from the tables and on the pretext of an interest in astronomy conceals herself behind a curtain to keep an eye on what is probably going on in the garden. His mind far from orchidacious matters Algernon kisses Poppit. Meanwhile, also absent from the card tables – she claims to have mislaid her handkerchief – Diva is prowling round in search of the lovers. She does not realise the guilty pair are in the garden so, thwarted, she steals a *marron glacé* and returns, having failed to find any evidence of illicit passion. Miss Mapp comes out from behind the curtain sated with what she has seen, saying merely, 'Aldebaran! So lovely!' Mrs Poppit tells her daughter that Mr Wyse thinks that leaf-mould would do the trick. Silently, within her bosom, Miss Mapp exclaims 'Liar!'

All this is magnificently consistent. Everything we know about Susan Poppit, her ample dumpling proportions, her lavish luncheon parties, her MBE nestling like some alpine hut upon her refulgent bosom, her selenotropic lawn walks to succour an orchid and steal a kiss, all incline us to believe that orchids are her thing. She is not the snowdrop type. Even though I have never knowingly encountered an odontoglossum, I seem to see some great quilted purple trumpet.

Talking of snowdrops, Lucia despised them. Well, we must of course allow Benson to know best. After all Lucia is his creation, and yet I can imagine her recalling Coventry Patmore:

> . . . And hails far spring
> With uplifted spear.

Elizabeth Mapp uses them. In a gesture which mingles menace and girlishness in equal proportions she fixes a few snowdrops to Major Flint's buttonhole, one of those fairy touches that, strain as he might, in the end enslave him. His golfing partner and sometimes friend, Captain Puffin, sees through Miss Mapp's wiles perfectly. 'Powerful woman', he remarks. Major Flint, 'Major Benjy' as she cooingly calls him, recognises her powerfulness but is disarmed by her oft-declared intention of saying goodnight to her 'sweet flowers'. Encountering her one day when she has successfully disputed the price of suet with her butcher, he speculates about what she has been doing: 'Fairy errands, I'll be bound.' Wisely Mapp lets this pass; she makes no mention of her suet success. Miss Mapp uses her garden and even the butterflies in her garden as a way of indicating her ladylike and feminine sensibilities. Major Benjy mistakes the manner for the matter, something which Mapp's arch rival, Lucia, would never do.

And like Mapp, Lucia uses her garden, her love of flowers, to advertise *her* niceness. At a crucial moment in her eternal war with Mapp, Lucia enrages Georgie by pretending to be absorbed in sketching her dahlias before the frost destroys them. The war is no less deadly for being conducted in such an essentially ladylike way. Lucia is as sedulous as any vestal in keeping the flame of culture burning. Anything, even a glut of tomatoes, is useful to her. Inviting her friends to a seemingly endless recital of Mozart she hopes to refresh them in the interval with tomato salad. Lucia is going through one of her austere plain living phases. Used to a more sumptuous table at Lucia's and dismayed to find just how much Mozart piano music there is and seeing no end to it or the tomatoes, Lucia's little circle is pushed to the very brink of revolution. Thus another twist is applied to the plot, another triumph for Lucia prepared. And of course gluts of tomatoes and jam making and planting out broccoli where you should have planted phlox . . . all these remind the reading gardener of the passing of the seasons, of man having but a short time to live, and other such sweetly melancholy thoughts. And if Daisy Quantock had not got into such a muddle over her seedlings, would she have been inspired by her spirit guide, Abfou, to found the Riseholme museum?

Mallards under Miss Mapp's regime and Mallards House under Lucia when she was seeking to turn all Tilling into her fief – a pretension hotly contended by Mapp – is as all the world knows, in reality Lamb House, Rye, in East Sussex, home of Henry James and later of E. F. Benson. Benson wrote therefore of what he knew. He once, according to Iain Finlayson in his fascinating book, *Writers in Romney Marsh*, while seated in the secret garden with the vicar, saw the ghost of a man in a black cloak. Probably this is why the garden strikes the reader as being so real. It is also the reason why I will make no effort actually to visit the garden and see it for myself. How can you visit a place that you already so thankfully inhabit?

As a flat-dweller making do with, these days, just two window boxes and several green hells formed by too many pot plants, I find I sigh and long to do a little gardening again. Via the enchanted pen of E. F. Benson this frustration is kept within the limits of safety. I can enter his secret garden whenever I like, and so, of course, can you.

Winter Flowers

ARTHUR HELLYER

There is no need for any garden to lack flowers in winter. Even the smallest can have snowdrops, winter aconites and hardy cyclamen and, with a little more space to play with, horizons expand to take in a number of fine shrubs. There could also be hellebores but I wrote about these at some length in the first issue of *Hortus* so I need not go over that ground again except to remind readers that there are some forms of *Helleborus niger* that actually start to flower before Christmas, of which the one variously known as 'Altifolius' and 'Maximus' is probably the best. Also there is the intensely deep purple *Helleborus atrorubens* which always starts to flower in January and is a most reliable plant but rather sombre in colour.

Shrubs are particularly generous with winter flowers. Viburnum alone can offer at least half a dozen in the top class. First to open of the deciduous kinds, almost neck and neck in November, are *Viburnum farreri* (*fragrans*) and the hybrids between it and *V. grandiflorum* collectively known as *V.* x *bodnantense*. Some gardeners complain that *V. farreri* flowers sparsely but in most gardens, including mine, it is reliable and prolific. It may be that there are some poor forms of this normally fine Chinese species around and it would seem to be worth buying in winter when one can select plants that are flowering well.

Because it is a hybrid, *V.* x *bodnantense* is variable and several forms have been selected and given names. 'Dawn' is the one that won an Award of Merit in 1947 when shown by Lord Aberconway, who had raised it at Bodnant, in North Wales. It is free flowering, carmine in bud but opening a paler pink. 'Deben', for which Notcutt's Nursery received a First Class Certificate in 1965, is a lighter pink, paling to white and the scarce 'Charles Lamont' raised in the Royal Botanic Garden, Edinburgh, is said to be deeper in colour than 'Dawn' but I cannot recollect having seen it.

All forms of *V. farreri* are more slender in growth than any of the *V.* x *bodnantense* varieties and much more likely to let their branches hang down to the ground where they readily take root and so transform a single plant into a thicket. It also has smaller flower clusters, light pink in bud becoming white when fully open, and

they are extraordinarily frost resistant. I have seen flowers encased
in ice which then emerged unscathed when the thaw arrived. I do
not find the flowers of *V.* x *bodnantense* so tough and that is probably
a result of the *V. grandiflorum* parentage, a distinctly tender shrub
only fully reliable in the milder counties or near the sea. All are
sweetly scented and cast their perfume far, as do so many winter
flowering shrubs.

   V. tinus is the familiar laurustinus, somewhat despised because it
was overplanted in Victorian gardens along with cherry laurels and
aucubas. Yet all are excellent shrubs in the right place – if not
overdone – and I certainly would not like to be without a few
bushes of laurustinus because, in mid-winter, it can be the most
attractive of all evergreens. It varies quite a lot, some forms shinier
in leaf, some pinker in flower and some earlier in flower. Unhappily
catalogues offer little help on flowering time. Some include 'Eve
Price' which has red-purple buds and pink flowers and can be
relied on to give some colour from November onwards and some
also offer *V. tinus* 'Lucidum' which has glossy leaves but is unlikely
to flower until March. I have seedling laurustinus bushes which are
showing bud colour in October and it is worth looking out for these
in nurseries though they will not bear any distinguishing name.
   Then there are quite a lot of witch hazels thanks to the many

hybrids between *Hamamellis japonica* and *H. mollis* collectively known as *H.* x *intermedia*. Here I have no hesitation in declaring my own favourite as *H. mollis* 'Pallida', a fine lemon yellow variety more penetrating in colour than the common deeper yellow type and a bigger flower into the bargain. From late November until mid-January it can be one of the brightest patches of colour in the garden and its sweet perfume carries a long way on a still damp day.

If there is room to spare I would plant ordinary yellow *H. mollis* for contrast and also one of the red flowered hybrids such as 'Jelena' or 'Diane' though I find the bronzy red colour more effective when branches are cut and brought indoors than in the garden. All these witch hazels dislike lime and dry soils and in time they can take up a lot of room but they can be pruned after flowering.

The winter jasmine, *Jasminum nudiflorum*, needs no recommendation since everyone knows and likes its cheerful yellow flowers which, in a sheltered place, can be there all winter. Though it loses its leaves in the autumn, one is not very aware of this since they are small and the stems are so green that it still looks like an evergreen.

Though usually listed among the climbers, it is really a sprawler but, planted against a wall or screen, it can be trained upwards to a height of at least 3m (10ft).

Chimonanthus praecox, the winter sweet, is another favourite but perhaps more with the writers than the with growers. To be frank it takes a little care and understanding to make it a complete success. It is slow starting and likely to take several years before it even starts to flower and then the more sun and warmth it gets the more flowers there are likely to be. This suggests a sunny wall as the ideal place for it but then there is the problem of pruning without destroying too much of the young flowering growth. The answer is to let it make a good framework of permanent branches and then prune annually to within a few inches of this each spring directly the flowers fade. There are easier things to grow and showier flowers than the pale citron yellow and maroon of the winter sweet but none with a sweeter, more far flung fragrance.

A rival on a still warm day is *Azara microphylla*, a small evergreen tree usually grown in Britain as a wall-trained shrub. The leaves are neat, the flowers little more than tuffets of golden anthers tucked in behind them but their vanilla fragrance can be powerful and well carried. Azara is not completely hardy and needs the shelter of a south or west facing wall in most places. There is an attractive silver variegated variety which is difficult to buy.

The shrubby winter flowering honeysuckles are as tough as you could wish and will make thickets quite rapidly as their long stems touch the ground and take root. The flowers are small, creamy white and not in the least eye catching but they are very sweetly scented, can be opening by December and still be around in March. There are two kinds that matter, *Lonicera standishii* and *L. fragrantissima,* and they are so much alike that there is no need to plant both. I would take whichever happens to be available.

All the winter flowering mahonias are magnificent evergreens but they vary considerably in hardiness. *Mahonia japonica* has never caused me any anxiety except that it spreads more widely than I can sometimes permit and it grieves me to have to cut out such handsome pinnate leaves. The flowers are pale by comparison with those of *M. lomarifolia* and less spectacularly displayed, in flat cartwheels rather than in erect shuttlecocks, but I do not find *M. lomarifolia* so tough and it gets too tall and gaunt with age. It can be cut back severely but takes a year or more to recover its shape. Then there are the hybrids between these two species, collectively named *M*. x *media*. Of these 'Charity' is available everywhere and is probably the best to plant, as handsome as *M. lomarifolia* and certainly hardier but without fragrance for my nose though some gardeners deny this. The one that certainly is sweetly scented is 'Lionel Fortescue' but with me it has been cut down in all recent hard winters and has now finally succumbed. I regret this since it is certainly a very handsome shrub.

There are numerous bulbs, corms and tubers which take advantage of the winter lull in competition to make a quick break, flower, seed and get out of the way before the summer crush. Top of the list for ease and satisfaction are the snowdrops, especially the numerous forms and hybrids of the British species, *Galanthus nivalis*.

These are problem-free plants able to thrive in sun or shade, colonising well even when they produce no seed, as is the case with the double flowered varieties and the admirable 'Atkinsii' which is top of my own list for vigour, display and reliability. It is also early, opening towards the end of January in a favourable winter but in this respect easily beaten by *G. nivalis* subsp. *reginae-olgae* which can be starting to flower in the autumn. The Greek and Turkish snow-

drops need more sun and warmth and do not, as a rule, spread so
rapidly. *G. elwesii*, with broad grey-green leaves is a handsome plant
but tall *G. byzantinus*, once so common, seems to have disappeared
from the catalogues even of bulb specialists. *G. caucasicus*, which, as
its name implies, grows further north in the Caucasus Mountains,
is variable but excellent in all its forms and there is a mid-winter
flowering hybrid between it and *G. hiemale* which does not yet seem
to have acquired a name of its own.

When it makes carpets of growth covered in February with golden
flowers rather like buttercups wearing green ruffs, *Eranthis hyemalis*,
the winter aconite, is the most cheerful of February flowers. It can
also be an indefatigable plant and I know one garden in which it
even competes successfully with ground elder. Yet in forty years I
have failed to establish it, why I do not know. Because of this
persistent failure I hesitate to give advice about it but the little

tubers which the nurseries and garden centres offer do often seem to be rather shrivelled and so it would seem wise to start them growing in pots or trays of peat compost and only plant out when growing strongly. The best colonies I know all grow in light shade but there is no uniformity, so far as I have been able to observe, about soil. Of one thing I am certain. Once a good colony of winter aconite has been established it should be left completely undisturbed.

The early crocuses and irises are all lovely but so fragile that, outdoors, they tend to be battered by rain. The ideal seems to be to grow them in pans and bring them indoors when the flower buds appear but that is cheating so far as the purpose of this article is concerned. Of the really early crocuses I would give pride of place to *Crocus tomasinianus* because it naturalises so well in short grass which in turn protects it from splashing. The pale lavender type seems to be the fastest spreading but there are richer colours such as 'Taplow Ruby' and 'Whitewell Purple'. *Crocus imperati* comes several weeks earlier and there is always a special fascination in watching those rather drab parchment coloured buds expand into violet flowers each with a glowing orange stigma in the centre but it needs more care than the 'tommies'.

The best truly winter flowering iris is *Iris unguicularis*, a sturdy perennial which makes so much foliage that the short stemmed flowers tend to get lost among it. The remedy is to keep it a little starved in a warm sunny place and gravelly soil. This both shortens its leaves and increases its flower production and, at its best, it can be very beautiful. Typically the colour is light lavender but there is a white variety, a deeper purple likely to be called 'Mary Barnard' and an excellent free flowering lilac variety named 'Walter Butt'.

Of the bulbous irises the two best to flower outdoors in January-February are *Iris histrioides* and *I. reticulata* in that order of flowering. *I. histrioides* is plump and blue, very lovely but easily smashed by rain. *I. reticulata* is more slenderly built, deep violet-purple in the wild form, sweetly scented and better able to withstand the weather. There are also numerous garden varieties such as light blue 'Cantab', plum purple 'J. S. Dijt' and 'Clairette' which combines light and dark blue.

The hardy cyclamen for mid-winter flower is *Cyclamen coum* and, though a small plant, it can provide the hottest colour of all in December and January, a rich magenta set off by rounded deep green leaves. It is a variable plant and there are forms with silver marbled leaves and also with white flowers but what I have described is the commonest wild form, hardy, fast spreading and reliable. There will not be any colour to rival it in intensity until *Rhododendron mucronulatum* begins to flower, which in my garden would be unlikely to be until early February.

Illustrations from *The Illustrated Dictionary of Gardening*, ed. G. Nicholson

Sir Cedric Morris, Artist-Gardener

BETH CHATTO

I first met Cedric Morris about thirty-five years ago, when I was half his age, and he was the age I am now. This is how it came about. Staying with us one summer weekend was a family friend, Nigel Scott, an impulsive, exciting person, gifted with a charm that made him friends wherever he went. He was also an enthusiastic plantsman. He did not know Cedric, but knew of his famous garden. Why shouldn't we go over and see it? It would not have occurred to Andrew and me to invite ourselves, but Nigel had no such qualms. He rang Benton End, and off we went, winding through narrow Suffolk lanes between drifts of Queen Anne's lace, innocent of what lay ahead, unaware that this day was a turning point in the lives of us all.

We arrived, walked across the gravel yard, knocked at the old wooden door and entered a large barn of a room, the like of which we had never seen before. Pale pink-washed walls rising high above us were hung with dramatic paintings of birds, landscapes, flowers and vegetables whose colours, textures and shapes hit me as though I were seeing them all for the first time. Bunches of drying herbs and ropes of garlic hung from hooks on a door, while shelves were crammed with coloured glass, vases, jugs, plates with mottoes – a curious hotch-potch, remnants from travels in years past. Filling the centre of the room was a long, well-scrubbed refectory table, and round it a rim of heads turned towards us. From the far end of the table a tall lean figure rose immediately, hand outstretched, informal and courteous. This was Sir Cedric Morris, artist and famous gardener, elegant in crumpled corduroys, a soft silk scarf around his long neck upon which was a fine head crowned with short-cut waving hair. His tanned face creased into a mischievous grin. Without fuss, a space was made, chairs were shuffled round on the bare yellow brick floor, three more mugs were found, Cedric poured tea and the conversation resumed. I took a deep breath, and listened, feeling incapable of any worthwhile contribution. I was the wife of Andrew Chatto, fruit farmer and grandson of the publisher. Andrew's real interest and life-long study was finding the origins and natural associations of garden plants so that we might know better how to grow them. I was also the mother of two small daughters: much of my time was spent teaching myself the art and

crafts of home-making. I was already influenced by Andrew to appreciate species plants as well as cultivars, but my knowledge was much
more limited than Andrew's who knew and recognised plants through
his studies.

Tea finished, the party broke up. Nigel, Andrew and I were invited
into the garden. It was not a conventionally designed garden with
carefully selected groups of trees and shrubs leading the eye to some
premeditated feature or walk. There were surprisingly few trees or
shrubs. Before Cedric's time it was probably a kitchen garden, and was
surrounded by still sound brick walls, the enclosed area divided into
rectangles by straight and narrow paths. Low box hedges had been
planted along the path edges. Some years later I was pleased to see these
disappear and better use made of the space and time required to keep
box in good condition. A few ancient fruit trees were dotted around.
Among them a tall cherry made the principal feature, wreathed with
ropes of wisteria; sadly, it all collapsed one night in a wild storm. The
other remarkable feature was a vast, spreading medlar (*Mespilus ger-
manica*) whose umbrella-like head covered a wide area, valued by
Cedric for those precious plants requiring shade and shelter from the
drying winds.

Dotted here and there were pillars of old-fashioned roses and several
huge clumps of sword-leafed *Yucca gloriosa*. The rest was a bewildering,
mind-stretching, eye-widening canvas of colour, textures and shapes,
created primarily with bulbous and herbaceous plants. Later I came to
realise it was probably the finest collection of such plants in the
country. But that first afternoon there were far too many unknown
plants for me to see, let alone recognise. You may look, but you will
not see, without knowledge to direct your mind. As you become
familiar with more plants and plant families your eye will pick out the
unfamiliar ones and so add to your pleasure and knowledge. Walking
behind the three men, pricking up my ears (I knew perhaps one Latin
name in ten) I felt like a child in a sweet shop, wanting everything I
saw. Ecstatic, I knew I must grow such plants in my own garden.

It is no exaggeration to say that at Benton End not only the plants,
but the people too were 'characters'. Larger, more intimidating, more
intriguing than any, was Arthur Lett-Haines, always called Lett. An
inventive, introspective painter, he and Cedric had lived together
since the end of the First World War. He ran the household. I doubt if
Cedric could boil an egg; he rarely wrote a letter. Lett organised and

taught in the East Anglian School of Painting and Drawing, which he and Cedric founded, and of which Cedric was Principal. He practically gave up his own work during the latter years of his life to foster Cedric's talents and promote his work. He cooked for the students, who were of all ages and from all walks of life, and for numerous visitors, complaining eloquently as he stirred the pot with one hand, a glass of wine in the other, producing at the end of it memorable dishes.

Lett introduced me to Elizabeth David's books (the three of them had been friends for many years). He sent me into the garden to find wild strawberries beneath the rose bushes, he showed me how to make salad on a chill March evening with blanched pink and cream leaves of sea kale. But it was Cedric who gave me a little type-written catalogue, produced by Kathleen Hunter, who supplied seed of unusual vegetables long before they appeared, in colour, in much grander catalogues. Most of them were not new; in fact they could all be found in *The Vegetable Garden*, published in 1885, written by Messieurs Vilmorin-Andrieux, of Paris, beautifully illustrated with fine line drawings describing all the different kinds of vegetables and salads grown in the latter half of the nineteenth century when gardeners were expected to know how to provide a wide variety of fresh food for the kitchen all the year round. In a way, my interest in unusual plants began in my kitchen garden. Growing unusual vegetables and salads was good training when eventually I came to organise a tidy nursery.

A few months after that first visit we were not surprised when Nigel went to live at Benton End. He looked like a Viking, with his narrow face, handsome hooked nose and sharply jutting eyebrows. By nature a pacifist, Nigel volunteered to fight in Finland in the last war, arriving there without proper clothing or equipment to deal with the terrible conditions. Eventually he escaped back to England via Norway and spent the rest of the war in a minesweeper in the Mediterranean, occasionally being dropped off to spend a few days climbing in the southern Alps, where his interest in species plants began. When peace came he attempted to settle down in a West Country nursery, but he was not equipped for organised routine. The atmosphere at Benton End was, by comparison, relaxed. Nigel added his own aura and fitted into the scheme of things as they were. During his time there the garden expanded and blossomed to the peak of its

Drawing of Sir Cedric Morris by Glyn Morgan

development and fame. This takes nothing away from Cedric as its creator; in Nigel he found a companion who shared his enthusiasm for plants to its fullest extent. They worked together, often from dawn till dusk.

It was about this time, the early fifties, that Cedric's work as a breeder of bearded iris was at its peak. He was the first person in this country to produce a pink iris. One of these was first shown in 1948, on the Gold Medal stand at Chelsea of Messrs Wallace, then of Tunbridge Wells. It was admired by Queen Elizabeth, now the Queen Mother, and she allowed it to be called 'Strathmore', after her own home. The names of Cedric's irises were usually preceded by Benton. I have an old Wallace catalogue containing Cedric Morris introductions in 1951 and '52 with romantic names like 'Benton Damozel', 'Benton Ophelia', 'Benton Fandango'. This last-named variety was a plicata type, meaning the pale silk-textured petals were lightly 'stitched' with fine veins, deepening in tone towards the ruffled edges.

On a few rare occasions, when the iris season was at its best, Cedric and Nigel prepared some of the newest varieties to take to one of the Iris Society shows in London. Can you imagine the performance involved for them to arrive with flowers intact? They had no car, so someone would offer to drive them to the station in Ipswich. Cedric would have hated every minute. He loved to have his plants admired and appreciated but he was not competitive and had no time for pot hunters.

It would be a pity if the records show Cedric only as a famous breeder of iris. Those of us who knew him and his garden over the last thirty years cannot adequately express our debt to him for introducing to us such an amazing collection of unusual plants, primarily species plants rather than cultivars. Today the National Council for the Conservation of Plants and Gardens is doing valuable work, with many specific genera being cared for individually in separate gardens. To us, Cedric's garden appeared to contain them all! An exaggeration, perhaps, but over the span of a long lifetime he collected, preserved and increased a wealth of plants never before seen together in one place. It was practically impossible to take him a plant he did not already possess, although it was tempting to try to do so.

One winter evening after dinner, sitting alone at the table with Cedric and Nigel, I was stunned to hear Cedric say I would never make a good garden where we were living, in our first married home. My heart dropped to the brick floor while my mind struggled to assess what this meant. We had been pouring ourselves into this garden, battling with chalky boulder clay, while I taught myself to propagate plants from the precious screws of paper full of seed, berries or cuttings I had been given by Cedric as well as generous earthy bundles of roots, tubers and bulbs. We were still far away from the ideal we admired in Cedric's garden, where no season was boring, where each time we visited we found fresh plants we had not noticed before. Several years were to pass before circumstances opened our eyes to the inevitability of building a new home and starting a new garden, but the seed had been planted in the dark of that winter night.

Today the great majority of plants established in our garden at White Barn came originally from Benton End. Certain ones in

Irises at Benton End, 1946. Photograph © *Country Life*

particular bring Cedric vividly to life in my mind: the many kinds of *Allium*, in flower and seed; the lime-green heads of euphorbia, in particular *Euphorbia wulfenii*, which billowed at the base of a deep Suffolk pink wall; fritillaries, large and small, plum-purple, soft chestnut, or pale lemon-yellow, with speckled or netted insides, looking as if they had been flung into sweeps and drifts among other plants whose season was yet to come! 'How do you get so many?', I would ask when I was still cosseting only two or three of these rare bulbs.

'Scatter the seed', he would say. So I did. But I had to learn, as he had done before me, to nurse the young seedlings for some years before they appeared 'like weeds' in my borders. Old fashioned roses, hellebores, old double primroses, and lace-edged primulas; alas I have almost lost those. There could be pages more.

Cedric abominated salmon-pink: 'Knicker pink!', he would snort. But he loved soft, 'off-beat' shades where the pink was sometimes greyed with tiny purple veins. His interest in breeding, never far beneath the surface, led him to produce an oriental poppy far removed from the bright scarlet and crimson of the species. Its flouncing petals were ashen-pink, with a central velvet knob deep in a pool of dark purple-black blotches. We always called it 'Cedric's Pink', but now it has become officially known as *Papaver orientale* 'Cedric Morris'.

Another poppy which seeded all over the place at Benton End, with magic effect, was Cedric's selection taken from the wild scarlet poppy of the fields. I think he was aiming to get a lavender-coloured poppy; occasionally he succeeded. Translucent, crumpled petals reflected the soft dove-grey of rain clouds, faintly suffused with pink. Others, in shades of pink, were heavily veined with crimson. Or again, shadowed, shell-pink overlapping petals were edged with a thin dark rim.

Recently I was brought a pan crammed with seedlings of these poppies, preserved by Mary Grierson, whose minutely observed paintings I greatly admire. We sat and indulged in nostalgic memories while she told me how much she owed to Cedric and his garden. It was he who set her on her career as a famous botanical illustrator.

It was not always dream-like. Meal times could be electrified by sudden squalls and conflicts, but the roof never fell in. We sat and waited, suffering with our idols, seeing them as human beings, our bonds of shyness shattered by the storm.

Sometimes there were nightmares. Nigel died, suddenly and tragically. Would summer ever be as bright again? Not long after Nigel's death Millie Hayes found refuge at Benton End. Slender as a flower on a stem, with huge dark eyes and expressive hands, she devoted twenty years of her life, helping to run the household, caring for the two handsome, naughty, darling old men who coloured our lives until eventually the light of each was blown out.

Daisy Chains

KAY N. SANECKI

Personal garden diaries abound, but few record the plants assembled, fewer still describe the fun. The Countess of Warwick not only described her garden but detailed the provenance of some plants and, with elfin gaiety, told how she made them her playthings. Here was an intelligent society lady indulging her delight in her plants with seemingly total absorption throughout the 1880s and 90s. Her garden was an escape from London, a fantasy, 'very Arcadian' and light-hearted.

But during the same period, her sociological concern and her awareness of the impoverishment of rural communities drove her to become an enlightened pioneer for the training of young people in rural husbandry. A staunch socialist, her strong belief in co-education led her to found Bigods School, supported by a grant from the Essex County Council, in 1897, where children from the age of eleven years were taught the basic scholastic subjects and agricultural and horticultural skills. About the same time her Needlework School was started in Essex, where girls were apprenticed in dressmaking, millinery and embroidery, and a shop was opened in Bond Street, London, to provide the market outlet. While on the one hand she allotted corners of her garden as sequestered nature reserves, on the other she enlisted her social contacts to support enormous national schemes.

Frances Evelyn Maynard (1861–1938), an acknowledged beauty of her day, was chosen by Lord Beaconsfield and Queen Victoria to marry Leopold, the Queen's youngest son. But following amicable discussions between the Prince and Daisy (as she was always known), she married his Equerry, the debonair Lord Brooke, heir to the earldom of Warwick. Her extravagance, her flouting of the moral standards of the day, her notorious involvement with Edward, Prince of Wales, all mask her true achievements. As a philanthropist and outstanding educationalist her foresight in initiating the training of women in horticulture and agriculture was visionary.

She outlined her ideals in the *Women's Agricultural Times*, July 1899, Vol. 1 No. 1, the official monthly publication of her Agricultural Scheme for Women, saying: 'Whatever direction this advent of trained and cultured women may take, that is whether they settle

The Countess of Warwick in the 1880s when, newly
married, she began to make her garden at Stone Hall

down to rural life either as married or single women, or ... as lecturers or teachers, it seems reasonable to hope that ... their influence must have a salutary and energising effect upon rural England ...' Lady Warwick demonstrated her practical concern in a period of economic deprivation in rural areas, coupled with excessive commodity imports that could be home produced. (About £30 million per year was going to foreign markets for butter, eggs, cheese and poultry.)

Away from the London social scene she escaped, often accompanied by friends, to her gardens in Warwickshire and Essex. At Easton Lodge near Dunmow, Essex she set about making a garden tucked away on the estate, near the village of Canfield, in her late teens when she became Lady Brooke. She had inherited Easton Lodge from her grandfather when she was three years old, and had been brought up there, but claimed her inheritance when she married in 1891. Later, she wrote a delightful record of it, listing all the plants she grew, adding details of how they were arranged. Meanwhile her philanthropic activities continued, extending to work for crippled children and fighting for qualified nurses during the nights in Poor Institutes. And on a national scale, she launched the Lady Warwick Agricultural Association for Women: LWAAW.

In a letter to W. T. Stead, editor of *Pall Mall,* a friend and supporter of hers, she wrote (1898): 'My agricultural scheme for women is developing rapidly on one side, viz. a hostel in connection with the Oxford University Extension College at Reading and I found a house holding about 50 boarders with charming gardens for experiment. I have secured the support of £200 from Lord Wantage, and the Huntleys, Palmers and Suttons, all Reading people, have come forward with sympathy and support, and money, and we hope to start off at the beginning of next term with a dozen students ... Mr Sutton has given the free use of his wonderful seed trial grounds for the students, which will be invaluable, and there is a splendidly equipped dairy, too.'

The first hostel was opened in October 1898 in a spacious house, Coleyhurst in Bath Road, Reading. Practical work was undertaken also at Wharton Robinson's Nursery at Calcot and Mr Parfitts' fruit farm, and poultry-keeping was taught at Mr Ernest Brown's poultry farm at Theale. Much seasonal work was continued in the surrounding countryside during the summer vacations. Expansion was rapid,

Gardening at the Lady Warwick Hostel, *c.* 1900. The new, thatched-roofed potting shed had working space for forty students and was also used as a venue for parties

The kitchen garden at Lady Warwick Hostel, *c.* 1900

and a year later two more hostels were opened, Maynard Hostel and Brooke House, providing accommodation for fifty students and ten teaching staff.

Meanwhile the LWAAW ran the *Women's Agricultural Times*, of which Lady Warwick was the Editor, and organised a Registry which published particulars of posts vacant, working in conjunction with the Women's Institute in London and various provincial women's employment bureaux. Prospects for work in South Africa and Canada were incorporated in the training schemes less than two years after the hostels had been started. Advisers from the Empire were enlisted and a small Executive Committee supported Lady Warwick in all this work. In addition there was a General Committee of about sixty distinguished members, all of whom she appears to have been capable of spurring into action: principals of other colleges, professors, Sir Cecil Rhodes, Sir Winston Churchill, Mrs Asquith, Mrs Garret Anderson, A. W. Sutton and M. J. Sutton, peers, peeresses, friends and supporters, all under the able Chairmanship of J. Marshall Dugdale.

The pioneer scheme soon outgrew its premises. In 1901 an appeal was launched for £30,000–£50,000 with HM King Edward VII as Patron. Lady Warwick addressed a meeting at the Mansion House, in the City of London, and within two years sufficient funds had been accumulated to purchase Studley Castle, Warwickshire with its 340 acres, for £25,000. Late in 1903, warden, staff and forty students moved to Warwickshire to a badly neglected estate, but with a fine range of lean-to glasshouses in a one-acre kitchen garden. Two 100 ft greenhouses were transported from Reading and re-erected by the students and remained until well after the Second World War. Potting and marketing sheds were built, a dairy equipped and the BDFA made the College a recognised centre for their examinations. A poultry department and apiary were established also on what, even at the time, were very slender financial resources.

Good trees including cedars, cryptomerias, hornbeams and a fine *Fagus sylvatica heterophylla* (*laciniata*) formed the basis of the Pleasure Grounds. A remarkable avenue of *Sequoia sempervirens* planted in the 1860s lined the curved and rising approach drive. A ruined orangery presided over a rose garden, which flourished on the Warwickshire clay. Studley College was thus established, and with the advent of the First World War was put in the control of a Board of Governors working under licence from the Board of Trade. For the following half century it flourished as a training establishment for women in agriculture and horticulture, with a strong practical basis. In 1929 following a public appeal it became freehold property. Her Majesty The Queen Mother, then Duchess of York, visited the College and received purses: the total amount subscribed was £13,000, of which £5,000 came from the Treasury. Lady Warwick lived to see her enterprise flourish, with modern laboratories, residential wings, a hundred students, large residential staff and trained women working at varying levels in agriculture and horticulture – a high proportion of which fulfilled her original dream, many working abroad. As a result of changing attitudes in education, and the withdrawal of Government support, Studley College was closed in the mid-sixties, following the Pilkington report.

In 1898 during the height of her various activities she wrote: 'Do you therefore wonder that once again I have evaded London? And if you do, then wander across the Park with me to the garden that I love, my playground far from the busy haunts of men . . . Where many generations that are passed and gone have brought their contribu-

Studley College: strawberries and bell glasses depict the
intensive cultivation methods of the day (1905). The frame
enables four bell glasses to be carried at one time

tions of marl and leaf-mould to bequeath to me the delights of my garden today.' To the south-west of Easton Lodge was a small ancient building known as Stone Hall, and it was there that she made her fantasy garden. (Much later the garden behind Easton Lodge was created, work being given to sixty men, all of whom were provided with board, food and recreation while they dug over ten to twelve acres on which Harold Peto designed a garden, noted for its *treillage*.)

At Stone Hall the Countess admitted that 'thro' the great oak roof the ivy has found its way, and is creeping down slyly and furtively below the black beams. Presently, but not yet, I shall need to set some limit to its pretty encroachment'. Apparently there was much decorative carving in the form of birds and animals – 'a very Noah's ark of shapely beasts' adorned the interior of the little Hall. Occasionally, parties were arranged for children and dogs at which 'high revelry' abounded. Over many years Lady Warwick assembled her 'Garden Librairie' at Stone Hall, and had books 'liveried' in green and gold. They were housed on 'oak shelves with quaint casings' – Gerard's *Herball*, a most perfect edition of Parkinson, and a complete set of Redouté's works: *Les Roses*, *Les Liliacées*, *Histoire des Plantes Grasses*

Studley College: students working in the vinery, *c.* 1906

and *La Botanique de J. J. Rousseau*, were counted among her treasures.
Later, books written by W. H. Hudson, whom she greatly admired,
were added to keep the library up-to-date.

Sitting there in an old green tapestry chair among her treasures,
bird watching through the latticed windows, she mused upon the
limitations of human achievement. She wrote: 'From the outer world
the faint sounds of reapers [could be heard] which tells us of a fine
harvest time, and yet it tells of anxious hearts and heavy; for in this
country the fortunes of our farmers have fallen on evil days . . . in
spite of ceaseless and anxious efforts it is still but poverty which rocks
the cradle, nowadays.'

No plan survives of the garden at Stone Hall, but it comprised a
rose garden, a sunny slope encircled by distant trees, a lily garden,
a winding shrubbery walk leading to the rock garden, with a pool fed
by a trickling cascade fringed by bamboos, iris and montbretias and
full of 'greedy goldfish'. The rocks were enveloped in ivy with a mass
of pink aubrietia below and tiny clinging *Arenaria balearica* mixed
with the variegated foliage of *Vinca elegantissima (major)*. There was

Studley College: students in the plant houses, *c*. 1905.
Duck boards were used to keep students' feet dry

soft green of *Omphalodes verna* below with sheltered crannies traced by fronds of *Cystopteris fragilis*. Elsewhere there was a living sundial, the gnomon originally of yew, the figures of trimmed box, encircled by the words *Les heures heureuses ne se comptent pas*. They were outlined in baby sprigs of box, by a friend.

Friends helped to create a Garden of Friendship where, sentiment-ally, the donor's name was inscribed on a heart-shaped label accom-panying each plant. The list reads like Debrett: HRH The Prince of Wales donated *Thalictrum adiantifolium*, phlox and asters, *Megasea cor-difolia* (bergenia) and *Anemone japonica*, *Helenium pumilum*, *Helianthus multiflorus*, *H. angustifolius*; the Duchess of Leinster contributed cam-panulas, aubrietia, spreading sage, *Tradescantia carnea*, *Lychnis chal-cedonica*, *Stipa pennata* and *Malva moschata*. Lord Randolph Churchill gave poppies, scabious, hemerocallis, azaleas and larkspur, *Trollius fortunei* and *T. loddigesianus*. Baron Ferdinand de Rothschild, the Countess of Listowel, Viscountess Curzon, Lady Cloncurry, Mrs Vyner, Mr Spiro, the Duke of Sutherland, Mrs Arthur Paget, the Earl of Chesterfield, the Countess Howe and others all seem to have clamoured for a place in the collection. Within this Garden of Friend-ship a small sanctuary was created – perhaps today it would be more prosaically considered a conservation area – and nesting boxes were introduced (G. B. Shaw laughed at them!). Later, an area of the sanctuary was dedicated to the memory of W. H. Hudson. London and local friends congregated for the little ceremony of dedication performed by R. B. Cunningham, one of Hudson's intimates. Thirty years later in her memoirs the Countess wrote '. . . [made] a sanctuary there at a time when nobody seemed to realise either that wild life has any rights, or that a suitable place should be reserved for it, beyond the reach of sportsmen!'

Individually-made pottery labels were designed for some parts of the garden. These took the form of *fleur de lis* for the Lily Garden, while in the Border of Sentiment the 'dear old herbs and flowers' were labelled with 'quaint meanings and emblems of bygone times'. Each label was a swallow in form, the flower name on one wing, the emblem on the other – the white clover for memory, the blue salvia for knowledge, veronica for fidelity, the violet for love, and many more. The Countess of Warwick's confessed favourite garden was her Shakespeare Border, which represented 'the work of many winters' evenings in hunting for quotations and reducing them, when found,

Studley College: students relaxing on the front lawn, *c.* 1905

to these label limits – delightful pottery butterflies, twixt green and brown, on each wing of which is the text, with reference to the play from which it comes'.

The form of the labels in the Rosarie is not recorded, but scattered everywhere were reference quotations for roses, from the Holy Bible, hymns, the classics, Shakespeare, Tennyson, Shelley, Keats, Browning and Burns. The Rosarie was richly planted and heralded by the 'flippant motto' *Peu de choses mais roses*. Damasks, Bourbons, Chinas, Provins and many more abounded, while 'standard fir stems' were festooned with climbing 'Pink Rover', 'Fair Rosamund', 'Mme Plantier', 'Gloire de Dijon', 'The Garland', 'Persian Yellow', 'Félicité et Perpétue' and 'Crimson Rambler'. The centre of the rose garden was marked by a rose tent enveloped by 'Crimson Rambler' and 'Félicité et Perpétue', within which the Countess used to rest, and felt it 'a joy to be experienced'.

Most of the roses listed have seemingly gone out of cultivation or are not commercially available today, but it is of interest to note some favourites that have remained, such as 'La France', 'Spong', 'Village Maid', 'Painted Lady', 'Stanwell Perpetual', 'White de Meaux', 'Mrs John Laing', 'Jules Margottin', 'Baroness Rothschild', 'Maiden's Blush', 'Francesca Kruge', 'Marie van Houtte', 'Mme Falcot', 'John Hopper', 'Mme Georges Bruant', 'Blanche Moreau', 'Général Jacqueminot', 'Mlle Bonnaire', 'Victor Verdier', 'Magna Carta', 'Emperor', 'Bardon Job', 'Paul Neyron', 'Empereur du Maroc', 'White Bath' ('Shailer's White'), 'Pomifera', 'Little Gem', 'Coupe d'Hébé', 'Homère', 'Fabvier', 'Little White Pet', 'Perle d'Or', 'Clothilde Soupert', 'Fellemberg', 'Hermosa', 'Charles Lawson', 'Souvenir d'un Ami', and 'Sir Joseph Paxton'.

Of her climbing roses, only the first three are thought to be no longer grown: 'Pink Rover', 'Dundee Rambler', 'Fair Rosamund'. All the others continue to be favourites: 'Gloire de Dijon', 'Mme Alfred Carrière', 'The Garland', 'Félicité et Perpétue', 'Austrian Copper Briar', 'Persian Yellow', 'Blairi No. 2', and 'Crimson Rambler'.

The lovely rose garden which she enjoyed at Warwick Castle, her other home, has recently been re-created by Paul Edwards, and was opened to the public in 1986. Alas, nothing remains of Easton Lodge or Stone Hall. The house was commandeered for use by the RAF during the Second World War, and the whole estate has since been developed.

In her memoirs, *Life's Ebb and Flow*, the Countess of Warwick relates how after some years she returned to look at her Garden of
Friendship and found it overgrown, and 'there came a flood of sad
memories, but many souvenirs had survived. And there were new
friends – the garden was alive with birdsong!'

English Bones, American Flesh

ROBERT DASH

ROBERT DASH   *Breaking Corms.* Oil on canvas, 78″× 78″. 1986

My garden is at the far eastern end of Long Island, in New York State, in a town settled in 1656. It is set amidst fields continually farmed since that time and one would need a maul and sledgehammer in order to separate it from its profoundly English influences. Yet a wedge struck with equal force might be needed to pry it from its continuous involvement with the patterns of Abstract Expressionism, a largely American form of painting.

Painting is closely related to gardening but closer still is poetry. I frame poems like canvases and daily see work by Douglas Crase,

John Koethe, Marjorie Welish, Donald Britton, Peter Schjeldahl, John Ashbery, Barbara Guest, Gerrit Henry and many others. Winter, for me, has now become the 'sure season' when 'sounds skip long distances' and 'the outside light contracts, the inside one expands /Out of necessity' (Douglas Crase: *The Sure Season*). Autumn is, very definitely, when 'Canada geese zoom in to land and /sleep, a murmurous, feathered herd' (James Schuyler: *To a Watercolorist*).

Further, there is much else that went towards the making of my garden: a love of Indian paths, rather like the secret walks small children think to make, (which counts a lot for how one moves through my garden); an admiration of the roan beauties of abandoned farmland pierced by red cedars and laced and tied by dog roses, honeysuckle and brown, dry grass; the memory of a meadow of a single species of short, grey-leaved, flat-topped, open-flowered Golden rod whose October display was feathered by hundreds of monarch butterflies. I have a stubborn Calvinist belief in utility which causes me to plant vegetables among flowers, use herbs as borders and berrybushes as ornamentals. This brutish littoral, continental climate leads me to choose only such plant material which has infinite stamina. There are recollections of an ancestress who planted hollyhocks at the gate and lilacs out back – but all gardens are a form of autobiography. Moreover, as a painter, I am predelicted towards shape, mass and form and have learned that the predominate colour of all gardens is green and all the rest rather secondary bedeckment. Finally, there is something else, too: a sign on my gate which reads No Callers. (A fierce addiction to privacy, in a democracy, is no small sin, which is why my windbreak is thicker than it need be.)

Madoo, which in an old Scots dialect means My Dove, is the name of my garden of 1.91 acres and I have been at it now for twenty years. I have gone about it as I would a painting, searching for form rather than prefiguring it, putting it through a process more intuitive than intellectual. The blunders are there to learn from; the successes, more often than not, are the result of bold throws. I started from the house and went out towards the edges, often revising solid achievements until they seemed made of finer matter, like marks and erasures of work on paper which sometimes may be torn and fitted again in collage. Black pine, privet and Russian olive form the windbreak, pruned to show their fine trunks and branches, husbanded at their base by a carefully controlled invasion of Golden rod, chicory, Joe Pye weed and milkweed among which I have planted a variety of thalictrum, rhododendron and kalmia. *Lonicera flava* go up white birch. Pebbled areas, through which soar *Lilium canadense*, have brick setts for easier walking and small trickles of santolina, rue, and grasses. I am particularly fond of *Molinia* 'Windspiel'.

Although I like white on white (the Duchess of Edinburgh clematis on a white fence over *Rosa* 'Blanc Double de Coubert' and I like to whiten white by throwing *Clematis paniculata* over yew and holly), the major push is for green on green. I have never cared much for all grey gardens or all blue gardens, indeed I am not certain that they are ever successful, colour being too quixotic to control in that fashion, full of lurking betrayals so that sky blue becomes sea-blue or slate blue and then not blue at all. The air over my garden from whose several points I can see the Atlantic surf is full of a most peculiar double light, rising and falling, and is itself one of the heroes of my landscape, kinder to foliage and bark than to flowers at any rate. Wild air will always do the painting. I have increased the atmosphere's multiple shimmer by putting in four small ponds above whose surfaces small mists sometimes gather. In contrast I have made darkness with a copse of twisted, pruned Arctic willows and another of a spinney of Black pines, the former underplanted with a mix of epemedium, woodruff, Japanese wood anemones and ferns and both washed with the littlest of spring bulbs. Paths are of brick, pebbles or setts or grass and alternate curves with strict, straight geometries the better to bound, heighten and confine the predominantly relaxed, semi-wild, superabundant atmosphere I like.

A meadow garden has been quite successful. Formerly it was lawn giving a rather dull view from the dining table, made duller by summer heat and inevitable drought. America is no climate for lawns. I did not starve the soil to make the meadow but plunged in robust, thrusty perennials through the grass in pits carefully nourished with well-rotted manure and much moss peat: monardas, peonies, Scotch broom, *Rosa rugosa*, Michaelmas daisy, buddleia, globe thistle, daylilies (of course), sewn tightly into the now, mostly timothy and volunteered milkweed, Queen Anne's lace, chicory and Golden rod. It is roughly oval with a backing of Nootka cycpress, cryptomeria and rhododendron, whose darks perfectly outline the brighter foil of the foliage.

To my way of seeing, a garden is not a succession of small rooms or little effects but is one large tableau whose elements are inextricably linked to the accomplishment of the entire garden just as in painting all passages conduce to the effect of the whole. Lack of keyed strength in any one of them may lower the pitch and thrift of the finished canvas.

A muting of a too perfect area is often in order, no matter how lovely it might be. Just so I have found those recent silvery clematises are too huge a cynosure to be acceptable to the general garden and I have taken them out. One can very definitely have too much of a good thing unless it be some grand ground cover like *Lamium* 'Nancy' whose very modest performance excludes it from the egregious. The subtle is more alluring. The quieter painting enters the heart and stays there while those of tremendous, immediate impact have long since dwindled away.

I do not paint in the way that I garden or garden as I would employ the brush although the process is often the same. Both are arts of the wrist, the broadest, largest sort of signature, if you will, highly idiosyncratic, the result of much doing, much stumbling, and highly intuited turns and twists before everything fits and adheres to the scale of one's intention. A good tree must often be moved to a more reticent spot when it begins to dominate and thus ruin the total orchestration. Beautiful tunes don't end up as symphonies nor do witticisms write books. Certain flowers may emblazon a room but be abusive to a fine garden. For that reason and that of stamina and the ability to take the brunt of the climate (I am in Zone 7, whose average lowest temperature is 0° to —10° F). I choose older varieties of the plant kingdom whose foliage and blossom are, more often than not, circumspect and discreet.

I am now becoming more geometric. In front of the Winter House and Winter Studio I have just installed a brick path I call a view-swiper. It's 120 feet long, (flying out to the potato fields and to the ocean, bringing all that fine view inside the purview of the garden as if it were mine), eight feet wide at the near end, six at the far, with eighty roses ('Frau Dagmar Hartopp') on the sides. The far border will have other, taller rugosas and daylilies mixed with teasels. The site is but a narrow spur attached to my property, surrounded by changing crops whose patterns of growth and tilling are overwhelmingly seductive, requiring but the simplest sort of anchor to moor the peninsula. My canvases now have changed, too, and are rather like foliant form held very close to the eye. Both gestures, then, are new for me, and the feeling from both is a bit scary, akin to someone in the middle of a new high-wire act performing over a slowly withdrawing net. The air of gardens and paintings now seems to me to be filled with a wild, deliciously cold oxygen through which I can still see the first plain view of the working barns I converted, twenty years ago, grey above a blowing field of grass. That verdure, it seems to me, was the very soul of the place 'working backwards, year by year' until it 'reached the center of a landscape'. (John Koethe: *The Near Future.*)

The English bones with which I began now seem entirely covered by what I have done, but that is the way of flesh.

ROBERT DASH *Spring Light.* Oil on canvas, 78″ × 78″, 1986

Sissinghurst:

Maintaining a garden in perpetuity

PAMELA SCHWERDT

A garden is a living, changing thing, so to what extent it should be slavishly 'preserved' is difficult to decide. The alternatives range from on the one hand stopping the clock so completely that the garden becomes static, to on the other imposing so many changes that the original concept would be hard to recognise.

It is not only the actual choice and siting of plants which keeps a garden alive: there is that atmosphere or 'feel' associated with a place which it is equally important to perpetuate.

This article is about the *running* of the garden at Sissinghurst Castle. The history and the making of the garden by Vita Sackville-West and Harold Nicolson during the 1930s, its gift to the nation by Nigel Nicolson in 1967 and its present-day administration by the National Trust are all well recorded elsewhere.

Sissinghurst is not a formal garden of the most rigid kind, though it has a well-defined framework formed by buildings, walls and hedges. Added to this, most parts of the garden have their own particular planting theme of colour or type of plant. These broad ideas had settled down after the formative years of the 1930s, and apart from a few changes made soon after the war, have remained the same. This means that, while the White Garden will always remain white, the herb garden will be filled with herbs, and the rose garden will be planted predominantly with roses, there remains freedom to adapt the planting to take advantage of changing circumstances. It also allows for the introduction of new plants – provided they are in keeping with the style of the place – thus continuing the experimentation with the arrangement of plants which played an important part in the formation of this garden.

Originally each part of the garden had its one main period of flowering, the family going to whichever part was at its best. Now, however, with the numbers who come here, we have added plants to extend the season both before and after the peak periods. The possibility of coming upon interesting plants round every corner helps to spread people out.

In the orchard, spring bulbs start the season with a carpet of daffodils; roses take over after the rough grass is cut; and by autumn, when the leaves have turned, a succession of colchicums flower from August to late October. The White Garden's prime time will always be in early July when *Rosa longicuspis* covers the central support with its white flowers, filling the garden with scent. But flowering in the White Garden starts in April with tulips and wallflowers and goes on well into October when dahlias and michaelmas daisies are still in flower. Continuity of flowering is greatly helped by the use of half-hardy perennials. They are a very valuable group for furnishing, where there is a glasshouse with a small amount of heat for over-wintering. Most flower for the whole summer, needing no staking and comparatively little dead-heading. Many of our most decorative silver foliage plants are best classed in this group as well as a number of beautiful plants from South Africa.

The Lime Walk is an exception, as the borders are so full of bulbs that it is not possible to plant for the summer. This means that the only colour after the bulbs comes from the scarlet impatiens in the urns, planted after the forget-me-nots are cleared. These are shown up against the green background of the trimmed hornbeam hedge and pleached limes. The herb garden needs quite a lot of attention to keep it going throughout the year; several of the short-lived annual herbs like coriander and chervil need to be sown two or three times during the summer.

The garden is staffed by a team of six full-time gardeners and we are kept busy throughout the year, for though the garden is only six acres in area, it is what in present day jargon is termed 'labour intensive'. Narrow paths and awkward steps coupled with the fullness of planting make passage difficult and restrict the use of machinery beyond the usual mowers and hedge trimmers. Our small tractor can circumnavigate the garden but access inside is restricted mainly to the use of wheelbarrows and carrying-sheets.

Any jobs that can be done during winter to speed the pressing tasks of summer are given priority. The staking of roses is done in autumn to last the year, as are the pruning and tying in of wall shrubs. Hazel sticks, for staking perennials, are cut in winter; with their ends pointed they are tied into bundles ready for the following year. The walls are wired for tying in and, in the case of clematis, large-meshed wire netting is fixed above the plants to provide an inviting 'ladder' which they can climb with little assistance, ensuring they are well displayed the following season.

We aim to have completed the winter work of pruning, tying in, replanting, forking and mulching by the time the garden opens again in April. So far this has proved an impossible target, and usually continues well into April. By this time the grass is growing again and so are weeds, so mowing and hoeing jobs vie with spring planting and early staking.

Gardens of small dimensions can soon get out of proportion. Shrubs need to be kept from getting too large by careful shaping, which is often best done soon after flowering. Hedges become too tall and wide, blocking entrances or leaving no planting space. From time to time they need to be cut back by more than their usual annual clipping. In the case of yew it is possible to rebuild a hedge entirely over the span of several years, cutting back hard to the main framework to stimulate new growth. Best results have come from cutting the top and one side first, then following with the same treatment to the remaining side after four or five years. Box does not always respond as readily so we have renewed the majority of box hedges during the last twenty years, raising the plants from cuttings. This severe cutting back of hedges can be done in spring or autumn, though it is best done in late March or early April, giving the whole summer for the new growths to come. Deciduous hedges are easier to cut back in winter when the leaves are off.

The main time for the annual cutting of hedges begins in early August, starting with the yews. There is only one hedge which gets the luxury of two cuts in each season and that is the hornbeam in the Lime Walk. The growth is too much to leave for a whole summer, so the first cut is done after the bulbs have died down, the borders been cleared of rubbish and the urns replanted. A hedge cut as early as this will have secondary growth so by early September a second cut is needed. Secondary growth rarely comes if hedge cutting is postponed till about mid-August, but this is not always acceptable in confined spaces. The box hedges are done last, often as late as October, as it is difficult to use lines to get the right levels in either the rose garden or the White Garden until after the visiting season. Wherever possible electric hedge trimmers, run from a generator, are used, but box is best cut with shears.

We need to have enough plants to draw on should some emergency arise like those caused by the two hard winters in the early and mid 1980s. The first killed all our ceanothus. Cobaeas and maurandias helped us to cover the bare walls. With our mildly heated glasshouses plus some supporting cold frames we can raise the large majority of the plants that the garden needs, leaving only the occasional tree, roses and bulbs to be obtained elsewhere. Many herbaceous plants can be divided and replanted in one operation, but the ones which are rather slower to get established are taken to the nursery area for a season and grown on in pots. This means that they can be planted out in the summer as soon as the old group has finished flowering. This gives them more time to become established, leading to better results the year after replanting. The old recommendation to replant an herbaceous border entirely every five years can give very uneven results, as some plants take a long time to settle down again. We have found that individual treatment is better, though it does lead to some awkward bits of digging. If several adjacent groups of plants need attention at the same time the opportunity is used for slight adjustments in arrangement to make sure of planting on fresh ground. This is particularly important in the case of roses of all kinds, which can easily suffer. Michaelmas daisies enjoy frequent division and doing this as often as every one or two years will give good quality spikes which are less prone to mildew. On the other hand, plants like acanthus, dictamnus and peonies can go quite happily for twenty years or so without needing attention. Hemerocallis and kniphofia both repay the trouble of lifting one plant from the group a year in advance, dividing it and potting it up to be ready to replace the group the following year. Some plants are renewed from root cuttings, others from stem cuttings or by division, and all annuals and biennials and a few perennial plants are raised from seed.

Sadly, seed catalogues seem to offer an increasing number of mixed, at the expense of single, colours. Because of this it has been necessary to step up our own seed harvesting to ensure we have the varieties which we need to follow our own colour schemes.

Plants new to the garden are usually first grown in the nursery bed for a year. This gives us a chance to learn their capabilities and flowering times and to provide a sample to help select future planting sites, ensuring they will have neighbours that enhance them. Sometimes a new plant may never seem quite right for the garden, in which case it will be discarded. We keep a 'Great Thoughts' book about the garden, adding comments and ideas to it throughout the season. This can be referred to when we are doing winter work. The choice of varieties plays an important part in the performance of the garden, some plants lasting far better in leaf or flower or giving colour at a different time. We need the best possible value from everything. To achieve this we try to grow plants well. We feed and spray them at the right times and stake them so that they display their flowers for as long as possible, even after dead-heading, persuading them to reward us with a second flowering. We prune for future growth as well as present quality, and endeavour to water at timely moments to help later flowering plants to do their best when autumn comes. It is a race to be ready by autumn to start the gardening year again with preparations for the following spring.

The impact of visitors on this garden is profound, affecting not only maintenance but also the visual appearance of the garden itself. A picture in a gallery does not intrinsically change however great the crowd. In a garden, the people are, so to speak, *within* the picture.

During Vita Sackville-West's lifetime the Tower, which contains her writing room, was never open. It was not until after her death in 1962 that the public could go to the top, thus gaining the only over-all view of the garden. Sadly, only a very few years after she died the white pigeons which had burbled peacefully on the ledges moved away, and no amount of bribery with corn would bring them back.

Numbers of visitors have increased vastly. The figure of about 11,000 was recorded in the year of Vita Sackville-West's death, rising to 20,000 by the time the National Trust took over in 1967. This number has increased steadily, until in 1986 we recorded the huge total of almost 140,000 pairs of feet. Some limit on numbers may one day have to be set. Garden-lovers come here from all over the world, the frequency of their visits being influenced by distance. They are knowledgeable, keen and interested, bringing notebooks and pencils to write things down. This makes the legible labelling of plants necessary and rewarding; it is a costly and time consuming task but one which brings the additional benefit of saving enquiries. Litter is on the whole a very minor problem provided that anything dropped is quickly removed as litter tends to breed litter.

The garden had been open daily for many years before the Trust took over. As numbers increased, the morning opening time was made later on weekdays to allow for work to be done. After the total for 1980 shot up to 125,000 it was decided to remain closed on Monday each week, both to rest the garden from wear for a day and to relieve it from the additional pressure of Bank holidays. This also gives a chance for the gardeners to tackle jobs which are difficult to do with people about. Bulky and messy operations like watering, spraying, carting and staking, treating the lawns and using noisy machines are all saved up for Mondays. The closing date of 15 October allows not only for the routine autumn jobs of turf patching and high-ladder pruning to begin but also permits building maintenance to be done before winter weather sets in. Since 1967 the roofs of almost all the buildings have been redone, brickwork repaired, walls repointed and paving relaid.

When the garden was first laid out for family use, it was not necessary to have foundations for the paths. A much-needed programme of relaying the paths was completed in the 1970s, using the original brick and York stone wherever possible, but adding paving in certain places which had not stood up to the increased wear. Land drains were added at this time as the soil is heavy and impervious to water, being sticky when wet and like concrete when dry. Wear on grass can be helped by adequate drainage as turf is soon ruined by a combination of feet and puddles. Wear comes not only in much used entrances but also in what we have come to call 'admiration patches'. These are unpredictable and arise where visitors are attracted to some group or combination of plants which is particularly successful at any one time, due perhaps to the weather or the maturity of the group. In a small turf 'nursery' we raise grass from seed to match the grass in the garden enabling us to have a supply at hand for patching to use when the conditions are right.

All gardens need a constant process of renewal, and Sissinghurst, because of its need to preserve certain elements and accommodate a growing number of visitors, is no exception.

Gardens in Fiction

The Aspern Papers

NANCY-MARY GOODALL

Henry James set this story in Venice. What follows is no more than is
relevant to the garden. Two shy, mysterious American ladies, the
Misses Bordereau, aunt and niece, live in a 'sequestered and dilapidated old palace' on a quiet canal. They possess a garden behind a
high blank wall 'figured over with the patches that please a painter'
and also some jealously-guarded secret papers which the hero intends
to obtain. Seeing 'a few thin trees and the poles of certain rickety
trellises' over the wall, he decides to use the garden as a pretext and
to get himself taken in as a lodger.

He gains admission, meets the niece, 'a long pale person' of uncertain age, sees the garden from an upper window and decides that,
though shabby, it has 'great capabilities'. He tells her he is doing
literary work, *must* have a garden, must be in the open air and cannot
live without flowers. It is already April, but he says: 'I'll put in a
gardener. You shall have the sweetest flowers in Venice'; and that he
would 'undertake that before another month was over the dear old
house would be smothered with flowers.' The ancient aunt is rightly
suspicious but needs money, so she offers him some empty rooms on
the second floor at an extortionate rent. He takes them. Has he not
already said that his tastes and habits are of the simplest, and added
the irritating words: 'I live on flowers'?

Anyone with a knowledge of gardening may feel that Henry James
has prepared a horticultural time-bomb here. His hero will never be
able to supply enough flowers from a neglected garden to smother a
large Venetian palace in the space of one month; indeed, he is already
running two weeks behind schedule when 'Six weeks later, towards
the middle of June' – so his first visit must have been at the end of
April – he has furnished his rooms, moved in with a manservant and
started to spend part of every day in the garden. The ladies will have
nothing to do with him, he never sees them, but he had told himself
that he would 'succeed by big nosegays. I would batter the old
women with lilies – I would bombard their citadel with roses. Their

door would have to yield to the pressure when a mound of fragrance should be heaped against it' – a tall order for any gardener. We sit back to watch him come unstuck.

Let us try to follow the timing. As soon as his rooms are arranged – and as this involves engaging his servant as well as the ordering and delivering of a boat-load of furniture, it must have taken at least a week – he 'surveyed the place with a clever expert and made terms' for having the garden put in order. But the 'Venetian capacity for dawdling is of the largest, and for a good many days unlimited litter was all my gardener had to show for his ministrations. There was a great digging of holes and carting about of earth.' After a while our schemer grows so impatient that he thinks of buying flowers – but he suspects the ladies will be watching through their shutters and contains himself. 'Finally, though the delay was long,' he 'perceived some appearances of bloom', he had 'had an arbour arranged' and, in it, worked and 'waited serenely enough till they multiplied.'

By July he was no nearer to obtaining the papers or even seeing the ladies, but as he sat in his arbour 'the bees droned in the flowers', though which he does not say, and he was spending the hot evenings floating in his gondola or at Florian's eating ices. Then, one evening, he comes back early, enters the garden's 'fragrant darkness' and finds the younger Miss Bordereau 'seated in one of the bowers'.

Now comes the bombshell, and it is not for the hero but for us. He says: 'I asked her why, since she thought the garden nice, she had never thanked me . . . for the flowers I had been sending up in such quantities for *the previous three weeks* . . . there had been *a daily armful*' and he would have liked 'a word of recognition'.

Gardeners may well ask how this was possible. Even if work on the garden started immediately, although this seems unlikely among 'Venetians with their capacity for dawdling', if, say, the 'clever expert' was able to find an unemployed gardener by the middle of May, the process of taming a wilderness can take weeks, and we have been told that the garden was 'a tangled enclosure' and had been 'brutally neglected'. We are not told how big it was nor what plants had survived from earlier days, although Miss Bordereau had said 'we've a few but they're very common', while the reference to rickety trellises leads us to suppose that there were at least some climbing roses and jasmine. There was only one gardener to clear the 'unlimited litter', dig his holes, 'cart earth about' and get his plants established – and he may also have had to 'arrange' the arbour. How on earth had he done it?

With his orders to provide 'big nosegays' we can imagine him, by the end of May, working from dawn to dusk, feverishly preparing the soil and sowing annuals – work that should have been done in March or April – and planting anything he could find that would produce flowers suitable for cutting. What would he choose? 'Digging holes' suggests that he put in a number of shrubs, but which? So many shrubs that are useful for flower arranging have finished blooming by July: lilacs, philadelphus and so on, likewise wisteria and blossoming trees – and few shrubs produce much in their first year anyway. Would oleanders or hibiscus have fitted the bill? The irises which grow so well in Italy would also be over, with the peonies, oriental poppies, lupins and the rest of the first flush of perennial flowers. He must have relied heavily on whatever was supplied in pots by the local shops and stalls or perhaps by nurserymen in the Veneto. But we are speaking of late Victorian Venice, not England, today. Did they sell bedding plants in boxes? Could he, at this late stage, obtain sweet peas, carnations, stocks, lilies, potted or boxed and ready to flower? In England sweet peas should be sown, and gladiolus corms planted, in March. Would these be available in Venice as late as May? Sweet Williams should have been planted the previous autumn, and are hardly Italian flowers.

Classic Italian gardens are not known for masses of flower colour but for architectural design, topiary, stonework, ironwork and water, the contrast of light and shade, for cypresses, yew, bay, box and marble, and while Venice has many pots and window boxes these are mainly of small plants, trailing geraniums, marigolds and the like. Such colour as there is in Italian gardens seems, at least in these days, to come, apart from roses, mainly from such things as azaleas, fuchsias, geraniums, Paris daisies and petunias grown in containers that are set out at strategic points as they come into bloom. You could not pick armfuls of flowers from them, and if you did they would take weeks to recover, while a gladiolus or lily, having bloomed, has shot its bolt and can be picked no more.

More is to come. After a talk with the younger lady during which they 'wandered two or three times round the garden' he dares to mention the all-important papers. She takes fright, hurries away and does not reappear, and after four or five days he tells the gardener 'to stop the floral tributes'. The cutting of armfuls of flowers has lasted for very nearly *four weeks*. In a later scene, between our hero and the ancient aunt, she thanks him for the flowers: 'You sent so many . . .' 'I suppose you know you could sell them – the ones you don't use.' And he replies: 'My gardener disposes of them and I ask no questions.' It is quite a jolt to realise that Henry James saw flowers as something to be used or disposed of, and that he imagined that once a supply of flowers – the only ones he names are lilies and roses – has been turned on, it flows like a fountain that cannot be turned off. His hero even turns to the younger Miss Bordereau and invites her to 'come into the garden and pick them, come as often as you like: come every day. The flowers are all for you.'

Even if the garden were fairly large – and he says at one point that he 'wandered about the alleys smoking cigar after cigar' – it must have been remarkable. This is a famous novel, written by a master, and the plot takes many fascinating turns: but we are amazed to find the niece still picking flowers weeks later, her hands full of 'admirable roses'. Surely most of the roses grown at that time bloomed in June and early July only. What repeat-flowering roses would we have found in Venice then?

Could it have been done? Or, and I may well be wrong, are there only two possible explanations: either that gardener, whose name is never mentioned, and who was never given a word of praise, was an unsung hero of horticultural literature, a genius who given an acre in England could have supplied Covent Garden; or – dare I suggest it? – fear it may be the case – Henry James, that legend, that great wordsmith and story teller, was as horrid as his hero who, in all the long days that the novel records, never touches a flower, never lends a hand by so much as dead-heading one rose, and, like his hero who pretended to love flowers so much but knew only two by name, was a townee and a beast, and unworthy to write about flowers?

Origins of the Ornamental Herb Garden

ALLEN PATERSON

It is, I suppose, inevitable that in attributing the origins of any art form or cultural development, credit should be concentrated, at least initially, upon a few well known names. In gardens, it is Brown and Repton, Robinson and Jekyll.

But deeper inquiry begins to show that Brown did not invent the *jardin anglais*, nor Jekyll, the herbaceous border. Such significant figures, one often finds, are apt to be less seminal than central. They were perhaps paradigms, they personified their time, in their time and, for those that came after, their style evokes it. It does no harm either if, for posterity's memory (apt to be fickle anyway), something acts as an *aide-mémoire*. 'Capability' has been an unforgettable nick-name, while to have your old boots painted by Sir William Nicholson makes a statement which mere professional expertise cannot.

As a contribution to garden history it is interesting to search out the roots of a current craze, the herb-garden, without which no garden today seems complete. Clearly it speaks, or its plants do, to the contemporary mind. But to what part of it? Herbs are so linked in our literature with times past that it is inevitable we should look to those more or less distant periods for clues which remain valid today.

It can be reasonably asserted that cultivation of herbs goes back to man's earliest horticultural activities, as a convenient addition to, and development from, collecting simples from the wild. Such beginnings are hardly garden-making – though perhaps not far removed from the little plot outside a lot of kitchen doors today.

Initially there were no distinct 'herb gardens' as separate from any other type of garden: all gardens were 'herb gardens'. All gardens grew medicinal and culinary herbs with, perhaps, ornamental herbs preserved for their abnormality, such as those with striped leaves.

But actual garden plans available to us from the distant past are lamentably few. There are the Pharoahs' tomb paintings and papyri which elegantly depict gardens in the somewhat confusing convention of two and a half millennia ago where every aspect faces the viewer. Palms are clearly differentiated from cypresses but little else is offered to the plantsman. Later, the younger Pliny's literary powers and love for his gardens have made it possible to draw conjectural plans and make elaborate models of such a Roman patrician's villa in the first century AD. Pliny's use of formal hedging is well supported by the recent and continuing excavation and recreation *in situ* of the third-century contemporary Roman palaces at Fishbourne in Sussex and at Piazza Armorina in central Sicily. Earlier excavations at Pompeii and Herculaneum give further details of the smaller courtyards within the villa complex, or of Roman town gardens. Our ideas are greatly helped by surviving wall-paintings depicting such gardens in their heyday. These seem to offer elements of the expected 'traditional' herb garden. The area is relatively small in size, walled or hedged around; it has a regular arrangement of beds, sometimes raised, sometimes sunken; arbours or bowers are covered with climbers.

But conscious arrangements of plants elude us. It is clear from lists compiled by Theophrastus, Dioscorides and others that given collections of herbs were grown. Moving well into the Christian era, it is also demonstrated by the list of plants which Charlemagne ordered should be grown in the imperial lands by every city of the Holy Roman Empire. The decree dates from his coronation in AD 800 and names eighty-nine plants.

In *Medieval Gardens*, John Harvey describes the Charlemagne list and discusses its origin. Throughout his book, Mr Harvey is at pains to trace the threads of ornamental gardening in his period to the mid-sixteenth century and finds it significant that the two plants which head the decree are ornamentals: the lily (*Lilium candidum*) and roses (in the plural). Neither were of great economic importance at the time but were presumably important in the symbolism of the Church and used in its decoration, for although the Empire's title was later to fall into disrepute, at this stage it was both Holy and Blessed by Rome, though centred on Aachen.

This significant list can be divided into categories. There are nuts, including almond and walnut; fruits, including quince, medlar and figs; salads, such as parsley and alexanders; pot herbs, including mint and savory while 'physical' herbs have savory, fennel, poppy and rosemary, etc. While this is a perfectly logical grouping it is but one of several arrangements possible; *all* the plants here picked out from the divisions have or had at the time clear herbal uses,

including even the lily and the roses. It seems just as probable that
the list, drawn up by a monk, brought together plants which, while
not yet crops in the agricultural sense, were produced on a garden
scale and were of use. In other words they are herbs in the full sense
of the word; that many were and are considered beautiful as well is
the sort of bounty that churchmen in that age would have expected.
This, in a less religious age, we are delighted to discover and rashly
presume to be fortuitous. But again, how they were to be grown and
arranged at that time is not discussed.

No search for early herb gardens could possibly omit the Church,
inheritor and preserver of classical learning as well as, in erratic
periods of liberalism and enlightenment, the initiator of new learning.
Ironically, for two or three hundred years each side of the millennium
the two great rival religions of Christianity and Islam were virtually
the only sources of Western garden making.

Islam had two European footholds, in Sicily and, much more
importantly in Spain where an enviable culture was vigorously
pursued. Its effect upon northern Europe was greater than it is
generally given credit for. Equally, the compressing eye of history is
apt to forget that much of Spain was Moorish, and Islamic for 600
years – as if Britain had been French since the Renaissance. How
different the course of garden design would have been in that case!

Spain, Islamic then, with its filigree threads of connection with
the distant East, insinuates into the thoughts, ideas and innovations
of gardens as much as in other areas of learning. Many of the greatest
Moorish gardens in Spain at, for example, Medina Azahara near
Córdoba and at Toledo no longer exist, while those of the well-
known Alhambra and the Generalife at Granada are restorations.
Yet their architectural surroundings remain intact and sufficiently
magnificent for us to gain a clear idea of what there must have been.
Courtyards, their ground plans patterned Persian-carpet-like with
geometric flower beds, pools and water-courses, were meant not
only to be enjoyed from within, but to be looked down upon from
above. Surrounding windows and, frequently a central pavilion,
offered various points of view. Though grander, in essence such a
plan is not greatly different from patrician medieval gardens throughout Europe.

Both John Harvey and Teresa McLean, in her *Medieval English
Gardens*, refer to, and describe from, the somewhat thin records

5 *Iris Biflora.*
Twice-flouring Floure de-luce.

available – tantalizing glimpses through the mists of time – the enclosed royal herb gardens in Britain as at Windsor Castle and Clarendon Palace, near Salisbury, Wiltshire, in the thirteenth century. At Clarendon the herb garden made for Henry III's Queen is noted as being paved in 1247.

But perhaps it is generally not to the gardens of the great we should look for herb gardens except that through dynastic inter-marriage, royal gifts and interchange of courtiers and men of letters they can be considered as entrepôts with styles, fashions and know-ledge as the commodities traded.

To return to the Christian Church might be more profitable, if only because, before the birth of printed books, this is where almost all literature had its base and where for centuries records were relatively safe from pillage and loss.

A remarkable survival exists in the well-documented plan pre-served at the Abbey of St Gall in Switzerland, near Lake Constance. This dates, amazingly, from around AD 820–830 soon after the death of Charlemagne and, as Teresa McLean says: 'It is a diagram of an ideal, not of an actual foundation and it amounts to an extended, Christianized, edition of a Roman villa estate with a wealth of gardens.' The plan shows in great detail how a major religious institution should be laid out according to the Rule of St Benedict as a self-contained and self-sufficient community. It thus has farms, orchards and gardens. Next to the physician's house is a square infirmary garden. Each of the sixteen beds is labelled with its herbal occupant. Mr Harvey also discusses St Gall and lists the plants as 'Kidney bean', savory, rose, horse mint, cumin, lovage, fennel, tansy or costmary, lily, sage, rue, flag iris, pennyroyal, fenugreek, mint and rosemary. Inevitably however, translation leaves some room for discussion.

Some way off is the kitchen garden whose eighteen narrow beds again in two ranks, hold onions, garlic, leeks, shallots, celery, parsley, coriander, chervil, dill, lettuce, poppy, savory, radishes, parsnip, carrot, colewort (cabbage), beet and black cumin (*Nigella sativa*). With only a few exceptions the plants grown in the kitchen garden can equally be considered 'herbs' as those in the infirmarian's garden. Such difference of site seems to indicate the main emphasis of use – not necessarily any exclusiveness of, say, rosemary to the infirmary or poppy to the kitchen.

The quantity of herbs grown in medieval times frequently seems to move them into the category of field crops. For the Royal Palace at Rotherhithe in 1354, 14 lbs. of parsley seed (cost 5s 10d), 12 lbs. onion seed, and 72 lbs. of hyssop are recorded. Twenty years later the Bishop of Ely's garden in Holborn had 32 lbs. of parsley seed, and 8 lbs. each of hyssop, savory and leek seed. Such stores could, of course, have been for culinary flavouring, rather than subsequent growing. For, to quote Teresa McLean again: 'Herbs had a culinary importance that is hard for us to grasp because we have been able to supplement our starch with a whole range of different foods and tastes. They are no longer the redemptive kitchen force they once were.' However, as modern food becomes more and more homogenized, that necessary 'redemptive force' takes on a new importance today.

The formal plans of St Gall are not vastly different in essence from kitchen gardens today, though closer to the large establishments of great country houses of a century ago when, similarly, a whole community was fed from them. Nor do they differ greatly from the lay-out of the early physic or botanic gardens. They are all, ultimately, gardens cultivated for their produce, but this does not mean that aesthetic considerations are absent, merely that they are secondary to the main aim.

The search for early productive herb garden patterns, then, begins literally to take shape: enclosed areas holding a pattern of regular beds in which plants are grown that are accepted as herbs. But continued search for gardens with more overtly ornamental aims throughout the Middle Ages is necessary. Verbal descriptions, then as now, are open to various interpretations but fortunately pictures show either a type of garden which exists or one which is considered to be an ideal of the 15th century.

Paintings by Jan van Eyck, Roger van der Weyden and Hans Memling, with books of hours and illustrated calendars by lesser masters, often show gardens as background to the main theme. The subjects, whether religious or depicting contemporary life as led by royalty and nobles, are invariably staged in a castle or palace. Still the gardens are the ageless geometric plots – sometimes raised, sometimes flat and set in grass or gravel.

On other occasions the enclosed gardens are as devoid of design as the most banal suburban front garden today – a central bit of grass with a narrow flower border all round, though the more imaginative will train roses or other climbers on the surrounding fence. The charm, the beauty, comes from the mastery of the painting and the depiction of elegantly caparisoned people, dead and dust these 500 years. Horticulturally, the one aspect of delight is the fact that their gardeners had no access to selective herbicides and that the grass is studded with daisies, wild strawberries and dandelions. Such 'flowery meads' are today being again encouraged under the aegis of meadow gardening: this is both sensible and delightful but not of particular relevance to the herb garden search, though again, as if to emphasise the all-encompassing use of plants all three of those had medicinal uses.

While, in most cases, northern gardens offer little design to excite us there is no doubt – if the paintings can be taken as guides – that there was strong interest and appreciation in the simple beauty of wild plants. Here is our real connection with times past, here the real continuum, because there is never a plant depicted in plot or flowery mead that is not a herb, medicinal or culinary, flavouring or food. Equally we can relate to them because with few exceptions those plants have not been changed over the intervening centuries. Only parsley has been accorded much Western plant breeders' attention; only curly parsley would give a reincarnated medieval any problems with identification. Fortunately his nose and his taste buds would tell him. 'French' parsley remains unchanged. (It is amusing to note that the traditional garnishing role of parsley in Britain to emphasise the freshness of meat on butcher's slabs is assured: the parsley is often now plastic!)

If early northern gardens offer plants without design, those in the south tend to the opposite: design without plants. Indications of the *giardino segreto* show vine-covered arbours and walks but the emphasis seems to lie, not surprisingly, with the need for shade from a hot southern sun. Native evergreens – bay, cypress and pines – are used for this same reason but also as architectural components in the design, clipped into buttressed hedges, cones and obelisks. Where there are 'flower'-beds their outlines are frequently etched, equally architecturally, with low clipped shrubs and the spaces filled similarly with plants of contrasting texture. In other words they are elementary knot gardens, patterns on the ground.

However, Georgina Masson's description of a 'rare jewel, a

13 *Hyacinthus Peruanus.*
Hyacinth of Peru.

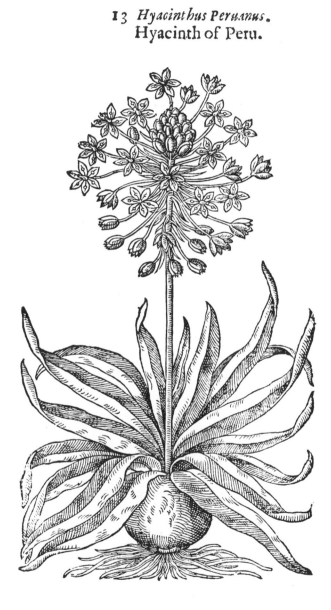

Tuscan garden of the second half of the sixteenth century preserved in all its original charm' moves us on. There are two small, enclosed gardens at the Villa Capponi either of which could be a pattern for an ideal herb garden today, leaving the choice of plants, as always, to the current owner. 'At the Western end of the terrace [is] the little walled garden room ... with its flower-filled box parterres, gurgling wall fountain and battlemented walls festooned with roses and wisteria. This little room is probably the most enchanting example of the Italian *giardino segreto* in existence. The hot sun beating down into this enclosed space distils a veritable bouquet of flower scents mingled with the spicy tang of the cypresses, whose dark spires frame the rolling panorama of the Tuscan landscape.'

There is no doubt that this is the pattern we have been seeking: enclosure, warmth, aromatic scents, water. Just as the English landscape school turned to idealized views of the Roman *campagna* for inspiration to embellish great estates in the eighteenth century, so for herb gardens we look similarly south, coveting a kind climate which encourages civilized enjoyment of life outdoors and makes possible the cultivation of a wide range of lovely plants. The English garden designer, Cecil Pinsent, worked on the lower terraces at the Villa Capponi in 1930, but there is no reason to believe he changed the upper garden.

There is a further strong strand to the herb garden web, that contributed by emergent science and medicine of the High Renaissance. Close to the Villa Capponi, and only twenty years earlier, were set up the first physic or botanic gardens. Those of Pisa and Padua date from the 1540s, supporting schools of medicine at their respective universities, are the first in a famous line which continues to the present.

It was clearly desirable for practitioners of medicine when it was based almost entirely upon plants, to be able to recognize plant species used to treat the sick. The difference in effect on a patient, for instance, between woody nightshade, black nightshade and deadly nightshade was then, as now, dramatic and only too permanent. Illustrations in the herbals generally available were often poor and of little help.

The botanic garden pattern quickly spread throughout Europe – to Florence, Bologna, Montpellier, Leiden, Paris and, in 1621, to Oxford. The Oxford Physic Garden (it changed officially to Botanic

Garden only in the nineteenth century) was founded by Henry Danvers, Earl of Danby. For, 'He, being minded to become a benefactor to the University, determined to begin and finish a place where learning, especially the faculty of medicine might be improved'. It is significant, as an indication of how such a garden should be regarded, that Dr Clayton, the first Regius Professor of Physic at Oxford, commented on 'the furnishing and enriching whereof with all useful and delightful plants'.

England's second such establishment was the Chelsea Physic Garden, founded by the Society of Apothecaries in 1673. Though walled round less grandly and in red brick rather than the golden stone of Oxford, in the eighteenth century it became far more central to the development of gardens and gardening. From 1722 to 1771, it was in the care of Philip Miller, whom Linnaeus referred to as *Hortulanorum Princeps*, and who, as Peter Collinson said, 'raised the reputation of the Chelsea garden so much that it excels all the gardens of Europe for its amazing variety of plants of all orders and classes and from all climates as I survey with wonder and delight this 19th July, 1764'. Miller's great folio, *Gardeners' Dictionary*, whose first edition came out in 1732, and his *Gardeners' Calendar* (1734) describes plants and their cultivation in minute details and in entirely practical terms.

Because the Physic Garden remained in the care of the apothecaries until 1899 and has changed little in this present century, it can be used as a typical example of such early gardens whose *raison d'etre* was, as their very names make clear, the growing of herbs. Yet it is equally important to remember firstly that the word 'herb' was a broadly inclusive one and that the terms 'physic garden' and 'botanic garden' were synonymous. (At Chelsea an existing stone in the east wall is dated 1684 and reads *Giardino Botanico Chelsieano*.) There is also in existence a fine plan of the physic garden dated 30th March, 1753. Its elegantly written legend declares it to be 'An accurate survey of the Botanic Gardens at Chelsea, the Whole carefully Survey'd and Delineated by John Haynes'. The small print adds 'Price 2/6d plain and 5s colour'd'.

From Haynes's map it is clear that Philip Miller's Chelsea Physic Garden was a working garden laid out to facilitate research and observation: for use but also for delight, as the writings of many visitors show, from John Evelyn onwards. Two-thirds of the $3\frac{1}{2}$

acres is down to long narrow beds to facilitate cultivation and ease
of approach. Two 'wilderness' areas hold woody plants and those
which could not satisfactorily be classified. A large central pool and
the surrounding high walls offer further diversity of habitat and in a
strip of ground between the river and the south wall is a nursery.

Early plates of the circular walled garden at Pisa show central
ornamental knots, but at Chelsea, though a few urns stand outside,
the ornament and the delight comes from its multiplicity of plants,
old and new, common and used for centuries, rare and with unknown potential. It seems to exemplify, almost 200 years in advance,
Vita Sackville-West's dictum that gardens should have the maximum
formality of design with maximum informality of planting. The
succeeding editions of the *Gardeners' Dictionary* indicate Philip
Miller's broad and developing interests in the diversity of plants
that might be legitimately grown in such a garden, and how they
might best be cultivated.

Chelsea, then, through its books and its plans – and the fact it
is still there with much of its lay-out and even more of its atmosphere
intact – offers much to the search for herb garden style. On the site
of Miller's 'place where the physical plants are grown alphabetically'
(as Haynes's legend asserts) the present herb garden, formed around
an enormous bay tree, groups plants according to their uses –
culinary herbs, historic medicinals, current drug plants, dye-plants,
species used in perfumery and so on. It forms a useful pattern for a
herb garden of today where the role is predominantly educational
yet where, in a highly concentrated space, the sensual effect is also
of importance. There is a nice link with the distant past: a record
exists (quoted by Mavis Batey: in *Oxford Gardens*) at Lincoln College,
Oxford, of a payment 500 years ago 'for mendying the seat under the
bay-tree'. The same could be needed today at Chelsea.

In the hub of the 18th century the Physic Garden held what was
probably the most comprehensive collection of plants in the western
world. But other 'curious gardeners', in the complimentary eighteenth century sense of the phrase, in that period had fine and
fascinating collections – Peter Collinson, quoted above; Dr Fothergill; the Princess Augusta, mother of King George III; Lord Petre.
Royalty, aristocrats, rich merchants with contacts in the colonies,
all were interested in what new plants those colonies could offer.
Several of these people, as well as Philip Miller himself, com-

missioned John and William Bartram in America to scour the east
coast for new species and the Bartrams can be considered the first
professional plant collectors. Though their own garden in Philadelphia was described (as might some nurseries today) as 'not well
laid out' and 'jumbled about in heaps', contemporary American
ornamental gardens show a continued use of formal patterns.

Back in Britain, a garden using arrangements of the Bartram
introductions is still something of a mystery. As we all know, in
general terms 17th century formal patterns banished flowering
plants because of their unfortunate but natural propensity to grow
irregularly, and the new Brownian style which brought the park to
the very walls of the house had equally little place for them. Flowers
joined vegetables and herbs in walled kitchen gardens out of sight
of the naturalistic, if not natural, landscapes seen from the house.
Here the pattern of planting within the walls followed the eminently
successful pattern of the botanic or physic gardens, where con-
venience of cultivation and close observation were combined.

It is perhaps surprising that the craze for medieval models in
architectural forms – the lighthearted Gothick of Walpole's eighteenth-century Strawberry Hill and the heavily serious ecclesiastical
Gothic of the nineteenth century – did not attempt to put buildings
into a suitably 'period' context, beyond a bit of 1850s topiary.

However, there are well documented exceptions to the fashionable flowerlessness of the 18th century. Those charming west-country
pictures of Thomas Robins show, both in the views and their frames,
the obvious pleasure taken in ornamental plants. Even better
documented and, in part, existing still is 'Mason's Garden' at
Nuneham Courtenay in Oxfordshire. Created by Lord Nuneham
(afterwards Earl Harcourt) who had temporary anti-establishment
tendencies, it was a product of literary associations and late 18th
century sensibility. The Chaucerian *Romaunt of the Rose*, Ariosto's
Orlando Furioso, Marvell and Milton were evoked, combined with a
current cult of the perfection of Nature. Jean-Jacques Rousseau who
actually stayed at the invitation of the Earl in the village, became
the presiding deity. Paul Sandby's charming watercolour of the
scene shows a floral miscellany of hollyhocks, lilies, sunflowers
edged with clipped santolina, box or teucrium, while honeysuckles
and roses clamber about the trees. It is all, in one sense, a full century
before its time and Nuneham can be seen to provide a continuity of

growing old-fashioned flowers and herbs as ornamental plants in a sophisticated planned garden. It is a link between John Parkinson and William Robinson, and halfway between them in time.

Thus, in the context of herbs and herb gardens, we see again that the thread of continuity is in the individual plants which, virtually untouched by the plant breeders, would be immediately recognized by reincarnations of gardeners from all times past. Throughout the ages they have been grown by peer and peasant alike, though in situations as different as the extensive stillroom of the great house is from the humble cottage kitchen, where they were subsequently put to use.

It was of course, this 'humble cottage garden' which has been credited with providing the spur to a return to flower gardening, via two of those easily remembered names mentioned above.

William Robinson's *The English Flower Garden* was first published in 1883: edition followed edition at a rate to be the envy of every garden writer before and since. As a fierce diatribe against what Robinson saw as the artificiality of Victorian carpet bedding and clipped shrubberies, *The English Flower Garden* gained the adherence of Gertrude Jekyll, whose own numerous books kept up the crusade. It is easy both to over-simplify and to exaggerate the Robinson-Jekyll axis: the importance here lies in two particular facets. These are the acceptance of plants, particularly herbaceous plants, as things of beauty in their own right, and in their use in complementary associations.

While Victorian architectural historicity and mock medievalism made little attempt to plant gardens in period, the same was not true of Miss Jekyll's gardens. But the model was a very different one. This was the discovery of an aesthetically acceptable vernacular tradition in the fifteenth to seventeenth century yeoman's house of south-east England, often fallen by disrepair to the category of cottage by the late nineteenth century. Yet it often retained a bit of ground in which a tumble of flowers and vegetables, fruit bushes and apple trees grew in happy profusion. Seen through the eyes of artists such as Helen Allingham and Myles Birkett Foster the 1880s became the golden age of the cottage garden in which pretty pinafored children smile sweetly from a bower of hollyhocks and honeysuckle.

With Edwin Lutyens as architectural collaborator, Gertrude

‡ **14** *Colchicum variegatum Chienſe.*
Checquered Mede Saffron of Chio.

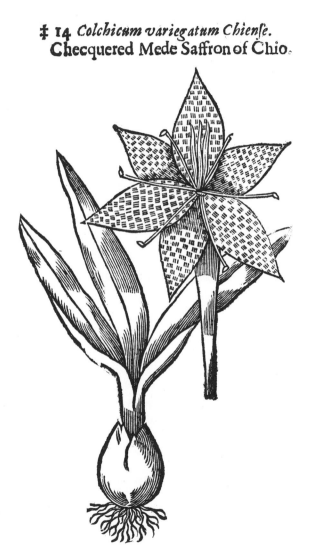

Jekyll turned this picturesque idyll into a highly sophisticated reality. The vernacular motifs of old Sussex farmhouses were adapted to produce houses which today we would consider rather grand, the miscellany of plants each side of the garden path became intricately planned borders, equally so. But in spite of their Edwardian grandeur, the simple, uncontrived, old-fashioned flowers – Miller's plants, Parkinson's plants, Gerard's plants – were re-established in the planned ornamental garden. That so many of them are herbs, in the original broad sense, makes this sequence of events important in tracing the trends towards today's renewed interest in them.

As always, it is easy to exaggerate the effect of certain individuals upon any trends in art and it would be a mistake to see Miss Jekyll and her work as an act of spontaneous creation, especially during the lifetime of Charles Darwin. In fact she was following lines set in the mid-nineteenth century by Ruskin and William Morris. We must remember that Miss Jekyll, who in many ways seems so close to us in time, was born in 1843: the Victorian age had a further fifty-eight years to run. The idealism of the Pre-Raphaelites led to William Morris's Arts and Crafts Movement with its emphasis on traditional workmanship and traditional methods. Certainly this is a part of Miss Jekyll's own Munstead Wood to which she refers again and again.

While, through her, it is possible to talk of a 'Surrey School' of vernacular architecture and gardening to match, it is equally valid to look at a post-William Morris 'Cotswold School'. Again, it is easy to forget how many of today's smart and tidy, visited-to-death Cotswold villages were but a tumble of tired cottages at the turn of this century. Even many of their lovely manor houses were in sad decline. William Morris founded the Society for the Preservation of Ancient Buildings in 1877. Neglect through periods of agricultural depression had brought fine buildings to the brink of ruin but at the same time it had also preserved them, and the plants in their gardens, until, just in time, they could be appreciated, rescued and restored.

In the context of the Arts and Crafts Movement many herbs became popular. Some practitioners returned to plant-based dyes for their 'aesthetic' clothes: more lasting have been the motifs of William Morris prints and wallpapers in which marigold, honeysuckle, corncockle and chrysanthemums continue to cover acres of wall and sofa throughout the western world.

But where are the herb gardens themselves? Although the late 19th century interest in 'old-fashioned' plants was in place (a Parkinson Society even flourished briefly in the 1890s) this form of 'old-fashioned' garden did not yet exist. For still, at the turn of the century, no ornamental herb garden had yet been planned and planted. Nor, it must be remembered, did any such garden remain from an earlier time. The style, if indeed there had ever been one, was apparently lost.

However, all was in place for its creation, if not re-creation: plant-lore had been researched in the herbals, the plants themselves had been rescued from cottage gardens and, in 1901, came Reginald Blomfield's *The Formal Garden* which offered thoughts on suitable architectural frames. Some owners of truly historic houses made efforts to put them into a setting which would emphasize their period: the analogy with re-setting historic jewels for the same reason is inescapable. The example of Broughton Castle in Oxfordshire has all the elements of the 'old-fashioned' garden. Developed by Lady Gordon Lennox in the early 1900s, it had borders of herbaceous plants, topiary shapes with even a sun dial cut in yew and, at last, a separate herb garden. If there is any doubt of this latter, long-sought-for fact, it is utterly dispelled at the garden's entrance, where spelled out in santolina are the words 'Ye olde herb garden'.

It is perhaps therefore surprising that Gertrude Jekyll, the most influential garden designer of the last 100 years, offers relatively little to the specific herb garden scene. A sketch does exist for a little herb patch for Knebworth House in Hertfordshire in 1907, showing a quincunx of circular beds with a few permanent herbs in each. Clearly the effect, with its lavender, sage, southernwood and roses, but no annuals or biennials, was not intended as a comprehensive herb garden. It was ten years before Miss Jekyll produced another herb garden design. This was in 1917 for Barrington Court, Somerset, and here the 'typical' herb garden at last appears. An area 100 feet by 30 feet is enclosed by 10-foot high walls on three sides and a yew hedge on the fourth. Within, are eight rectangular beds, each 14 by 8 feet (an area the size of many complete herb gardens today). The range of plants is small but they are used on the scale that the monumentality of the garden demands. Thus one bed requires a dozen feet of 'chervil sown, 18 thyme, 3 lavender, 18 pink pinks'. Other beds also combine a couple of culinary herbs with cottage garden flowers such as mignonette, *Campanula persicifolia* and white phlox. Roses ('Zéphirine Drouhin' and 'Jersey Beauty'), jasmine and honeysuckle drape the walls. The small number of species used reflects the fact that there is so much else at Barrington Court that here the simple statement of a scented summer spot is all that is required. That some of the plants are in fact culinary herbs is rather by the way.

For Boveridge Park, Cranborne in Dorset, a smaller plan exists dated March, 1920, and for Burningfold, Dunsfold, Surrey (December 1923) a design which is clearly for kitchen use. Here, a 40 by 20 foot plot has lavender hedges on two sides. There are two clumps of fennel, a long line of parsley, 10 feet of tarragon: 14 herbs in all. No indications are made of successional planting and it seems that Miss Jekyll made no further essays into this specific field. It has been left to her successors to do so.

Despite her lack of herb garden designs, Miss Jekyll's influence did move into herb garden design. Writing in *The Education of a Gardener* (1962), Russell Page asserts: 'I can think of few English gardens made in the last fifty years which do not bear the mark of [Gertrude Jekyll's] teaching, whether in the arrangement of a flower border [or] the almost habitual association of certain plants . . .' These, to provide scent, for grey foliage, for their flowers are in so many of her 'garden rooms'. The connection with that ideal 16th century garden at the Villa Capponi again comes to mind.

It now becomes possible to see the 1920s and 1930s as the period when the growing and cultivation of herbs began to develop as an interest in its own right. But not only in Britain. Indeed, as has been indicated, Jekyllian herb gardens were somewhat half-hearted. An infusion of new blood was needed and it came – or came back – from America. Just as aspects of New England vocabulary and figures of speech maintain the language of the seventeenth-century founding fathers, so there are remnants, sufficiently clear for authentic re-creations to be possible, of herbal use in garden and kitchen, in stillroom and in chemist's shop. Over three centuries the settlers had brought seeds and plants from the 'old country' (not by any means only the British Isles), they adopted native plants used by the native peoples and in doing so revitalized a herbal tradition which in industrial northern Europe was in decline. The distance and

5 *Primula veris minor.*
Field Primrose.

isolation of the new country necessarily maintained it. The Puritan ethic which lay at the root of much early colonial thought was led to reassert itself, as industrialization and 'civilizing influences' softened the pioneer spirit. Religious sects seeking again the simple life sprang up, tending to move westward but, wherever they settled, a pattern of subsistence farming became established at least at first. It meant a return to plants of the garden and of the wild woods and fields; thus to herbs.

Such a sect were the Shakers which grew from tiny beginnings when Ann Lee and eight followers embarked at Liverpool in May 1774 for New York, first settling in Albany, New York State. By the mid-1800s the sect's members numbered six or seven thousand. Because of their avowed intent to keep separate where possible from 'the world' they had to be relatively self-sufficient and this self-sufficiency extended quickly to medicine. Soon the sale of home medicaments from introduced or local plant species developed into the Shakers' predominant method of support. They became one of America's main suppliers of medicinal and culinary herbs and soon expanded to the production of seeds as well. A vast range of plants were collected in the wild, later grown for trial and then as crops. What had been garden was now farm but from the beginning a separate ornamental aesthetic garden was unknown. It would have been considered unnecessary and at variance with the Shaker ethic. However, it is valid to emphasize the American Shaker experience because it carries into our own century the sequentially archetypal herbal tradition and brings together its threefold strands of collection in the wild, the setting up of botanic or physic gardens for study and the cultivation of the rarer plants, and field-scale herb production. It does so in a country where pre-18th century garden patterns still existed and which were ripe for rediscovery. This American contribution can be seen to have influenced a younger contemporary of Miss Jekyll's and who in turn has been credited with the invention of the modern herb garden. Like those other attributions mentioned above, it is an exaggeration but not an untruth.

Between the wars Eleanour Sinclair Rohde (1881–1950) moved herb growing into a new genre of ornamental herb gardening. Her books, *Old English Gardening Books* (1924), *Old English Herbals* (1922), and *Rose Recipes* (1936) treated these then somewhat esoteric subjects in a popular but serious style for the general reader. Her thoughts on the practical use of plants are especially clear in *Gardens of Delight* (1934), where historic herbs are often put to new and visually attractive uses. Many of these ideas have become a part of the common currency of gardens in the succeeding half-century. So it is surprising today to read in Miss Rohde's *The Story of the Garden* (1932), discussing John Parkinson's seventeenth-century contribution to the evolution of gardening, that:

> From his garden of pleasant flowers he leads us to the kitchen garden, full not only of 'vegetables' as we understand the term, of strawberries, cucumbers and pompions, but also a vast number of herbs in daily use, many of them never seen in modern gardens. Besides the familiar thyme, balm, savory, mint, marjoram, and parsley, there are clary, costmary, pennyroyal, fennel, borage, bugloss, tansy, burnet, blessed thistle, marigolds, arrach, rue, patience, angelica, chives, sorrel, smallage, bloodwort, dill, chervil, succory, purslane, tarragon, rocket, mustard, skirrets, rampion, liquorice and caraway.

Now, fifty years later, the majority of these are back into commerce and the general garden scene.

The final chapter in *The Story of the Garden* was written by a founder member of the Garden Club of America, Mrs Frances King: it has a short passage highly significant in this search for the original of the ornamental herb garden. The Mission House in Stockbridge, Massachusetts, was built in 1739 (pre-dating the Shakers by half a century) and was the first house of substance in that town. It was restored as a museum in the 1920s and its garden laid out to match. Mrs King describes the Mission House garden:

> It is close to the street and near one side of the lot. Between it and the highway is a small fenced-in herb garden. Behind the house is a little yard with wood-shed, well and well-sweep and grape-arbour . . . Between street, house and barn is the old-fashioned garden with its straight walk lined with fruit trees and flower borders, its vegetable plots, bush fruits, and casual rose bushes and beds of striped grass.
>
> This garden of the Mission House is not a restoration but a recreating of an early American garden as it was supposed to exist. We have no actual authorities to turn to for such gardens, but must build on what we think those gardens were.

The success of the Mission House and renewed interest in Americans' early years led to many projects throughout the eastern

States. Further south the Garden Club of Virginia was founded in 1920, a banding together of a few garden clubs formed in the decade before. The Club soon became concerned with the decay of important homes and gardens dating back into the earliest years of the Commonwealth of Virginia. The first in a line of major restorations it supported was at the fine Tidewater House, Kenmore, which had been the home of George Washington's sister Betty.

Seventeenth and eighteenth century American gardens are invariably formal in effect with box-edged parterres, brick-paved walks leading to charming little gazebos (which may in fact turn out to be the 'necessary house'). 'Parterre' however is too grand and daunting a term for what, even at the Governor's Palace at Williamsburg, is a series of charming garden rooms on a domestic scale. They hold a diversity of plants: ornamental natives, florists' flowers of the period, such as hyacinths, tulips and daffodils and inevitably those herbs which can be incorporated into a regulated scheme – rosemary, lavender, santolina and germander. The room-like enclosure of so many of these gardens, both large and small gave the impression of being herb gardens even when, in most cases, that role is not a conscious intention. The point is, of course, that broad extension of the word 'herb' in pre-industrial societies which made most garden plants literal grist to the herbalists' mill and, conversely, flowers to that of the ornamental gardeners'. Here with such plants and planting we see an interrelation of house and garden, of use and of delight, which is the hallmark of civilized domesticity.

This is the American contribution to both garden design and garden history, a domestic form almost lost in Britain from which it had apparently originally come. It provides a firm foundation on which to base a herb garden ethic today, which Miss Rohde appreciated.

Again, then, the 1930s can be seen to be the meeting place, on both sides of the Atlantic, of interests which led to the present passion for herbs. Belief that modern medicine was throwing out proven remedies of the past led to the formation in England of the Society of Herbalists by Hilda Leyel and from it the Culpeper shops as retail outlets (the first was opened on St Valentine's Day, 1927 in Baker Street, London); they still flourish and the Society is now The Herb Society, an educational charity which serves more than

2 *Polygonatum minus.*
Small Solomons Seale:

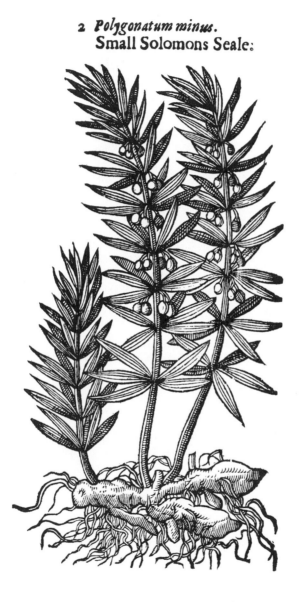

medicinal interests. In 1933 the Herb Society of America was founded.

Any trend in gardens has to be supported by the availability of those plants which are considered suitable for it, whether it be tropical annuals by the vanload for carpet bedding or specimen trees for an arboretum. In the 1930s intending herb growers soon were able to be supplied by a range of plants, the lack of which Miss Rohde had complained about only a year or two earlier, from nurseries such as the Seal Herb Farm, in Kent. This was begun by Dorothy Hewer in 1925 and continued by Margaret Brownlow, both significant names in the world of herbs, although the farm no longer exists.

It is suitable therefore, that at nearby Sissinghurst Castle, Vita Sackville-West should have planted a herb garden that is now, under the care of the National Trust, one of the best known in the world. It is also one of the most beautiful. As with Sissinghurst's other garden rooms – here literally planted above the foundations of the ghostly chambers of this vast Elizabethan mansion – it combines great artistic sensitivity of planting with cerebral formality of design. Reference to Sissinghurst brings us full circle, for this great house was in its heyday in the time of Gerard and Parkinson, when its population was like that of a small town that had to be relatively self-supporting. What would grow was grown. Here again, like the famous Sissinghurst rose which the Nicolsons found surviving in the ruins when they bought the Castle, the herb garden plants themselves are the real link with that age. Though now in careful graduations of colour and height, form and mass, they are the same tansy and tarragon, sage and sorrel, that the garden's first makers grew in their simple clumps or rows.

The woodcuts reproduced in this article are taken from
a 1636 edition of Gerard's *Herball*

The Azores: Garden Islands of the Atlantic

DAVID SAYERS

Nine islands sitting in mid-Atlantic, half way between Lisbon and New York, caressed by the Gulf Stream, largely unnoticed by the outside world: these are the Azores, forever green, made of patchwork fields, little villages and small towns of basalt and whitewash, cobbled roads and several thousand working horses. Each has its own character, influenced by size, topography, location and settlers. The largest of them is São Miguel, 62 km long. Most interesting botanically are São Miguel, Pico, Faial and the westernmost islands Flores and Corvo.

All manner of plants and crops may be grown: oranges, tea, vines, bananas and many other fruits and vegetables, while flower gardens delight in begonias, bromeliads, palms and exotic shrubs, as well as the usual annuals and shrubs seen in Britain.

There are references to the Azores from Plutarch to early Arab maps, but once the Portuguese rediscovered them in 1432 the first settlers quickly followed. Most came from the Alentejo and Algarve districts of Portugal, followed by people from Flanders.

Soon, the native laurel forests were cleared and animals and plants imported to create a thriving agricultural economy. The islands' position on the sea lanes, however, brought visitors. First pirates, then, later, American whalers, crews of merchant shipping, cable companies, and naval crews during the Second World War. Now every year over 600 pleasure yachts take a welcome break in Horta harbour from the long Atlantic crossing, and packaged tourists are beginning to find Faial and São Miguel.

In the early nineteenth century São Miguel was a major producer of oranges, supplied mainly to England and St Petersburg, when as many as ninety English sailing schooners could be seen waiting to load. The most successful exporter was a Bostonian, Thomas Hickling (d. 1834), who established in the Vale of Furnas the Terra Nostra garden, planted with many species from North America, China, Australia and New Zealand. The gardens remain his living memorial and must be among the most tranquil anywhere.

A series of canals and pools surrounding the fine house and the many trees, coupled with the naturally high humidity, create shade and cool for the green mosses that cover the paths. New Zealand tree ferns stand reflected in still water, frogs sun themselves on the lily pads, giant tulip and plane trees shade podocarpus and hide rarer magnolias, sterculia, cinnamomum and cupressus trees. Dark, wide crowned *Metrosideros excelsa* turn deep red with flowers in midsummer to add another moody tone. Camellias, both bushes and trees, abound, and formal hedges are of neatly clipped azaleas. Steep banks are retained by blue hydrangeas, and in shady places the ground is covered with agapanthus and green chlorophytum.

The vegetable garden is sheltered by 2.5 m tall hedges of evergreen oak, eugenia, camellia and pittosporum. Bordering the paths beneath the plots are low trimmed hedges of shiny leaved tea bushes. Behind, sweet corn grows tall between French beans while dahlias line side by side with cabbages.

Gardeners here are gentle, patient people undertaking tasks long ago accomplished elsewhere by chemicals and machinery. Lawns are rhythmically scythed, and lichens go on smothering all before them. Even the air layers of rhododendron and melaleuca seem to have a permanent look about them. Nothing appears ephemeral; only rarely are new plants added, and removal is by storm alone.

The surrounding hills are densely clothed with a Japanese conifer, *Cryptomeria japonica*. These are frequently planted, for they can be felled on a thirty-year cycle, and often they are grown in belts around meadows to provide shelter for cattle out to graze the year round. Beneath these forests the ground is thickly covered with 2 m-long stems of Himalayan *Hedychium gardnerianum*, a tremendous problem for the foresters and a great threat to the little that remains of the native flora. Introduced as a garden ornamental it has escaped and naturalised aggressively and now covers many hectares of São Miguel. Large stands of tree fern high up in inaccessible places give a tropical effect. By the lake is what was once a fine garden where, in the shade of oaks and other trees, extensive wide walks edged with low azalea hedges take one between large beds of old camellias. *Gunnera manicata* was introduced here and that too has escaped and is rapidly invading pastures while local scientists research a herbicide to kill it. Nearby there are hot springs with occasional sulphurous smells, and as the evening darkens an unremitting crescendo from unseen multitudinous frogs adds a sense of witchcraft to the bellowing steam rising eerily against black trees.

Further east is Pico da Vara, 1103 m, the highest point on São Miguel where one can find remnant laurel forest. Largely cleared for cattle grazing, only pockets are left of the impenetrable thickets that once covered all the islands. Although related to the Madeiran forests, it is different, with fifty-six plants unique to the Azores. The laurel shrub-forest is dominated by *Laurus azorica*, *Erica azorica* and *Juniperus brevifolia*. With these may be found *Viburnum tinus* ssp. *azorica*, *Ilex perado* ssp. *azorica*, the shrubby *Euphorbia stygiana* which grows to more than 2 m tall, and others. With careful searching one may find the curious parasitic yellowish green *Arceuthobium azoricum* sprouting from the woody branches of junipers.

Pico island has the most interesting remaining native flora. There are relatively large patches of remnant forest, now rapidly disappearing under foreign investment to increase pasturage. This is a tragedy, for the Azores are highlighted by the World Wildlife Fund in their current campaign 'to save the plants that save us' and the land is not really suitable for pastures made of alien grasses needing high fertiliser input.

The island's summit, Pico, rises straight from the Atlantic to a height of 2351 m. Driving upwards for the first 1500 m along farm tracks one passes through intensively grazed fields and patches of laurel forest. One of the loveliest shrubs here is *Vaccinium cylindraceum*. Hardy in sheltered gardens in England, it grows to about 2.5 m tall and prolifically bears racemes of red buds which develop into 12 mm long pink to almost white pendulous flowers. The young foliage is tinged red; altogether it is a splendid shrub, and another species found only in the Azores. The next 800 m must be done on foot, at times following a barely perceptible trail through the grass and volcanic cinders covered with mats of two most lovely plants, *Thymus caespititius* and *Daboecia azorica*. The thyme has soft foliage and flowers of a lavender pink which clashes a bit with the bright pink-red of the daboecia. In summer extensive areas of hillside are covered with these flowers and the effect is spectacular. The final ascent is a scramble up a perfect cone, where the rocks are hot and steam issues from little crevices. The view is extraordinary: in one direction little Faial and nothing else but a deep blue sea to the horizon. Turn around, and there are puffy white clouds building up against the summit and covering the land below.

At 1043 m Cabeco Gordo is the highest point on Faial. Nearby is an enormous crater or *caldeira* about 2 km across and 400 m deep. The floor is largely covered by *Juniperus brevifolia*. Now a nature reserve, many endemic Azorean plants are found here; pink and wine red *Daboecia azorica* scatter through the grass along with a yellow creeping Jenny, *Lysimachia nemorum* ssp. *azorica,* and in bare patches *Centaurium scilloides* is locally common, a delightfully pretty white flowered relative of the gentian. Included in Aiton's 1789 published list of plants cultivated at Kew and sent back by Francis Masson in 1776, it could be one of the first plants from the Azores cultivated in England.

On the western point is Ponta dos Capelhinos, the location of the last eruption in 1957/58 when nearby villages were destroyed and fields were covered in ash above the height of the boundary walls. Faial gained another 2.4 sq km and thirty years later the grass *Arundo donax*, tamarix and Hottentot fig (carpobrotus) and evening primrose (oenothera) are only just beginning to colonise.

Further west out into the Atlantic are two remote and tiny islands, Flores and Corvo, the latter with only 300 inhabitants. During July the tiny meadows, yellow with buttercups, are surrounded by hydrangea hedges in full flower. It is a remarkable sight, to see blue hedges running out in all directions and marking off fields in squares, rectangles and many odd shapes. Everywhere one looks there are views of green hillsides and lines of blue hydrangeas. Around the harbour on Corvo, growing in the porous volcanic rocks and exposed to sea spray, are substantial populations of *Azorina vidallii*. Previously named as a *Campanula,* it is a dwarf shrub with terminal rosettes of dark green shiny leaves and numerous rather waxy bell-shaped flowers, wider than those of a bluebell. The colours varied on Corvo from deep pink to white and since I have only seen white-flowered plants in cultivation, I hope my seed collection will provide some good dark coloured forms.

Returning home from a few days away and going into one's own familiar garden it is always an anticipated pleasure to see what is in flower, what changes nature has brought about. It is the same with a visit to the Azores, whether wandering around a town, a village or through native laurel forest, for the archipelago is really a series of friendly, timeless island gardens.

Small Courtyard Gardens in Charleston, USA

ROSEMARY VEREY

There is a charm about the small gardens of Charleston which keeps them in your mind long after you have left. When Loutrel Briggs went there in the mid 1930s, his talent as a garden designer inspired in him the realisation that much could be done to bring back the beauty of those town gardens hidden behind walls and fences, gardens which had seen their heyday in the eighteenth and nineteenth centuries, but which had suffered great fires, the earthquake of 1886, hurricanes and floods, and war damage when the old city had been besieged during the Civil War. He spent each winter there for the rest of his life and became actively involved as an adviser on historic preservation. He helped restore old gardens to their original design and created new gardens where today his individual mark is still apparent.

Years before Briggs went to Charleston, other botanists and gardeners had been inspired by the natural vegetation, the majestic Live oaks with their festoons of grey Spanish moss, the cabbage palmettoes and snowdrop trees (*Halesia carolina*), the beauty bushes (kolkwitzia) and sweet-smelling wild olives (*Osmanthus americanus*).

John Lawson made the first known record of plants growing wild in South Carolina, where the mild climate, sunshine, fertile soil and sufficient rainfall combine to establish an enviable range of natural vegetation. The naturalist Mark Catesby went there, and by 1748 had published two great volumes, *The Natural History of Carolina, Florida and the Bahama Islands*. Soon after this the Bartrams, John and William, father and son, were lured south from Philadelphia to find plants for their own garden and to send seeds and specimens to their English patrons, Peter Collinson, Dr Fothergill, Philip Miller and Sir Hans Sloane.

Turning to the first volume of *Curtis's Botanical Magazine* (1787), it is exciting to find *Rudbeckia purpurea*, the purple cone flower, depicted as the second plate and described as native to the warm climate of Carolina. But it was the French botanist, André Michaux, who made the greatest contribution to the already flourishing gardens of Charleston in the eighteenth century. He had been commissioned to go there by his government, with instructions to send back plants of

interest to France. This he did, but of the 6000 plants he is said to
have shipped, only a few survived the ravages of the French Revolution. However, he imported a wide range of exotic plants, which soon
became established in the gardens of Carolina, and these are still part
of the backbone planting in Charleston and further afield in this soft
southern climate. There is the crape myrtle, *Lagerstroemia indica*, with
its long-flowering summer blossoms and pale, patterned trunk which
stands out against the dark green of the native hollies. He introduced
the ginkgo and the china berry, *Melia azedarach*, the silk tree, *Albizzia
julibrissin*, and also two of our most important present-day garden
plants, *Azalea indica* and *Camellia japonica*.

There are other written reminders that gardening and the study of
botany was a fashionable pursuit here, for 'upwards of fifty young
ladies attended classes, for the purpose of acquiring a regular knowledge of this delightful science, many of whom are making the most
flattering progress.' The fashion for Gardeners' Kalendars had
travelled from England and in 1796 Martha Logan wrote reminders

A typical decorative wall in a public garden in Charleston.
The recessed arches and coping are characteristic

for each month. Her November entry reads, 'Trim your monthly roses: and at the full moon, open their roots and dung them.' She must have been a relaxed character, for later she remarks, 'What you neglected last month may be successfully done in this.'

Contemporary newspapers have advertisements for 'the best sort of seeds', lemon trees with lemons on them, and camellias covered 'with buds ready to burst into their wintery bloom'. An advertisement with a difference appeared in December 1786: Peter Crowells had arrived from Haarlem and was selling 'rare and curious bulbs which have never appeared in this country before.'

Near Charleston are the grand estate gardens, Middleton Place and Magnolia Gardens. It is an inspiring experience to walk in these gardens of lush vegetation, but you must not neglect a stroll through the carefully planned streets of old Charleston, where many of the homes and public buildings date from the mid 1750s, when this colony was under royal jurisdiction. Behind the fine doorways, white porticos and balconies with slender, elegant columns, and the wrought-iron gateways individually designed, lie small gardens, carefully planned, inviting in their half mystery, as you wonder if you may enter and observe, partake of their excellence, walk in their paths.

Here Loutrel Briggs was inspired to make new gardens, of necessity quite small and often of an irregular shape. Creating a garden in this limitation of space is the challenge of making a beautiful picture, framed by high walls, overhanging trees, carriage houses and other immovable structures. An artist may find it easy to fashion a landscape with long vistas and a variety of elements, but to be confined by space, putting thoughts into perspective, demands a strength of discipline, the ability to see from all angles, to appreciate in all directions, to create a picture within the smallest and most unpropitious corner. Each device which the designer employs (for that is what he is doing) must be moulded into a perfect whole.

This allows him to use jewels, so small and precious that they would be overwhelmed and lost in a larger, more spacious setting. He must be conscious of this finely focused painting, its feeling of intimacy, remembering how it will be seen, enjoyed, from the windows and by the visitor as he arrives. He must study the reflections, the shafts of light at each hour of the day and each season. There must be a feeling of peace, of interest in every mood, but dominating all, there must be the essence of tranquillity, no agitation or urge to move on.

Mrs Whalley's garden is just 30 × 50 ft. The perspective is
altered by the careful positioning and clipping of the box
balls which echo the shape of the shallow, round pool

It should inspire the beholder with a sense of completion and satisfaction.

There should be a limitation of flowers, in fact there will be,
because the choice in these special conditions will be dictated by the
elements and microclimate created by the proximity of the surrounding houses, the walls casting shade but reflecting warmth and keeping
away the wind. Pierced walls help the air to circulate, and this is
important in winter as well as in summer, for as cold air sinks the
frost will stay unless it is moved on, encouraged away by a breeze.
Hot days need a special cool area with appropriate surroundings, so
when evening brings relief from the high temperatures there are the
seat, the pool and the evening-scented plants awaiting you. In the
same way, there should be framed views from inside, views to be
enjoyed during hot days in summer and bleak days in winter.

Shadows are important, daytime shadows and those cast at night
by specially-sited lights. In this small area much more thought must

be given to every detail. The fence should have its own character, the reflecting pool be in just the right place, the paths must have movement made with varying materials, with stone and bricks laid in different patterns, some lying flat and others on their sides, giving just a touch of differing levels. All must flow, yet be separated quietly into the suggestion of rooms.

For me all these ideas came together in one particular garden, Mrs Ben Scott Whalley's, the ground plan of which was laid out by Loutrel Briggs, but which now owes its special quality to Emily Whalley's feel for plants, perfect eye for scale and, even more important, her decision after a devastating storm – typical of the hazards of gardening in Charleston – to replant and turn the existing three circular sections into seven individual gardens, which help to conceal the fact that this is a tiny narrow plot, 30 by 50 feet.

Walk from the street through the narrow passageway, where a line of *Eriobotrya japonica*, clipped as a tall hedge, screens her house from the neighbours and provides a honey-like scent in midwinter. Ferns grow at the feet of these loquats. Beyond, the path winds you on, and in this very shady area is a planting of evergreen foliage shrubs and ground coverers. There are holly ferns, fatsias, tall camellias and an upright podocarpus contrasting with trim box balls. Bleeding heart (*Dicentra spectabilis*) grows by the stone statue of a girl spilling water into a shell. The first small lawn, surrounded by a patterned brick path, is flanked by the two main borders; one is in full sun and the other mostly in shade. The colours are soft at all seasons – pink tulips in spring, pale blue irises, snapdragons and salvias. Roses and vines climb the white scalloped picket fence, and plumbago is allowed to spread. White impatiens are tucked in between white azaleas; alyssum, begonias and parsley share a pot. Everywhere the planting is original, and overflows.

Even the round pool has an unexpected touch: it is only one and a half inches deep and becomes a magnet for the birds to bathe in. Round the pool are more box balls, wood violets, ajugas, myrtles, more fatsias, and four varieties of fern. Beyond and furthest from the house is an almost enclosed area where Mrs Whalley's favourite azaleas, camellias and blue hydrangeas are thickly planted.

This could be my dream garden, with its thoughtful planting, a pool for reflections, a seat among the scented flowers, and shadows. There is another essential quality – the sense of continuity and peace.

A Glance at Chinese Gardens

NANCY-MARY GOODALL

The Chinese have always believed their mountains to be the homes of the Immortals. Over two thousand years ago the great emperors started to copy the mountain scenery with lakes and rivers within their vast hunting parks, hoping to attract those magical beings who might come down to visit them and, perhaps, teach them the secrets of immortality. This dream of the mountains was later expressed in gardens influenced by the three different but compatible religions. Tao, the Way, is a faith involving innumerable spirits, of animals, plants, the elements, et cetera, which seeks harmony with nature and a long life on earth. It is influenced by *Yin* and *Yang*, complementary but not opposing forces. *Yang* is male and positive, *Yin* is negative, yielding, feminine; they imbue every aspect of life where antithesis can be found and are reflected in gardens in deliberate successions of contradictions: light and shade, stone and water, open and enclosed, vertical and horizontal, mass and void. Buddhism deals with man in his relationship with God and has its own heavenly hierarchy, while Confucianism, a philosophy concerned with moral symmetry and man's position among and behaviour towards his fellow men, includes a great respect for ancestors and age.

Tao priests and hermits roamed the mountains seeking herbs for life-prolonging drinks, the Buddhists built monasteries in the mountains and, in monastery and temple gardens, evoked the Buddhist paradise of Amida. Confucian thinkers, often after lives spent in official positions, retired to the mountains or to the countryside of their youth, or to their gardens, there to live a simple scholarly life writing poetry in exquisite calligraphy and painting pictures of nature. They were often involved in garden making.

While Chinese designers could produce superb landscapes, such as the West Lake at Hanzhou, once believed to be the origin of the willow-pattern – an English Chinoiserie design of 1780 by Thomas Turner – or the Imperial retreat at Chengde, north of the Great Wall, the reality may seem congested and confusing. Unable to create vast mountain scenes in the confines of the town gardens of officials or rich merchants, the designers enlarged them by various means using tricks, sometimes even mirrors, in plans so labyrinthine

In the *Shih Tzu Lin*, Stone Lion Grove, a courtyard with many
typical elements: a raised octagonal bed, mosaic pavement, a gourd
shaped doorway, a filigree window, a cherry tree, bamboos and rocks.
Suzhou. Photograph: Nancy-Mary Goodall

Butterfly mosaic in a path. *Yiyuan* (Garden of Ease), Suzhou.
Photograph: Heather Angel

that the visitor is soon lost. Such gardens were intended to provide
a lifetime's entertainment and to a Chinese lady with bound feet
might represent her whole world. They were not meant to be rushed
through in half an hour.

If town gardens such as the Yu Yuan in Shanghai or the Shih Tsu
Lin, Stone Lion Grove, in Suzhou seem intolerably confused this is
partly because lakes, mountains and rivers are represented in miniature while the many necessary buildings – for these gardens were
lived in – are full sized and always set facing squarely to the south:
halls, studies and pavilions, all are connected by bridges and paths
that are often roofed and fenced and sometimes zig-zagged to foil evil
spirits who can only travel in a straight line.

The space in a garden is usually broken up into compartments by
walls that may be painted any colour, white, grey, yellow or red, and
which, if plain, may act as backdrops on which bamboos and trees
throw moving shadows that are part of the design. Doors and windows may be oblong or square but more often take geometric shapes
such as octagons, ovals or circles – the well known moon doors – or
may be shaped like a vase, a fan, a leaf, a gourd or pomegranate or a
flower. I have seen a window shaped like a teapot. Windows may be

filled with fretwork in wood or plaster, in abstract patterns or portraying flowers, birds and fabulous animals. In her book *The Chinese Garden* (1978), Maggie Keswick says: 'Notice what is framed.'

Much use is made of quotation and symbolism. Everything is given a poetic name, every courtyard and building, every rock and tree. Names are painted or carved over doorways and, on the doorposts, the two halves of poetic couplets which an educated Chinese would recognise and, if they are part of a quotation, would be able to complete. They are important in setting a mood.

The mountains were symbolised by grotesque rocks, full of holes and crevices, with no attempt to imitate natural strata and often stood on end. In the old days such rocks were carefully catalogued and named, their every nuance studied, the shape, striations, colour, even the note they made when struck. Emperors as well as lesser men have bankrupted themselves for rocks.

There are no lawns in Chinese gardens: grass carries unpleasant images of cows or of invading hordes from the Mongolian steppes. Instead there is paving, from large flagstones to intricate mosaics, like flowered carpets or with cheerful representations of lucky bats, or cranes, or turtles, or those most real and powerful entities, dragons.

As if this were not enough, gardens were often designed to express not so much real mountain scenery as the scenery in scroll paintings. In a famous Chinese novel, the *Hong Lou Meng* or *Dream of The Red Chamber*, translated by David Hawkes as *The Story of The Stone*, which gives a gripping account of the making of an enormous garden, someone is asked to paint a picture of it, an almost impossible task since the garden has been designed as a series of incidents along a winding route like the unrolling of a very long scroll. A seventeenth-century garden book, the *Yuan Yeh*, repeatedly likens gardens to paintings and white walls to the unpainted areas of a scroll. No detailed instructions are given but a series of beautiful scenes: 'The misty water stretches far, far away; the cloud-swept mountains fade in the distance, the fishing boats drift in the wind, the gulls glide gracefully'. The gardens were a triumph of the imagination.

The Taoist obsession with longevity and immortality and the Confucian ethic of respect for age embraced both rocks and old gnarled trees which are often miniaturised on the principle that, as the beef cube to the ox, so a diminutive mountain or tree contains the concentrated, and powerful, essence of the thing itself – hence what

A raft at dawn on the Li River near Guelin. Mountains are one of the most important influences on Chinese gardens. Photograph: Heather Angel

the Japanese call bonsai and the Chinese P'un'tsoi. Miniature landscapes appear in very old paintings and fit any receptacle from a large trough to a small dish; they are at their most charming when minute models of buildings are set among dwarf trees, rocks and tiny ferns.

A book could be written about the Chinese symbolism of plants which are not given garden space unless they have historic, religious or poetic associations. The peony represents the spring, health, distinction, promotion and passing exams, the pine stands for longevity and survival in the struggle of life, the bamboo for loyalty and Confucian rectitude, the plum for friendship and happiness, the magnolia – because its name Ah pin also means a jade hall – being the most auspicious to plant near a building. Puns are everywhere – and jokes: the Chinese are happy people – but impossible for westerners to grasp.

This brief glance at Chinese gardens may tempt you to deeper study and perhaps a Chinese garden tour. One returns more than a little dissatisfied with western gardens and their naïve emphasis on horticulture and plant collecting and what can seem, after China, a pathetic paucity of ideas.

From the Mountains of Heaven to the Sacred Peak of the East

Wanderings in search of China's wild flowers

STEPHEN G. HAW

This was my first experience of desert. Much of north China is dry, and often looks bare and inhospitable to someone used to the green fields of Britain, but from Lanzhou onwards the terrain had become increasingly arid and desolate. During a brief stop in Lanzhou I had witnessed one of the most extraordinary phenomena of this desiccated region, desert soil from the north-west blowing eastwards to add to the already immense deposits of loess in north China. When the sky suddenly darkened I had expected heavy thunder-clouds, but looking up had seen great sheets of yellow-brown dust blown at considerable altitude, and in sufficient density almost to obscure the sun.

The train had carried me onward from Lanzhou into the 'Gansu corridor', sandwiched between the rugged mountains edging the Tibetan plateau to the south-west and the desert hills of the Mongolian Gobi to the north-east. The corridor itself is largely semi-desert, with here and there enough water to allow some cultivation. At one stop an old man was ploughing with an ox and an enormous white *pianniu* (ox-yak hybrid). The water supply in this region is mainly from springs, underground streams and a few rivers running down from the Qilian Mountains on the south-west, where there are high peaks of more than 5,000 metres (16,400 ft.) and permanent snows and glaciers. That there is also some precipitation was demonstrated by a moderate snowfall during the course of my journey. It was late May, too late in the year for the train to be heated, so an uncomfortable day was spent wearing as much as possible against the cold. The discomfort was prolonged when the train became stuck on a steep gradient, and had to roll backwards and make several attempts before finally achieving sufficient impetus to carry it to the top of the slope.

On our right hand as we rolled north-westwards there were frequent glimpses of stretches of ancient wall. These are remains of the western end of the Great Wall of China, here not built of brick

The vast snowy mountains edging the Tibetan plateau tower above the
arid wastes of north-west Gansu province

and stone like the sections familiar to visitors to Peking, but constructed entirely of compacted soil. This 'stamped earth' construction technique has been used in China since at least as early as the late Neolithic period, and results in very solid structures capable of surviving for many centuries (and even millennia) in the dry north Chinese climate. Finally there was a view of the fortifications of Jiayu Guan, considered the most westerly major gate of the Wall, and the railway began to leave the corridor behind.

The route continued across increasingly desert landscapes for many more hundreds of miles. I broke my journey at Liuyuan, the station for Dunhuang, an oasis which was an important point on the old 'Silk Road' where there are magnificent Buddhist cave temples dating from as early as the fifth century. In this area the desert showed a diversity of forms; huge sand dunes rolled around one side of the oasis, while elsewhere there were vast shingle plains, or spectacular and eery moonscapes of black rock. It was amazing to find life even where the desert seemed most hostile; small geckos (*Phrynocephalus przewalskiii*) speckled with colours to match the grit of their environment would run up from underfoot where it seemed there could have been nothing to support their existence.

Even though I had long been a student of China I had not really expected to find such vast areas of desert and semi-desert. Images of rice-fields are so solidly connected with western conceptions of China that it is really only experience that can set them into a more realistic framework. The truth is that China is a vast land of extreme geographic diversity, which no single picture can possibly embrace. During the course of many long journeys around the country this was gradually borne in upon me, in a series of often quite startling revelations.

This particular journey through China's desert regions had as its ultimate object a visit to the great Tian Shan range, the 'Mountains of Heaven'. This is a long mountain range, divided into three major segments. The western Tian Shan stretch from Soviet Central Asia across the border into China as far as the city of Urumqi, the regional capital of Xinjiang (Chinese Turkistan). This is the longest and highest section of the range, some 11,000 kilometres (700 miles) from west to east and with some peaks near the Sino-Soviet border reaching to around 7,000 metres (23,000 ft.) or more. At Urumqi there is a gap in the range where the altitude drops to below 2,000 metres (6,500 ft.), so that this has always been an important point on the Central Asian trade routes. East of this gap are the central Tian Shan or Bogdo Ula, dominated by the great peak of Bogda Shan, 5,445 metres (17,864 ft.) high. On a clear day this mountain is easily visible from Urumqi's northern suburbs, a snow-covered mass towering above the dusty city. The most easterly and lowest section of the range is the Kharlik Tagh, north of the oasis of Hami, with a maximum height of 4,886 metres (16,030 ft.).

In the south-west the Tian Shan are connected to the Pamirs, and to their north lie several subsidiary ranges. These are strange names to capture the imagination – the Borohoro Shan, the Ala Tau, the Tarbagatai, and, more widely separated to the north, the Altai of the Chinese-Russian-Mongolian border region. These ranges have been little explored by western Europeans. Evidence of this is seen in the Latin names of plants from the area, liberally scattered with epithets commemorating Russian botanists and explorers. Many of the more widespread plants of this region are of course common to both the Russian and Chinese sides of the borders. The Mountains of Heaven are geographically and botanically part of Central Asia, and their flora has more in common with that of Europe than with that of China proper.

Excursions into the foothills of the range, both to the east and west of Urumqi, were not especially rewarding. The lower hills are very dry, supporting only semi-desert vegetation. The most notable plants recorded were *Rosa berberifolia*, a very unusual small rose closely related to *Rosa persica*, *Ixiolirion tataricum* and a tulip which was not in flower but was probably *Tulipa iliensis*. There were also considerable clumps of *Iris lactea* wherever there was a little more moisture than usual. Shrubby vegetation included several caragana species, *Halimodendron halodendron*, and some other roses, probably *Rosa platyacantha* (golden flowers) and *Rosa albertii* (white).

To the north of Mt. Bogda a rough track penetrates the range, leading to a lake at about 2,000 metres (6,500 ft.) altitude, where accommodation is available. It follows the valley of the river flowing down from the lake, climbing away from the arid lowlands to much lusher mountain pastures. The vegetation gradually changes during the ascent. More or less total desert beyond the foothills becomes semi-desert among the hills, with vegetation like that just described. Then a few elms (*Ulmus pumila*) begin to line the river. Next,

A lake at some 2,000 metres altitude in the central Tian Shan

Populus talassica appears, at first mixed with the elm, then dominant, and finally mixed with willows and spruce. At the level of the lake the last few poplars occur, leaving the higher slopes to the spruce alone. This is *Picea schrenkiana* var. *tianschanica*, tall and slim with pendulous cones. Undershrubs include *Sorbus tianschanica*, *Berberis ?heteropoda*, *Salix ?xerophila*, a spiraea, and a couple of shrubby honeysuckles, *Lonicera hispida* and *L. ?altmannii*. On higher slopes too dry for the spruce *Juniperus sabina* was common. *Clematis sibirica* scrambled among the shrubs.

The meadows were wonderful. I had arrived very early in the season, probably too early for the best of the flowers (the snow had only just melted at the level of the lake). The finest show was made by *Gagea filiformis*, of which there were great golden-yellow sheets.

The bright yellow stars of *Gagea filiformis*, abundant in damp areas on the slopes of the Tian Shan

Gagea albertii also occurred in slightly drier places. *Iris loczyi* had flowers which were usually mid-blue with white markings and darker blue veins, but sometimes varied to purple or reddish-purple. In clearings among the spruce trees were large clumps of *Iris ruthenica*

var. *brevituba,* covered with deep purple-blue flowers. The nodding bells of *Fritillaria walujewii* were rich claret-red inside and pale greenish-white outside. *Primula algida* was common in cooler areas, and there were also two pasque-flowers, *Pulsatilla campanella* and *P. ambigua.* Violets and androsaces, anemones and wild strawberries, and sheets of buttercups, dandelions and forget-me-nots completed the floral spectacle.

My stay in the Tian Shan was unfortunately only of a few days, but it was sufficient to allow me to form a clear impression of the flora. This was essentially similar to that of most European mountain ranges. Most of the common genera were the same, even if the species were often different. There was certainly little in common with most of the rest of China – no rhododendrons, no camellias (or indeed any Theaceae) and no lilies, with the possible exception of the mysterious *Lilium tianschanicum,* recorded by Russian botanists but not known to the Chinese. Even the people of this region are different, Uighur Turks, Kazakhs and Mongols, a complete contrast with China proper.

I have begun by giving an account of this area to stress that China is a constant source of the unexpected. Most gardeners associate the country with the work of a comparatively small number of collectors, whose main introductions came from Hubei, Sichuan and Yunnan provinces. There is no doubt that these are the richest areas in terms of numbers of plant species, yet a high proportion of plants collected there have failed in cultivation or are rare and difficult. Many of the best garden plants from China (in terms of effect and ease of cultivation) are from elsewhere. *Viburnum farreri* comes to mind, as do *Ginkgo biloba, Weigela florida, Forsythia suspensa* and *Prunus triloba.* Many other plants occur within the famous collecting areas but are by no means restricted to them. It must therefore not be thought that the areas covered by, say, Wilson, Rock and Forrest are the only parts of China of any great floral interest.

When travelling across the vast, intensively cultivated plains of eastern China it is easy to think that the natural vegetation has been virtually entirely destroyed. Here there are not even hedgerows to shelter a few wild flowers. It is possible to appreciate why Charles Maries, who collected in China in the late 1870s for the firm of Veitch, could have thought that there was nothing left in China worthy of introduction. But here and there among the cultivated

areas are wild places which for various reasons have escaped the
closest attentions of the industrious Chinese peasants. Often they
are too rocky and mountainous to favour agriculture, and in many
cases they also have some religious significance. In these isolated
places, which are frequently difficult of access and well removed
from major transport routes and centres of communication, there
survives a flora which rivals or surpasses those of Japan, Europe
and many other regions. If it does not compare well with that of
western China, it is only because the latter is exceptionally rich.

One example of such an isolated location with which I am particularly familiar is Mount Tai in the province of Shandong. For
two years I lived in this province, in the provincial capital, the city of
Jinan. This lies no more than 56 kilometres (35 miles) in a direct
line from the mountain. Communications were relatively good
between the two, and I was able to climb Mount Tai no less than
five times, at varying seasons. It rises almost sheer from the North
China Plain on its southern side, with lower hills stretching for
some distance to the north and east and a short way to the west.
The summit slightly exceeds 1,500 metres (5,000 ft.), which though
not remarkable makes it the highest point in any direction for
hundreds of miles. It is a large block of granite pushing up through
the limestone of the surrounding hills.

Mount Tai is the most holy mountain in China, the sacred peak of

Mt. Tai seen from the large temple situated at the foot of its southern face

Abies fabri *silvered with snow and frost on the summit of Mt Emei*

the East. Formerly it was worshipped by Emperors who personally travelled to the large temple at its foot and sometimes even made the ascent to its summit. It probably derived much of its national importance from its strong association with Confucius, who is supposed to have climbed it himself, though it undoubtedly was a holy mountain long before his time. There used to be temples to the god of Mount Tai in many towns and cities throughout the Chinese Empire. A proportion of the visitors to the mountain today still go for religious reasons, making offerings at the several temples on and around the slopes.

Much of the mountain is covered with woodland or scrub. The lower slopes suffered severe deforestation during the troubled period between about 1920 and 1950, and has since been replanted with a variety of trees, not all of which would originally have grown there. Many areas on the upper slopes have been comparatively little disturbed, however. The shrubby flora is especially good, and includes *Forsythia suspensa, Syringa microphylla, Viburnum sargentii, Deutzia grandiflora, Rosa multiflora, Rhododendron mucronulatum* and *R. micranthum*, at least three species of spiraea, *Elaeagnus umbellata* and *Berberis amurensis*. There are also several fine small trees, particularly *Prunus davidiana* and *Sorbus hupehensis*. Many fine old trees of *Pinus tabulaeformis* grow on the steep upper slopes. Attractive non-woody plants include *Lilium concolor, Iris lactea, I. ruthenica, Lysimachia clethroides* and the superb *Pulsatilla chinensis*, which must easily be the finest of all the pasque flowers but has unfortunately so far proved impossible to keep in cultivation.

This is just a selection of the most attractive plants of Mt. Tai. The many others include a few familiar from Europe, such as *Polygonatum odoratum* and *Valeriana officinalis*. Considering the very moderate height of the mountain and the modest area I was able to botanise, such a flora must be considered quite rich. It certainly compares well with that of many European mountains of similar size.

It cannot, of course, compare very favourably with what can be found further west. A single mountain in Sichuan may support more than a dozen species of rhododendron alone. This is certainly true of Mt. Emei (Omei), where I have personally counted at least twelve, and published floras record about fifteen. This mountain also supports such rarities as *Davidia involucrata*, among many other superb plants.

I have been fortunate during my two visits to Mt. Emei. The region in south-western Sichuan where it stands is notoriously damp, with almost constant cloud and mist. It is said that the sun is seen so rarely, that when it does appear the dogs bark at it! In summer, the monsoon brings several weeks of heavy rainfall. My first, very brief visit, was in May, and I enjoyed clear sunny weather throughout. I was only able to spend one night on the mountain, at a temple about 1,000 metres (3,300 ft.) up, and a second at a hotel at its foot. This did not give me sufficient time to climb as far as the summit, more than 3,000 metres (10,000 ft.) high, but I did manage to reach some 2,000 metres, returning by a different path.

The lower slopes of the mountain have sub-tropical vegetation, in which the family Lauraceae is strongly represented. The undergrowth is dense, with many ferns and exotic shrubs such as melastoma and strobilanthes. The trees are mainly broad-leaved evergreens, with some evergreen conifers such as *Cunninghamia lanceolata* and the palm *Trachycarpus fortunei*. This vegetational zone extends up to roughly 1,000 metres (3,300 ft.) altitude, and gradually becomes mixed with elements of warm temperate flora, including deciduous broad-leaved trees and shrubs. The davidia is one of these. In May, it had virtually finished flowering, with just a few of the white-bracted 'handkerchiefs' left on the trees.

Between about 1,000 and 2,000 metres the vegetation shows a marked change. The broad-leaved evergreen trees gradually disappear, and towards the upper part of this zone some *Abies fabri* occur among the predominantly deciduous woodland. With these the first rhododendrons are seen, and also hydrangeas, including the climbing *Hydrangea anomala*. There are extensive brakes of bamboo, of various species, from the lower part of this zone upwards. Herbaceous plants include several arisaema species, *Anemone davidii*, *Disporum bodinieri* and *D. sessile*, *Bletilla striata*, *Iris japonica*, *Primula obconica*, *Androsace ?henryi* and *Cardiocrinum giganteum*, this last still in bud at this time. Perhaps the most exciting find was a damp cliff dotted with pink and red flowers of *Pleione speciosa*. They were of particularly good flower-colour, with extensive blood-red markings on the lip.

At about 2,000 metres is a temple by a small pond called the 'Elephant Bathing Pool'. It is said that a Boddhisatva was passing by on his flying elephant, and stopped here to allow the elephant to bathe and rest (the pool, scarcely big enough for a large pig to immerse itself in, mysteriously grew to accommodate the elephant's bulk!). This marked the highest point reached during this visit. Tantalisingly, it was obvious that just above the rhododendrons were in full flower, as descending Chinese often carried with them a truss or two. But the upper slopes had to be left for another visit. After a slight altercation with a large monkey (a local kind of macaque), who was angry that, as the dominant male of his troupe, he had not been given the core of my apple, a break was taken for tea in the temple, before commencing the long descent.

My second visit was more leisurely, as I was able to spend about a week on the mountain, but there were less flowers as it was January. However, I reached the summit, easily distinguishing the numerous rhododendron species by their differing leaves. During the ascent the mountain was wrapped in mist, which on the upper slopes froze onto everything it touched, coating trees, bushes, bamboo canes and rocks with a thick layer of rime. Passing the night at a temple near the summit, I awoke to find water in a bottle in my room frozen solid, but the dawn was magnificent and the day remained clear and sunny throughout. Far below lay a sea of clouds, through which projected a myriad mountain peaks and ridges. To the south-west the flat top of Wa Shan was readily identifiable, and far away towards Tibet towered the great peak of Gonga Shan (Minya Konka). All over the summit ridges the ice began to melt from the rhododendrons, abies and *Arundinaria nitida*, sparkling like a million diamonds.

The next day immediately after sunrise the clouds rolled up over the top of the mountain. I ate breakfast with mist swirling in through doors and the unglazed windows. The descent was difficult, as the previous day's sun had melted the frost and snow covering the path, which had then refrozen into a sort of ice-slide. Even my solid mountain boots could not always grip on this surface. But eventually I passed below the frost line. Almost my last interesting find was a beautiful pink primula, growing on banks and cliffs by a river at quite low altitude, which to this day I have been unable to identify.

Other botanical excursions in China have taken me to several more excellent areas. In the hills near Kunming in Yunnan, I have seen *Camellia pitardii, Rhododendron spinuliferum* and several other rhododendrons, gentians (including two pink-flowered species) and a fine variety of other beautiful plants. On the Lu Shan range in Jiangxi grew *Hydrangea paniculata, Lilium brownii, L. speciosum,* hemerocallis, hosta, *Spiraea japonica, Buddleia davidii* and platycodon. Here I can describe briefly only one more particularly exciting trip, to the Koko Nor region of Qinghai province.

The great lake of Koko Nor, the 'Blue Sea', lies at 3,200 metres (10,500 ft.) altitude on the north-eastern corner of the Tibetan plateau. Towards the end of my two years' residence in China, I heard that it had become possible for foreigners to go there. The opportunity could not be missed. After negotiations with Chinese officialdom, I found myself in a minibus travelling along the Xining to Lhasa highway.

The lake in central Tian Shan

This is an inhospitable region, dry and very cold for most of the year. Even in early August, the time of my visit, there was sleet and hail as we crossed the mountain pass leading onto the plateau. There are no trees here, and the only shrub seen was a fine form of *Potentilla fruticosa,* with shining golden-yellow flowers. The yak-grazed pastures around the lake were a mass of colour, however, with the flowers of alpine herbs. These included half a dozen species of gentian, some blue and some white, *Leontopodium haplophylloides*, a small parnassia, several alpine asters, *Adenophora himalayana* (like a small campanula) and *Androsace mariae* var. *tibetica* (the *Androsace tibetica* of Farrer's *Rainbow Bridge*). Large areas were coloured red-purple by the flowers of *Pedicularis kansuensis*, and damp hollows were splashed with the gold of the flowers of another pedicularis, the unfortunately-named *P. longiflora* var. *tubiformis*. There is not room here to mention all the other fine flowers, but one must not be omitted. In dry, sandy areas grew rounded tufts of *Stellera chamae-jasme*, its deep pink buds opening to white, daphne-like flowers. This is a wonderful plant, and it must be eternally regretted that it is almost impossible to cultivate.

There are so many floral wonders in China. Although I have been lucky enough to travel there extensively, there are still many areas I have not yet been able to visit, and many I would like to see again. It is now quite easy to travel around China, though still not always very comfortable. It is not possible (nor, indeed, desirable) to collect plants there as was done until the last war, but although we already have many superb garden plants from China there are many yet to be introduced. It is to be hoped that, as contacts develop between Chinese and Western botanists and gardeners, more of these will find their way into cultivation in Europe.

Photographs by the author

Phyllis Reiss at Tintinhull

PENELOPE HOBHOUSE

Phyllis Reiss, a quarter of a century after her death in 1961, would undoubtedly be surprised to find that her strongly individual gardening tastes merit a thorough analysis. She was the sixth child of Colonel and Mrs Alfred Lucas of Hobland Hall near Great Yarmouth in Norfolk. In the family there was a keen tradition of gardening interest. A grandfather, Alfred, and his brother Charlie were both notable gardeners, the latter at Warnham Court near Horsham in Sussex. Colonel Lucas grew prize fruit and his wife was a gardener and beekeeper. According to the family Phyllis was an original child with individual tastes – ready to have a go at anything – and with a sense of humour which she retained all her life. A devoted aunt and a warm and welcoming hostess to people from every walk of life, at both Dowdeswell in Gloucestershire and later at Tintinhull House in Somerset, she and Captain Reiss were childless. This may be significant in that much of her emotional energy could be devoted to developing a gardening taste and style. Characterised by a natural modesty, Mrs Reiss never sought publicity – indeed, like her mentor Lawrence Johnston at Hidcote, she thoroughly disliked having her photograph taken – and if she were alive today might well disclaim her influence on garden styles.

What are the qualities that make her garden planning at Tintinhull memorable? A gifted amateur, she certainly had no formal horticultural training. She came from a family with a gardening tradition, but from a background that would have accepted the innate amateurism of her class and time. Most people of her background would have been expected to have absorbed a fair aesthetic sense, which would find expression in both their house decoration and their garden arrangements. It seems, although nothing is known of her schooling, that she travelled widely, and in Italy would have seen some of the great Renaissance layouts where interconnected garden 'rooms', extensions of the villa, reflected its scale and architecture. Lawrence Johnston when he first envisaged his garden framework at Hidcote must also have drawn on a similar experience. When Mrs Reiss discovered Tintinhull in 1933 she must have recognised not only the classical proportions of its compartmentalised garden areas, but also its almost uncanny similarity, on a reduced scale, to Johnston's inspired composition.

What made her different from many of her contemporaries was her architectural approach to garden layout, to plants and to the colour schemes she prepared for her borders. She went beyond the conception of beds and borders as pictorial compositions; instead she interpreted the garden in terms of spatial relationships, and saw plants as playing a structural part in the overall layout, as fundamental to the framework as walls, paving areas or ancillary buildings. By her, leaf and flower associations were not only considered from the point of view of colour harmony or contrast, but were also judged for weight and density to give balance to a whole or a part of any scheme. Thus, like an architect simplifying the materials with which he would work and which were appropriate to a particular site, she often chose to repeat a particular planting theme in another garden area, refusing to allow additional colours or types of plants to distract from overall unity of purpose. Her contemporaries, especially woman gardeners such as Vita Sackville-West, used pictorial rather than architectural compositions. The latter, the framework of whose own garden at Sissinghurst was created by her husband Harold Nicolson, originally planned the forecourt borders at Montacute House (a few miles from Tintinhull) with pale grey and silver foliage plants and pale flower colours. In the 1950s the National Trust invited Mrs Reiss to replace this planting with stronger, brighter colour blocks to anchor the towering Elizabethan mansion to its site. Margery Fish, a close neighbour at East Lambrook, collected hardy plants which she arranged to emphasise each specimen's particular beauty, rather than seeking any unity of garden design. With her, Mrs Reiss studied plants and their needs. They remained true gardening colleagues, but their gardening ethic was totally different.

Good gardens set an aesthetic standard and, if they survive, become inspirational to future generations. Mrs Reiss was not in any sense a professional designer yet her gardening style, as developed in her own garden at Tintinhull during nearly thirty years, has a simplicity and lack of fuss which make it memorable. Although colour schemes at Tintinhull are strict and many individual harmonies or contrasts are striking, and indeed often daring, the essence of her work lies in the way she used certain plants as architectural features to link the more pictorial and ephemeral seasonal colours. There is another salient

Tintinhull House, the west front

point which is worth making. The garden at Tintinhull is not large – perhaps hardly two acres if the kitchen area is included – and Mrs Reiss had only one gardener and limited resources. Its modest size – and the fact that within the whole garden each of the six geometric compartments could be a prototype for a self-contained garden – ensures that many of today's garden visitors who have small modern gardens, maintained without any outside assistance, can feel that Mrs Reiss's teaching has relevance to their own circumstances.

After the First World War every proper garden had an herbaceous border, some more successful than others, where hardy deciduous perennials were arranged to give pictorial effects as if on a painter's flat canvas. The effects of these compositions were revealed to the appreciative garden visitor as a series of images, sometimes glimpsed across a lawn from afar, at other times unfolding in progression during a garden walk. For the garden *cognoscenti* the Robinson–Jekyll school was firmly established; hardy exotic and native plants grew beside each other in natural-looking clumps and the bedding-out of annuals in ribbons or concentric colour circles had become unfashionable. In gardens such as Hidcote made by Lawrence Johnston between 1907 and the outbreak of war in 1914, cottage-type gardening was on a grand scale. A formal layout of garden 'rooms' with walls of yew, beech, and pleached hornbeam and lime provided a framework and

Tintinhull. Looking west from the house

background for tightly packed informal planting. Captain and Mrs Reiss were neighbours living not far away at Dowdeswell through the 1920s. Undoubtedly the Hidcote style helped form Phyllis Reiss's own tastes. In 1933 they moved to Tintinhull House, near Yeovil.

Tintinhull, where the original Jacobean farmhouse was added to in 1700 and a classical Queen Anne façade faces on to the garden, is as firmly balanced by its garden compartments as any architectural purist could desire. A series of garden 'rooms' is laid out to the west and north in such a way that a garden tour follows a logical route. A long axial stone path links three distinct garden areas. Off this to the north three larger rectangular areas at slightly descending levels are divided by tall yew hedges. In addition mature trees balance with the mass of the house and frame the skyline. Basically Tintinhull was a Hidcote in miniature: two acres instead of ten made it possible to follow the Hidcote theme with only one gardener. When Captain and Mrs Reiss came the basic layout was already established, although the final embellishment, the centrally placed pool garden, was still a tennis court until after the war ended in 1945. Then wide borders were designed in contrasting colour schemes to face each other over lawns and a central water canal.

Mrs Reiss read Gertrude Jekyll's books and may even have visited

Montacute. Mrs Reiss replanted the borders in stronger colours

her garden at Munstead Wood before her death in 1933. Nevertheless her own planting schemes, which often incorporated plants and plant associations taken directly from Miss Jekyll's teaching, remained simpler and therefore easier to follow and interpret. Where Miss Jekyll recommended complicated and sophisticated drifts of colour sequences which blended in the eye, Mrs Reiss kept each plant and colour group in sufficiently large blocks so that each colour remained distinct. She used pure hues such as reds and yellows in strong contrasting blocks which she linked by deliberately repetitive foreground planting of grey and silvery foliage. At the back arching grasses (*Miscanthus sinensis* in various forms) performed the same unifying function. 'Frensham' roses, spires of yellow verbascum, scarlet dahlias and *Achillea* 'Coronation Gold' were set in front of a hedge of dark yew. Elsewhere low-growing blue-flowered plants were massed effectively to make a carpet to frame pale pink shrub roses and magenta-flowered *Geranium psilostemon*. Perhaps the most frequently copied scheme at Tintinhull is a wide border where purple and golden foliage plants make a tapestry background for crimson roses and bright blue *Veronica teucrium*. Purple-leaved plum (*Prunus cerasifera* 'Pissardii') and *Berberis × ottawensis* 'Purpurea' with *B. thunbergii atropurpurea* contrast with gold variegated dogwood (*Cornus alba* 'Spaethii'). In search of continuity and to link the different garden 'rooms' together she planted the purple-leaved smoke bush (various cultivars of *Cotinus coggygria*) in more than one place but with different companions; similarly, groups of *regale* lilies were distributed in pots and beds to create different yet repetitive effects, and grey-leaved hostas and alchemillas edged beds and marked corners.

Perhaps fortunately, no detailed Reiss planting plans exist; instead comprehensive plant lists (made by Graham Stuart Thomas in 1954 in conjunction with Mrs Reiss) indicate plant and colour schemes while allowing a certain freedom of arrangement to those in charge today. At Tintinhull and Montacute all planting is 'mixed' in form. Every gardener knows or soon learns that this sort of gardening cannot depend on a blue-print. In mixed beds and borders small trees and shrubs with spreading canopies give height and architecture as well as seasonal flowers and foliage; beneath and between them, covering the ground, bulbs and perennials and drifts of annuals (or tender bedding plants) complete the composition. Almost yearly adjustments keep planting relationships in satisfying proportions. A gardener such as Mrs Reiss, having chosen and placed her foundation planting of trees and shrubs which structured the garden, composed and recomposed her less permanent planting schemes around them.

Some might call it luck that when she came in 1933 she found an almost perfect garden framework within which she could manipulate plants in their design roles. It seems equally fortunate for posterity that she could garden here for nearly thirty years and give the house and garden into the care of the National Trust, ensuring its future. Dame Sylvia Crowe, who took her first job after Swanley Horticultural College with Mrs Reiss's father Colonel Lucas at Hobland, first met her in 1922, when she was already married. They remained firm and affectionate friends. In *Garden Design* (published in 1958 and now reprinted) Sylvia Crowe discusses the qualities of Tintinhull and Mrs Reiss's use of plants. More recently she writes, 'One of Phyllis's strengths was that she knew just what plant was right in a particular place, and would not be seduced by novelty or extra colour'. Perhaps the secret of Mrs Reiss's garden planning lay not only in her capacity to see plants and plant colours in architectural roles, but more simply in her capacity for a limiting self-discipline – most gardens suffer from too many diverse plants placed in too many diverse schemes. Yet how many other gardeners could practice such restraint and not have a tedious garden? Tintinhull was restful but never dull.

A Flying Start at Sixty

DENIS WOOD

When a man retires from his profession or business at sixty or sixty-five and moves to a new garden, perhaps in some long-desired part of the world, he will find it hard to accept the slow rate of growth of some particular plants which he would like to have around him in his old age. When he was a young man he soon came to accept the slow tempo of growing things, and he knew that after thirty years in one garden, he would see his oaks 30ft. high from acorns, his Scots pines 40ft. high from forest transplants, and even his beloved arbutus and Judas trees 18–20ft. high from 2ft. These last are two of the particularly attractive and distinctive small trees, which are not only slow-growing but cannot be transplanted from the open ground in sizes much above 2ft.

But if he were to take action five or ten years before removing to his place of retirement, he could at least ameliorate the prospect of having to face these long intervals all over again. The action would be to buy young trees at the prescribed height of 2ft., put them into fairly large pots and systematically 'pot them on' over the five to ten years into progressively larger pots, then into small tubs and larger tubs or rough boxes. If a start were made in a 12 inch pot and the size increased by 3 inches every two years, the size of the container after six years would be 18ins. and after ten years 21ins. If *Arbutus unedo* is taken as an example, the rate of growth, according to that excellent book, *Trees for Town and Country*, by Brenda Colvin, Jacqueline Tyrwhitt and S. R. Badmin, is 15ft. in twenty-five years in its early stages in the open ground. This works out at about 7ins. in a year. I do not know how this rate would be influenced by a plant being grown in a tub, but it might be reasonable to estimate three-quarters of the rate, which is just about 5ins. in a year. So that, from a 2ft. start, plants after five years would be 4–4½ft. in a container 18ins. in diameter. At these dimensions they should be fairly easily lifted and planted out by two men. After ten years the plants would be 6ft. in containers 21ins. in diameter, and would need at least two men with ropes and greased planks to move them about, but 6ft. is a good deal better than 2ft. at the age of sixty-five.

The pots should have a drainage layer of shingle at the bottom, the growing compost should be 50 per cent loam, 25 per cent coarse sphagnum peat, 25 per cent coarse, gritty sand, reinforced by John Innes base fertiliser at the rate of ¾lb per bushel (four bucketsful). The containers would be best kept plunged, that is sunk into the ground, and the plants would have to be conscientiously watered, and as soon as the roots are round the continer, fed with a general fertiliser at least once a month in the growing season.

Magnolia grandiflora

Beside arbutus and Judas trees, there are other plants which could be treated in this way. The evergreen Magnolia, *M. grandiflora*, which although it can be obtained at from 3–5ft. and is not at all slow-growing, takes an unconscionable time to produce its glorious lemon-scented flowers in July. It would surely benefit from ageing in a wooden cask before being planted against the house wall. In mild climates *Magnolia mollicomata*, said to take only from seven to ten years to come into flower, is an improvement on its haughty relative, *M. campbellii,* which does not condescend to flower for twenty or thirty years. In warmer districts, the Monterey pine, *Pinus radiata,* which can only be supplied at a very small size but which, when once established, is fast-growing and majestically beautiful. The evergreen oak, *Quercus ilex,* is another which is usually only supplied in pots.

Some of the plants started in this way might end up as permanent tub-residents; for example, varieties of *Camellia japonica* and many different rhododendrons – bushes of 'Pink Pearl', 8ft. high in large tubs, are a considerable spectacle. Bay trees are generally kept in tubs and steadily become more massive each year, while Portugal laurels, *Prunus lusitanica,* can be treated in rather the same way, planted in tubs in as large a size as can be obtained – probably not much more than 3ft. these days – and pruned into shapes over the years. For more than two hundred years orange trees have been grown in large tubs, known as *Versailles caisses.* 1m × 1m × 1m high (a cubic metre) and having detachable sides in order that parts of the growing compost can be removed and replaced from time to time.

The most triumphant application of this procedure would be, instead of laying down port at the birth of a son, to lay down instead half-dozens of arbutus, cercis and magnolias and keep them going for 21 years, so that when the son or daughter comes into his or her new garden, they will have trees approaching maturity from 12–18ft. high. They would need a fork lift truck to transport them, but the hire of one of these should not be outside the scope of an adequate twenty-first birthday celebration.

New Roses of Victorian Times

HAZEL LE ROUGETEL

Over Queen Victoria's reign spread a great surge of development, following the introduction of four long-flowering roses from China between 1789 and 1824. These, crossed with old summer-flowerers of the west and subsequent hybridisation of new strains, produced a wonderful range of roses lingering into the autumn. As the nineteenth century progressed, so blooms became larger, their colours more varied, and competition to produce the most spectacular roses increased. This was an era of introduction and display, with breeders, nurserymen and exhibitors vying in rose promotion.

First to evolve from this China rose revolution were Portlands, probably from 'Slater's Crimson China', with Gallica and Damask strains. These were hardy, medium-sized, repeat-flowering, and eminent among them are 'Comte de Chambord', 'Jacques Cartier' and 'Marbrée', of varying pinks, bred in France between 1858 and 1869. Noisettes originated in South Carolina early in the century from a liaison of 'Parsons's Pink China' and R. moschata, to be further developed in the Paris nursery of Louis Noisette. These fragrant, clustered climbers, flowering long, were immediately acclaimed and two of note were 'Madame Alfred Carrière', almost white and tolerant of a northern aspect, and our own 'Alister Stella Gray', also known as 'Golden Rambler' (1894).

A third class sprang from the Ile de Bourbon where the old autumn Damask 'Quatre Saisons' had long been used for hedging. A chance cross with 'Parsons's Pink China' resulted in the first of the Bourbons, 'Rose Edouard', in 1817. Others were quickly developed in France. With lovely fragrance, they were soon widely acclaimed: blushing 'Souvenir de la Malmaison' for nostalgic association with the Empress Josephine; charming pink, cupped 'La Reine Victoria' and its paler sport 'Madame Pierre Oger', for example. Some grew tall as climbers: deep pink 'Zéphirine Drouhin' proved ubiquitous, and an earlier 'Blairi No. 2', pale pink deepening towards the centre, also displayed well on high while, unrivalled for scent and size of cerise blooms, 'Madame Isaac Pereire' was an irresistible Victorian charmer.

Other newcomers not readily falling into these three early groups have been classed as Hybrid Chinas and a trio in lasting demand have been 'Hermosa', most floriferous with small pink globular flowers, 'Perle d'Or' whose pointed buds were deemed ideal for buttonholes, and 'Cécile Brunner', coveted by florists for tiny, shell-pink blooms.

Selection of outstanding qualities of these new roses led to another class, and it seems appropriate here to consider a typical nurseryman of the time, one who propagated a vast number of these Hybrid Perpetuals. Among European rosarians of the nineteenth century England's William Paul and Thomas Rivers were revered. Both had extensive collections, bred new varieties and distributed them around the world. Both wrote books which ran to many editions: Paul's *The Rose Garden* (1848) was the more erudite, although Rivers's handy little *Rose Amateur's Guide* (1837), eminently practical, was widely read and quoted. It also provides glimpses of the activities of an eminent Victorian rosarian and of the achievements in his nursery at Sawbridgeworth in Hertfordshire.

He was often in Europe: in 1824, tempted by yellow Tea roses in pots at a Paris market; in 1843, enraptured by a Noisette 'Cloth of Gold' in Vibert's new nursery at Angers, and one May in Florence, astonished by an abundance of the old double yellow rose. Guillot of

Portland Rose: 'Marbrée' (1858) is an attractive
mottled pink, here grown with *Artemesia ludoviciana*

Lyon named a Hybrid Perpetual 'Madam Rivers' (William Paul gave it a 'delicate complexion') and another, 'Laffay's Rivers', was offered in the 1844 Sawbridgeworth *Catalogue*. With Laffay he shared a love of Moss roses, and claimed to have in his nursery all those currently grown in France. From Como in Italy came seeds of *R. multiflora* and others, to produce an unusually scented red climber and 'Rivers' Musk', described as 'rosy buff and very fragrant'.

At home he crossed a blush Ayrshire from Scotland with a maroon Gallica, to produce his acclaimed dusky 'Ayrshire Queen'. Always adventurous, Rivers encouraged his readers to experiment to try to create a yellow Ayrshire or a mossy Bourbon. Rich shades excited him and he maintained that his enthusiasm for roses was sparked off by a chance China hybrid in his collection – one, he said, to eclipse all dark roses known, and he named it 'George IV' (1820). It also caught the eye of Robert Buist of Philadelphia on a visit to the nursery, and for him it became one of the best sellers in America.

In 1833 John Claudius Loudon had favourably reviewed the Sawbridgeworth *Catalogue* as the most useful description of roses in the English language. Over the years, issues indicate changing trends: in

'Reine des Violettes' (1860), one of the most attractive
Hybrid Perpetuals, with purple/violet shading

1840 some 200 summer and 250 autumn roses were listed, twenty years later the former had been reduced to 40 and within another ten to 18, while 137 Hybrid Perpetuals were offered under colour headings. Selection could now be made from dark crimson, light crimson and scarlet, carmine, rose and pink, blush and flesh, to white.

Union Standards were available around 1840, 'two varieties of opposite colours on one stock having a pretty effect when in bloom at the same time'. One suggested association was of florid 'George IV' with blushing 'Duchesse d'Angoulême', a Gallica bred by Vibert in 1835. This fashion was replaced by emphasis on roses trained to form an eight foot pillar of bloom, suitable Hybrid Perpetuals being marked with a 'p' and including deep pink 'Baronne Prévost', carmine 'Jules Margottin' and 'Reine des Violettes', one of the loveliest of this class.

However, in the mid-century two reds were widely acclaimed: Rivers distributed 8000 standards and dwarfs of 'Géant des Batailles' (1846) around the country only three years after its introduction. Five were included in a consignment of 37 roses safely delivered after a three-month voyage to Thomas Lang of Ballerat, Australia, on 31 March 1858 and in the following year, American visitors at Sawbridgeworth were particularly impressed with this variety, reporting on large plots 'profusely covered with blossom, like a rich green carpet embroidered with superb bouquets of dark crimson roses'.

The 'Géant' seems unavailable today, but another firm Victorian favourite, 'Général Jacqueminot' (1853), has survived. Whereas the former's crimson was usually described as 'bright' (or 'fiery' by George Leslie of Toronto), the Général's was invariably 'brilliant' and, in the catalogue of David Day, Auckland, New Zealand, 1865, as 'most brilliant, crimson, scarlet, even surpassing "Géant des Batailles", the best in this class'. From American T. B. Jenkins, in *Roses and Rose Culture* (1892), came lasting tribute: 'In 1853 France gave us 'Général Jacqueminot', leader of the Hybrid Perpetuals . . . the great half-grown crimson buds have slept on the bosom of every belle since that day'.

Results of the great rose explosion had to be assessed, and one third of Dean Reynolds Hole's *Book about Roses* (1869) was devoted to showing them, an aspect on which he had much expertise, having conceived the idea of a National Rose Show. With Paul, Rivers and Charles Turner ('prince of florists') collaborating, an appeal was launched, St James's Hall booked, and the Coldstream Band secured for 1st July 1858, when 'half the nurseries of England poured their treasure' – so reported Dr Lindley in the *Gardeners' Chronicle*. The Dean's love of roses and his rapport with their growers led to his appointment as first President of the National Rose Society in 1876.

Rose shows were by no means exclusively for great growers and the Dean movingly described his visit to judge one staged by working men on Easter Monday in Nottingham. Having no roses out himself at the time he was sceptical, but was astonished to find, in an up-stairs room in an inn, 'Adam', 'Devoniensis' and 'Souvenir d'Ami' shown exquisitely, with the best 'Maréchal Niel' and 'Madame Margottin' he had yet seen, 'that Spring in Nottingham in ginger beer bottles'. After the judging he was taken to the allotments and learned that blankets had been taken from beds to insulate tiny glasshouses and protect most precious Teas from frost.

Two tea-scented Chinas, 'Hume's Blush' and 'Parks's Yellow', of the all-important China quartet, were responsible for the Teas. The first to be recognised, 'Adam', came from Rheims in 1833, and an early favourite with florists was 'Safrano', with beautiful saffron buds

Rosa rugosa typica introduced from Japan in 1796 but not used in gardens
for about another hundred years. Deep pink flowers,
splendid red hips and dark deep-veined foliage

'Hermosa' (1840), a China Hybrid, fairly small in growth
with pink blooms over a long period. Photographs: Hazel Le Rougetel

opening paler, grown extensively in the south of France for the winter
trade. In England, white 'Devoniensis' (1841) bred in Devonport
could reach 12 feet, but proved tender in comparison with the very
popular apricot-orange 'Gloire de Dijon' of like habit. 'Souvenir
d'Elise Vardon' gained superlative comment from all leading rosarians
and, although tender, was still included thirty years on as one of the
best Teas (*Journal of Horticulture*, 11 December 1884).

In the garden Teas could not compete with Hybrid Perpetuals, and
they were almost entirely grown in conservatories where their subtle
fragrance could be savoured and their inclined heads viewed to
advantage from below. In today's Tea revival some have proved surprisingly hardy and 'Safrano', 'Général Schablikine', coppery-red and
'Archiduc Joseph', of many pinky-purple coloured petals, are Victorians which have survived severe winters in Hampshire in the
1980s, well blanketed with bracken. Alternatively, they may be
grown in pots for winter cossetting.

Given hardy Hybrid Perpetuals and tender Teas, breeders took the
best from both and in 1867 the first Hybrid Tea, 'La France', appeared,
although the class was not recognised until 1884 and did not successfully compete with its parents until the early twentieth century.

Meanwhile, hybridists the world over were working to improve these latest roses, among them Henry Bennett in England, George Dixon in Ireland and Joseph Pernet-Ducher in France, the latter producing exciting new brilliant yellow shades through *R. persiana* and *R. foetida bicolor*. A further Victorian development was a class of Polyanthas, from a China hybrid and *R. multiflora*, of which 'Mignonette' (1880) survives today. They are important because through them evolved the Floribundas (now known as Clustered Roses), the other all-important class of the twentieth century.

Shirley Hibberd, first editor of both *Amateur Gardening* and *The Florist*, was also author of *The Amateur's Rose Book* (1864 and 1894), so may be taken to represent rose development in the latter years of the Victorian era. His wide knowledge covered both the decorative and the practical gardening aspect of roses. Ninety Teas were cherished in his rose-house at Stoke Newington and he gave good advice on growing under glass, as well as forcing in pots for house, conservatory or garden. He advocated them for 'a little bijou plunge ground in a sheltered nook near a window after potted tulips, hyacinths and alyssum have had their day'. An informative chapter on roses for indoor decoration stressed consideration of colour by day or artificial gaslight. The second edition of Hibberd concludes with a comprehensive 'Synoptical Catalogue' of fifty pages giving a brief description of some 2500 varieties – an excellent up to date survey.

Towards the end of the century, the concept of a more informal use of roses took shape, as Hibberd's discourse on hedgerow and wilderness roses shows. He suggested planting roses in the 'negligé style', letting Noisettes 'Ophirie' and 'Miss Glegg' form dense natural screens to hide unsightly landmarks, and planting clumps of Scotch roses and sweet briar in pleasure ground or park. He praised the use of *R. rugosa* as an impregnable hedge and included an illustration of one in Mr G. F. Wilson's garden at Wisley. He drew attention to the bonus of its spectacular fruit in autumn, and although this rose had been brought from the far East a hundred years before, it was only in the nineties that its potential became appreciated, when beautiful hybrids like 'Blanc Double de Coubert' arrived from France and 'Conrad Ferdinand Meyer' from Germany.

The use of roses as shrubs, with consideration of their whole form, foliage and fruit, as well as flowers, was another revolution in the rose world. Over the Victorian era emphasis had been on blooms of exquisite shape, shade and scent of roses bred, nurtured and exhibited by a diversity of enthusiasts, led by our rosarian Dean who loved best 'those Roses which are chosen for their more perfect beauty, like the fairest maidens at some public *fête*, to represent the sisterhood before a wondering world'.

Green Flowers for Green Fingers

STEPHEN LACEY

We are always on the lookout for things curious and uncommon: leaves with splashes and stripes, seedheads with horns and tentacles, branches arranged like cake-stands and flowers shaped like lobster's claws or burrowing field mice. To this list we might add plants which have forsaken the conventional spectrum of flower colours to exhibit blooms in shades of green, black and brown.

As it happens, sophisticated colouring is very much *de rigueur* at the moment and green, black and brown flowers are being embraced by every fashion-conscious gardener and florist worth his sea salt. Certainly, Oscar Wilde's green carnation wouldn't cause many raised eyebrows in St James's today. The trend has done much to bring obscure plants to light again and let us hope that when it dies away, they will not vanish with it.

As a plant lover, I am not a great slave to fashion. Plants are chosen on their own merits and become more or less permanent members of a mixed community. I grow the greens, blacks and browns for their eccentric personalities – comic, mysterious, sinister, retiring, exotic, or just plain odd – and for the element of surprise they bring to border schemes. So I am not going to encourage you to cast out your oranges and flame reds, your rich violets and crimsons, in favour of a new order based on restraint and sobriety; rather I am going to persuade you to absorb these quirky individuals into your existing plant groups and use them as part of an already well-stocked palette.

Green flowers are far more numerous than blacks and browns and are produced in virtually every month. In tone they vary from off-white to near-blue, but the majority tend towards yellow. When siting them, two general points should be borne in mind. First, they may need to be illuminated by their immediate neighbours if they are to be properly visible. This can be done either with a very bright backdrop, such as white flowers, or, funnily enough, by a very dark backdrop, like purple foliage. Second, they may be aggressive. It is a mistake to assume all greens are neutral and can be combined harmoniously with all other colours: the yellow-greens are real troublemakers and will clash ferociously with pinks and pinky purples.

In winter, when even the greens of leaves are scarce, a green flower is doubly precious. The first to appear is *Helleborus foetidus*. Once, when out riding in central Italy, I came across a disused road totally buried in the dark, fingered foliage of these hellebores. At home we have to content ourselves with tamer images, and fortunately *H. foetidus* is skilled at seeding itself into eyecatching positions – the most apposite in my garden is between the brick porch, leading to the front door, and a mound of white-variegated euonymus. The sprays of yellow-green, maroon-rimmed bells are silhouetted perfectly against the leaves, but you need to secure 'Bowles's Variety' for the best contrast. There is a form with red stems (actually not as dramatic in appearance as it sounds) called 'Wester Flisk'.

Oriental hellebores are also to be had in fine green-flowered seedlings. They don't display themselves wonderfully, it has to be said, but if you assemble some plum-coloured forms around them, they show up rather better. Cutting away the old foliage is also a sound policy. Helen Ballard (Old Country, Mathon, Malvern, Worcestershire) has a superior green clone which bears her name: and I am very covetous of her lime-coloured plant called *H. odorus* ssp. *laxus* which was illustrated in the January 1987 issue of *The Garden* (published by the Royal Horticultural Society).

The Corsican hellebore is far more boldly architectural than its cousins and can be trusted in prominent positions at the corners of borders or beside steps. Its pale green cups associate well with the bright blue flowers of *Brunnera macrophylla* and *Symphytum caucasicum*. Indeed, the partnership is satisfactory on several counts since all three ingredients also have a strong but distinct foliar presence, display flowers and foliage of contrasting sizes and shapes, and thrive in the same conditions of well-nourished semi-shade.

Equally imposing characters are the euphorbias. *E. wulfenii* takes all winter to transform its croziers of yellow-green bracts into giant bullrushes, and they are probably at their best in April. It is the ideal centrepiece for schemes of lemon daffodils and gentian blue scillas, and for stands of early orange tulips like 'Orange Emperor', but its glaucous foliage is available as a foil for strong colours all year. *E. characias* has bluer leaves, darker bracts (aptly described as 'lovebird green' by Margery Fish) and chocolate brown eyes, and is good in a sweep of damson and cream tulips like 'Queen of the Night' and 'Reforma'. I cannot see the point of paying out huge sums for named hybrids and clones like 'Lambrook Gold' and 'John Tomlinson', for if you grow *E. wulfenii* and *E. characias* near each other, you will certainly find your own exciting intermediate and idiosyncratic forms; but this is an heretical view to hold.

The flowerheads of *E. robbiae* are similar in effect. It seems a pity to waste a sunny position on this plant, which puts up with any amount of dry shade you throw at it, but I have never seen a better partner for it than the strange green-striped yellowish tulip called 'Humming-bird'. There are loads of other euphorbias with lime-yellow inflorescences worth collecting, including *E. amygdaloides* (in its purple and variegated leaved forms), *E. × martinii*, *E. myrsinites*, *E. nicaeensis* and *E. palustris*, but for colour the most striking must be *E. polychroma* (syn. *E. epithymoides*). The bracts are as shrieking a green as you can get without actually being yellow, and glow in the company of forget-me-nots and white-flowered, white-variegated honesty. Daring gardeners might try them in the front of an orange berberis.

There are two choices of green-flowered carpet to spread in front of your taller green, yellow, blue and white perennials. Barnhaven Nursery (Brigsteer, Kendal, Cumbria) has selected polyanthus seed in strains called 'Chartreuse' ('cream iced with pale green'), and 'Limelight' ('limey whites and yellows'), and these mixtures of subtle shades can either be used on their own, or stirred into pools of dark blue and purple polyanthus to make stronger images.

The other shade-loving carpeter is the dwarf *Hacquetia epipactis*. Because it is impossibly slow to increase and reluctant to be divided, you have to acquire several plants to make any sort of impact. The green ruffs and their central tufts of yellow are dazzling throughout April and look well with brunneras and yellow erythroniums, white pulmonarias and primroses.

Really exciting greens, proper jades and emeralds, lurk among the auriculas, but you have to grow them under glass to preserve the coating of farina with which they are dusted. The compensation for their absence from border schemes is their lemon scent, which would surely be lost outdoors. Brenda Hyatt (1 Toddington Crescent, Bluebell Hill, Chatham, Kent) sells seed and named plants.

I am always suspicious of the epithet 'connoisseur's plant'; it often means the plant looks like a weed. What connoisseurs see in the rose plantain, *Plantago major rosularis*, for example, I cannot imagine. I was given this plant early in my gardening career but soon threw it onto the compost heap. Apart from the fact that its leaves were always mildewed, I thought its knob of wrinkled green bracts coarse and grotesque. It vulgarised every group it was put into, and I would sooner grow a good-sized cabbage, which you could at least eat, when you were sick of looking at it. *Rosa viridiflora* is a similarly unappealing freak.

Aquilegia viridiflora is also likely to prove a disappointment to gardeners expecting something eyecatching and extrovert. Furthermore, it seems to have a delicate constitution which makes it unsuitable for the rough and tumble of the border. But there is no denying its beauty. The brownish green bells are scented and fritillary-like and the foliage is glaucous and dainty. I had it in a raised bed once, backed by a dwarf blue juniper and teamed up with mauve purple *Semi-aquilegia ecalcarata*.

As for the real fritillaries, the two green ones I have attempted so far are *Fritillaria pontica* and *F. acmopetala*. Both are hardy and easily cultivated, the former enjoying cool, moist semi-shade and the latter sun and good drainage. *F. pontica* is the greenest, its large bells only lightly flushed with yellow and tipped maroon. *F. acmopetala* has maroon blotches. Because of the presence of purple tones and because these are flowers that do require a discreet foil, I would suggest planting a purple-leaved berberis or cotinus behind them; ferny corydalis and dicentras are appropriately airy companions.

Two evergreen shade-loving daphnes have yellowish green flowers. *Daphne laureola*, the spurge laurel, opens its clusters of fragrant tubes in February but the flowers are small and badly displayed and don't really make much impression, even though the leaves are flatteringly dark. *D. pontica*, which performs in May, is more impressive. The effect is still scruffy but there are so many long flowers that a limy haze is created. Try a belt of those old scarlet cottage garden tulips in front of it.

I am forever enthusing about the sweet cowslip scent that pours from the untidy flower spikes of tellimas and this, together with the purple winter foliage of the variety 'Purpurea', is the main reason for growing them. But the flowers are lime green and it is worth showing them off; mine grow in front of black-green holly. *Heuchera cylindrica* 'Greenfinch', which Beth Chatto sells, gives a similar effect. Its long stems drip with pale green bells and it also has magnificent foliage, silvery and scalloped.

One of the most bizarre green performers enters the stage in May.

It is *Paris polyphylla*, the Himalyan relative of our native herb Paris or true love. The startling inflorescence is a cross between a large clematis flower and a jellyfish, and you really need to grow it among simple conventional plants like bluebells and Welsh poppies to capitalise on its ability to surprise. It prefers shade and well-drained soil, and the easiest way to acquire it is as seed.

Veratrum viride joins Paris in early June. I have not yet attempted to grow it myself, but have often admired it in other people's gardens. The vivid green candelabrum stands high above the broad pleated leaves, making it a truly sculptural border ingredient. It enjoys moist, rich living and looks well against a purple maple or plum in the company of hostas and alchemilla.

The tobacco flowers provide us with two green varieties. *Nicotiana* 'Lime Green' is the most popular, and its flattish stars are useful throughout the summer as a cooling influence in hot schemes of penstemons and lilies, crocosmias, bronze fennel and ligularias. But *N. langsdorfii* with its thin limy funnels filled with turquoise anthers is also desirable. I put it with blood red *Cosmos atrosanguineus* and the curious green and red *Alstroemeria pulchella*, which makes an unusual colour scheme for August and September. You could add the green-tasseled *Amaranthus caudatus* 'Albiflorus' and that flower arranger's delight *Moluccella laevis* to the group, but I usually use these annuals to tone down any blazing orange or scarlet bedding plants that I am currently playing with.

Several sea hollies do not bother to turn their thistles blue. *Eryngium agavifolium* is a stiff species with solid upright stems and rosettes of serrated daggers, the individual thistles being no bigger than thimbles. Actually, I may be describing *E. serra*, which is similar, for my plant did not come to me with a name. *E. eburneum*, which gardeners usually call *E. bromeliifolium*, has a more relaxed appearance with arching stems and grassy foliage. Sea hollies generally look more at home in the cracks in paving or springing out of gravel than in the border, and in such positions their skeletal shapes can be better appreciated. But they are also effective rising from a mat of low-growing plants like blue hebes or purple ajugas, artemisias or golden marjoram.

All the yellow-flowered kniphofias look very green until the buds are on the point of opening, but Beth Chatto's seedling 'Green Jade' preserves this delicate tone. I have just secured a plant after years of searching.

Four plants most suitable to pot cultivation, except in very favoured districts, have green flowers and can be enjoyed in isolation or gingerly dropped among your orange daylilies and pokers. *Eucomis bicolor* and the superior *E. comosa* look like pineapples on sticks and never fail to draw attention to themselves. Their only drawback is their revolting scent, which is beloved of bluebottles. *Puya alpestris* is a real stunner. For a start, the shape of the flower spike is extraordinary, like a besom with its head in the air, the tight clusters of yellowish buds pointing in all sorts of acute angles. And then there are the flowers themselves, upward facing bells of a unique sea-green with projecting orange anthers. It is difficult to find a source for this plant but it comes readily from seed so it is worth scouring seed catalogues as well as nurseries.

Ixia viridiflora is another plant of legendary beauty that is extremely difficult to find. Certainly it has eluded me so far. A number of bulb firms sell ixias in mixed colours but this blue-green, black-eyed beauty is in a class apart. The effect is of a cloud of tropical butterflies feeding on the stems. Cultivation is the same as for freesias, in other words a frost-free greenhouse and a dry summer dormancy. Flowering is in late spring.

There are two green-flowered galtonias for the late summer border (though it is wise to keep a few bulbs in the greenhouse during the winter as a safety measure). Slightly shorter than the familiar *G. candicans*, *G. princeps* bears bells in alabaster green. It is an interesting partner for apricot *Buddleia × weyeriana* and enjoys the light shade it casts. *G. viridiflora* is a touch greener.

This is by no means a comprehensive list of green treasures. Once you start rummaging through catalogues and nurseries you will turn up plenty of other candidates. And you will not want to restrict yourself to all-green flowers. What about those plants with green eyes (*Dianthus* 'Charles Musgrave' and *Primula bhutanica*), green spots (snowdrops and leucojums), and green smudges (tulips 'Spring Green' and 'Angel')? What about those plants suffused with green like astrantias, *Aquilegia* 'Nora Barlow' and *Zantedeschia* 'Green Goddess'? There is enough material to fill the entire garden with unexpected greenery. Imagine what a cool and refreshing place it would be, especially if we added quantities of bold foliage and glistening white lilies and roses and saturated the borders in peppermint scents. Perhaps we do need to throw out our strong colours after all.

Lawrence Johnston, Creator of Hidcote Garden

ALVILDE LEES-MILNE

To thousands of gardeners and horticulturists both professional and amateur in Western Europe, and even to some in Australia, the USA, Canada and Africa, the word Hidcote means only one thing. It means one of the most beautiful, interesting, haunting gardens in existence. Yet how many of these thousands of visitors, who go there year after year, ever give a thought to its creator?

Who was Lawrence Johnston? Where did he come from? Why did he choose a remote and cold Cotswold hilltop on which to make this remarkable garden? How, anyway, did he know so much about gardens? In fact, how could any one man in his lifetime create something so perfect? Perhaps it is time he was brought out a little into the limelight which he so much disliked.

Lawrence Waterbury Johnston was born in Paris on 12 October 1871. His father, Elliott Johnston, came from Baltimore, Maryland, USA, and must have died before 1887, for in that year Lawrence's mother, born Gertrude Cleveland, married Charles Francis Winthrop, son of a prominent New York family. Winthrop died in Paris in 1898. The Johnstons, who had Scottish connections, came from the north of Ireland. Lawrence Johnston's early life was spent in France. His parents evidently belonged to that cultured group of rather well-to-do Americans who in the late nineteenth and early twentieth centuries felt drawn to Europe, where they found more to satisfy their interests and where they often settled for good. In fact, they were what are often loosely termed 'Henry James Americans'.

So Lawrence must from an early age have been accustomed to being surrounded by beauty and culture. Walks in the streets of Paris, visits to museums, visits to *châteaux* and *manoirs* with exquisite gardens, all this and a great deal more must have made a lasting impression upon the small boy. Being in a foreign country he was educated at home by a tutor. He was always very close to his mother; when they went to Hidcote, she lived with him for nearly twenty years and was buried nearby. She seems to have been quite a character, and inevitably somewhat dominated her son.

There is no clear picture to be drawn of him in his early years, and there are a great many gaps in our knowledge of his life. When quite young he became a Roman Catholic, possibly through the influence of his French tutor. It is not known when he first came to England, but it was certainly before he was twenty. The first definite date in his life is 1894 when, after cramming at Shelford, he matriculated at Trinity College, Cambridge. He was then twenty-three. He received an ordinary second class degree in history in 1897, and left the university that year. The next landmark is 1900, when he became a naturalised British subject. In that same year he joined the Imperial Yeomanry as a trooper, and went off to the Boer War. What drew him into that mesh remains a mystery. A longing for adventure, perhaps, coupled with a way of seeing a new continent.

In 1902 he returned, and went to live in Northumberland. The reason for this was twofold. Firstly, when in South Africa he made friends with a young man called Savile Clayton, whose home was near Humshaugh. Secondly, he was suffering from weak lungs, and the bracing north country air was considered healthy. In Northumberland he became a student farmer, lodging with a landowner called George Ray.

Next comes the important date 1907. Lawrence was then thirty-six years old, and had presumably made up his mind where his real interests lay. It was in this year that his mother, Mrs Winthrop, bought for him a property in the heart of the Cotswolds, called Hidcote Bartrim. It consisted of about 280 acres of farmland, a tiny hamlet of thatched cottages, and a small stone farmhouse. There was a wonderful view from the escarpment over the Vale of Evesham away to the Malvern Hills. But the great attraction was a huge and ancient cedar of Lebanon and a clump of fine beech trees.

It was a strange choice, as in those days Hidcote was really remote, and one which could only have been made by someone with considerable vision and imagination. There is no doubt that his active interest in farming was a contributory factor to the acquisition of Hidcote, and perhaps the fact that this hilltop site was considered beneficial for his health. A friend who lived nearby remembered often seeing him ploughing. However, by then gardening had already become his chosen hobby. His interest in, and knowledge of, horticulture must have grown rapidly. Unfortunately, apart from a few very early photographs, there are no records to tell us how he planned the garden at Hidcote. Luckily Mrs Winthrop had a considerable fortune to draw on, and her son knew how best to spend it.

A wing for Mrs Winthrop was added to the little farmhouse, today known as the Manor, and other parts of the house were structurally altered with various embellishments. The farmyard was turned into a respectable courtyard and the cottages were renovated. Later Lawrence designed and built one or two more. He also converted a small barn in the courtyard into a chapel where sometimes he would have Low Mass said, or what the French call a *messe de chasse*.

Life in the country must have been very agreeable in the pre-Great War years, and from this point of view Hidcote was in an auspicious situation geographically. A few miles away at the foot of the escarpment lay Broadway. This lovely little town, as yet undiscovered by tourists, was in its intellectual heyday. A beautiful and famous American actress, Mary Anderson, had come to live there with her Spanish husband, Antonio de Navarro. They had a wide circle of interesting friends. Among others, Elgar, Sargent, William Morris and Burne-Jones were frequent visitors. The Navarros, too, were planning and planting a garden which today is of considerable interest and beauty. Writing in 1936 in her book, *A Few More Memories*, Madame de Navarro said: 'My Italian friends regard Hidcote as the most beautiful garden they have seen in England. Its wonderful blending of colours and its somewhat formal architectural character please them particularly.' Later she wrote of seeing Reginald Farrer's incomparable gentian blooming at Hidcote in November: 'It seemed too good to be true.' But of course this was sixteen years later.

Most of Lawrence Johnston's friends were passionate and knowledgeable gardeners. Here again he was fortunate in having several in the vicinity – Major Mark Fenwick at Abbotswood, the great alpine grower Clarence Elliott near Moreton-in-Marsh, Lord Barrington then living at Armscote and later at Nether Lypiatt where he emulated the tapestry hedges at Hidcote, Charles Wade, then at Snowshill, and George Lees-Milne at Wickhamford. Later the Jack Muirs came to Kiftsgate, which is at the end of the Hidcote drive. Here they created a garden which was to become a rival to Hidcote, though entirely different in character, and which to this day is still very spectacular, and of course immortalised by the great climbing rose that bears its name. Mrs Muir and Lawrence Johnston were able to help each other, and enjoyed many years of close gardening partnership. Then there was Norah Lindsay. Mrs Lindsay was probably Lawrence Johnston's closest woman friend, and though she did not live nearby was a constant visitor. She herself was no mean garden architect, and among her achievements is the parterre which she redesigned on the south side of Blickling Hall in Norfolk. She was gay, witty, amusing, and indeed wonderfully stimulating. Another, geographically distant, friend was 'Bobbie' James (the Hon. Robert James), creator of a great garden, St Nicholas, near Richmond, Yorkshire and, like Lawrence Johnston, an avid collector of rare plants. In fact his friends were legion, each perhaps contributing an idea here and there towards the eventual form of the Hidcote which we know today.

Little by little the garden grew, and the acres of rough pasture were turned into acres of botanical and horticultural interest. Lawrence Johnston's planting was entirely original. It was the very opposite of the conventional herbaceous border setting, so popular among his contemporaries. His blending of sophistication and simplicity was unique. Nowhere else, except perhaps at Sissinghurst, are unusual plants found growing in cottage garden-like settings. This conception of little gardens within a large garden was entirely novel, as were the tapestry hedges and many other schemes. There are no fewer than twenty-two separate enclosures within the garden at Hidcote, excluding the Beech Allée, the Lime Avenue and the Holly Avenue.

I have been told that a trainful of lime-free soil arrived from Surrey for the camellias, rhododendrons and other lime-hating plants. This was mixed with rotted sawdust and peat. Those extraordinary lines of hornbeams, looking like hedges on stilts, a *palissade à l'italienne*, appeared later, as did the two little brick and stone pavilions with their pointed, ogival roofs, each side the centre walk. They are said to be copied from something Lawrence Johnston saw in France. But who knows? Some think they have a Dutch influence. The great avenue of Huntingdon elms by the north approach, devastated by the catastrophic elm disease and now replaced by *Quercus cerris* and hornbeam, was a truly bold planting, as was the Holly Avenue leading to the courtyard entrance. One could cover pages eulogising the endless and enthralling innovations at Hidcote, but that is not the purpose of this article. Many people have described the garden, but perhaps no one better than Vita Sackville-West in an article for the Royal Horticultural Society's *Journal* of November 1949. Anyone who has read it can be left in no doubt as to the genius of Lawrence Johnston.

The Fuchsia Garden in spring is a mass of *Scilla sibirica*.
The beds are edged with box. The topiary peacocks at the
entrance to the Pool Garden can be seen in the background

The truth is that in spite of, or because of, its simplicity and bold
planting Hidcote has a sophisticated, continental flavour, which in a
way puts one in mind of gardens in the Isle-de-France.

Like all dedicated gardeners Johnston was both acquisitive and
generous. Yet he allowed no room for poor specimens and failures.
He believed in cramming his beds and borders with what he most
wanted so that there was less space for what he did not want, that is,
weeds. Therefore in each category of plant at Hidcote you will find
only the best. People began to send him plants from far and wide, and
as his knowledge grew, so did his collection.

In his day there was a large winter plant house for the more tender things, a place for the cultivation of lush, sub-tropical species of rare plants, which he had collected on his travels or had been sent by other connoisseurs. Unfortunately, when the National Trust took over the garden this house, proving too costly to run, was demolished and the collection dispersed.

For seven quiet years the garden grew, and Lawrence Johnston worked alongside his gardeners. For he was no onlooker. He dug, and planted, and pruned as much as they did. Then came 1914 and the Great War. All thoughts of gardening had to be laid aside. Johnston, who had never retired from the Army, was promoted a Major and immediately sent off to France. Owing to his friendship with Savile Clayton, his commission was in the Northumberland Fusiliers. Nothing much is known about his military career except that he was wounded at the very beginning of the War, and again later. At one point he was laid out with a lot of other bodies awaiting burial. By chance an old friend from Broadway, Colonel Henry Sidney, had been detailed to see to the burial ceremony, and as he passed Major Johnston, he not only recognised him but saw him move.

When Johnston returned from the War there was much to be done at Hidcote. Four years' neglect in a garden can alter it drastically. As things gradually returned to normal he began to think of going off plant collecting, and in 1927 and 1931 he undertook two enthralling expeditions. The first was with Major Collingwood (Cherry) Ingram on a four-months' trip from Cape Town to the Victoria Falls, during which time he climbed the Drakensburg Mountains. George Taylor (later Sir George Taylor, and Director of Kew Gardens) and Reginald Cory made up the party. The expedition has been splendidly recorded by Major Ingram in his book, *A Garden of Memories*. Lawrence Johnston, who liked his comforts, brought along his Italian cook and chauffeur valet. Major Ingram described Johnston as a typical bachelor, wholly dedicated to gardening, and says that of the four of them he was by far the most catholic in his choice of plants. He would collect members of any genus if they had the slightest claim to beauty. The result was a vast accumulation which he sent for the most part to Edinburgh Botanic Gardens. Many of these plants were later to go to Mentone where he had acquired a property and was making another garden. The second expedition was much longer, more remote and tougher. Johnston accompanied George Forrest on what was to be

Forrest's last journey to Yunnan in China. But unfortunately it proved too arduous for him; he fell ill and had to come home before the expedition was completed. Among other plants which he brought back was that lovely, tender creeper, *Jasminum polyanthum*, which he grew in his south of France garden. Later he gave a plant of it to Major Warre at the Villa Roquebrune and he, in 1938, sent a cutting to England. *The Botanical Magazine* featured it in an article that year. Although it was already known to Kew from seeds which Forrest had collected in 1925, this was the first published reference, and from then on every plant-lover wanted it. Johnston also collected the seeds of *Mahonia siamensis*, and *M. lomariifolia*. The former is tender but it grew very well in his Mentone garden where, just before his death in 1958, it was still looking superb. He also gave it to the Botanic Garden at Cambridge. *Mahonia lomariifolia* is less tender and does well in sheltered positions in this country. It is a spectacular plant with its whorls of golden flowers in the winter. It is thought that, among other species, the seeds of *Hypericum patulum* 'Hidcote' may also have been collected by him, but this is uncertain. Johnston also made several less adventurous journeys in pursuit of rarities for his gardens. The list of plants sent from his Mentone garden to Cambridge after his death is staggering. Unfortunately, few have survived.

He bought the Serre de la Madone, as his French property was called, in the early twenties, with a view to creating a garden which he might enjoy in the winter months. It lies in one of the hidden valleys running up behind Mentone to the foothills of the Alpes Maritimes, right on the Italian frontier. It is a perfect natural setting for a sub-tropical garden, and was already well planted with olive and citrus trees, and sheltered from every wind. Johnston became increasingly absorbed in this Mediterranean paradise, which he crammed with all the plants that could not grow in the cold Cotswolds. He had many gardening friends along the Riviera. Mrs Warre and her husband lived nearby at the Villa Roquebrune. They shared his tastes and had also created a magnificent garden on terraces overhanging the Mediterranean.

Much further west at Hyères lived in those days that renowned French gardener, the Vicomte de Noailles. His property adjoined that of another of Johnston's close friends, Edith Wharton. He often visited them both. Mrs Wharton, writing to Louis Bromfield in 1935, asked, 'Do you know a Spanish rose called Apelles Mestres? Lawrence

Johnston tells me it is the most beautiful rose in the world.' And again later she wrote for the address of a nurseryman near Mortefontaine, 'where we all went one day last summer, and Lawrence Johnston who was staying with me, very kindly ordered for me a very big and splendid magnolia, to be *mis en bac* and delivered in the spring. Neither he nor I seem to have noted the address, and Johnnie wants to be sure the *mis en bac* has been done'.

With the Vicomte de Noailles he planned a journey to Burma for 1938 but owing to the menace of another war it never took place. The Noailles had a squash court where Johnston spent many hours playing. He was also a keen tennis player and liked to get professionals to come and play with him both at Hidcote and in France. He was at the Serre de la Madone when the Germans invaded France, and was evacuated on that terrifyingly overcrowded ship which brought thousands of stranded Britons home in 1940.

During the war he remained at Hidcote, struggling to keep things going, and had some Americans billeted on him. Later his memory began to fail and he found the effort of managing the garden increasingly difficult. Also, he wanted to make suitable arrangements for its preservation after his death. An old friend, Lady Colefax, persuaded him he could not do better than give it to the National Trust. After many months of negotiation the deeds were finally signed, and in 1948 Hidcote Bartrim Garden became the first property the Trust acquired under the new gardens scheme. Johnston retained the use of the house for his life. Partly for tax and partly for climatic reasons he planned to spend most of the year in France, with three months at Hidcote. Although the arrangement was a great weight off his mind, it was a sad one for, as he remarked to an old friend, 'Hidcote is not my baby any more'.

Norah Lindsay died but her daughter Nancy, herself a keen plantswoman, adopted Johnnie, as his friends called him, giving everyone to understand that she was his 'seeing eye', and that she knew just what his wishes were. This assumption led to difficulties, and in 1949 the Trust decided to form a small committee of his local friends, capable of managing the garden in his absence. It consisted of Colonel Shennan, who was the chairman and whose son was Johnston's godson, Mrs Muir from Kiftsgate, Mr de Navarro, the son of Mary Anderson de Navarro, who had inherited his parents' house in Broadway, and, inevitably, Nancy Lindsay. At that time there were four gardeners. Three of them received £4 a week, and Hawkins the head gardener £4 10*s.* until he asked for a rise, and got £5. In 1949 Hawkins was allowed to exhibit some geraniums at the Chelsea Flower Show and won the Banksian Medal, but that seems to have been the only time Johnston bothered to exhibit anything and perhaps it was really to please Hawkins. In those early days of opening to the public, attendance was very small. Admission was only from 2 till 5 p.m. on three days a week, at a shilling a head. On an August afternoon in 1949 someone counted seven visitors. In June 1950 the admission charge was raised to 1*s.* 6*d.* and it was thought very splendid that one day in May a hundred people came. The story is very different today. In 1986 there were approximately 90,000 visitors.

What more do we know about the creator of this truly great and unique garden? He was a small man with fair hair and very blue eyes. One of his old friends described him as blithe. He was shy and modest. He was scrupulous. When visiting the Vatican garden on one occasion he could not resist picking a piece of water ranunculus. Whereupon, turning to a friend, he said, 'Excuse me, I must now go and light a candle.' He also hated publicity. Of the many plants for which we are indebted to him today only one or two bear his name, but many that of Hidcote. He endeared himself to all who knew him well, especially his staff. He was an avid reader of all horticultural literature, and his library contained a fine collection of books on this subject. He enjoyed painting and did a frieze for one of the rooms at Hidcote, as well as decorating the two little garden pavilions. He also decorated a room in the Florentine style for the Muirs at Kiftsgate. He collected old glazed tiles on his travels, which he used very effectively in the bathrooms, kitchens and garden rooms of his two houses. He had a number of French eighteenth-century lead watering-cans, which he would group in strategic corners of his gardens. His choice of garden furniture was faultless and included some lovely reeded iron seats and terracotta urns. He was inseparable from his pack of little dachshunds who went with him to France when he finally decided to leave England. He never married. Above all he loved his gardens. He died at the Serre de la Madone in 1958, and is buried beside his mother in Mickleton churchyard, a mile or two from his beloved Hidcote.

The Impact of American Plants on British Gardens

WILL INGWERSEN

Some years ago I gave a lecture in America on this subject, and during my research I made the interesting discovery that it is virtually impossible in England to stand in sight of cultivated land, with gardens around you, and *not* see an American conifer! This is very largely due to the introduction from California in 1854 of seeds of *Chamaecyparis lawsoniana*, sent to Lawson's nursery in Edinburgh. In subsequent years a great many forms have been raised and distributed. Den Ouden's comprehensive *Manual of Conifers* lists over two hundred named varieties.

The introduction of American plants on any considerable scale began early in the seventeenth century during the reign of James I, when John Tradescant the elder started to collect specimens through his business agents in Virginia.

During the sixteenth and seventeenth centuries the accent was very much on the introduction of trees. Interest in the smaller plants came later. In 1660 the Royal Society of London 'for improving Natural Knowledge' was founded. One of the first members to read a paper to the Society, in 1662, was John Evelyn. His subject was the need for the conservation of timber in Britain and the development of forestry.

Evelyn was of course the famous diarist who in 1664 wrote an expansion of his earlier lecture, the classic book *Sylva, or a Discourse on Forest Trees*. At that time the varieties of native timber trees were limited to English oak, Scots pine, beech, ash, silver birch and elm, plus some poplars and willows. Evelyn had also heard of the New England white pine as a tree which grew very tall. The Navy valued highly trees which were sufficiently tall to provide ships' masts in one piece.

In 1670 Evelyn enlisted the help of his friend Samuel Pepys, Secretary to the Admiralty, and persuaded him to instruct the captains of naval vessels sailing to America to bring back seeds.

The primary interest in exotic plants was in trees, and mainly for economic reasons. Once the flow of material began it was not long before collectors became aware of the wealth of smaller plants of immense potential amenity value and the flow became a flood for which we gardeners must be forever thankful.

It never ceases to surprise me that so many plants and seeds survived the long and hazardous voyage from America to Europe. On the long-drawn-out Atlantic passage there was danger of salt spray damaging cargoes stored on deck, while rats, mice and cockroaches took their toll of items stored below. These were not the only risks. Botanists asking for perfect specimens of fruit, flower and foliage to draw, required them to be stored in jars of rum. Sailors often found irresistible the temptation to tip out the contents and drink the rum. Nowadays such eighty day journeys are reduced to just a few hours, by air.

In the eighteenth century John Bartram of Pennsylvania came into the picture. He was a farmer and botanist and the agent of Peter Collinson, a London merchant who introduced him to Robert, 8th Lord Petre (1713–42) of Thorndon Hall in Essex. Even at a very early age Lord Petre displayed a vivid interest in plants and subscribed to collectors such as Mark Catesby and others. It was a severe blow to horticulture when, at the age of twenty-nine, Lord Petre died from smallpox. He did however leave a magnificent collection of trees at Thorndon, many sent by Bartram.

John Bartram also supplied the gardens of other great landowners. In 1765, George III appointed him King's Botanist. The American War of Independence interrupted the flow of plants but Benjamin Franklin, then American envoy in Paris, arranged for seeds to be sent to France instead of England. Bartram died in 1777, still packing boxes of seeds for Europe.

Since those distant days, of course, there have been other collectors of American plants, and the impact of these on our gardens has been considerable and important. One introduction was the tulip tree, *Liriodendron tulipifera*, which in nature extends from Nova Scotia southward to Florida. It is known to have been cultivated by Bishop Compton in London in 1688, and was probably first introduced some time before that as it is also recorded that a specimen of magnificent proportions was growing in a garden in Essex early in the eighteenth century.

One of the most popular trees to find its way to England – in 1688 – was *Acer negundo*, the box elder. It is to be seen in a great many gar-

Cornus florida. Introduced from the eastern United States, *c.* 1730

dens and is also used as a street tree, especially in one or other of its forms whose leaves are variegated with yellow and gold. There has been some confusion as to the origin of the specific epithet 'negundo', which is of Indian (Asian) origin, and one may be surprised that it became attached to a plant from North America. Those who are interested in knowing how their plants got their names would enjoy an article by the great taxonomist Professor W. T. Stearn in the November 1986 issue of *The Garden*, the journal of the Royal Horticultural Society, in which he throws much light on the matter.

For some reason, although it was introduced from North America as long ago as 1759, *Amsonia tabernaemontana* has never been appreciated as a border plant as it deserves to be. Related to the periwinkles (*Vincas*), it produces tufts of leafy stems up to 18 inches in height,

Calochortus venustus, from California

each stem terminating in a head of nice, pale blue flowers. Easily grown in any open position and well drained soil, it remains something of a Cinderella. It may be that some infuriated gardeners have thrown it away when it was sold to them, as it sometimes is, as *Rhazya orientalis*, a rather similar but much rarer plant.

I suppose the scarlet runner bean, *Phaseolus multiflorus*, is the most commonly grown vegetable in gardens large or small but not everyone knows that it was first introduced from South America in 1633 as an ornamental climber. I know of gardens where it is grown on poles at the back of a flower border for the sake of its brilliantly coloured flowers. The original introduction had very short pods which would be scorned now that the plant breeders have produced the long-podded modern varieties which are so much esteemed.

It was not until early in the nineteenth century that the very lovely calochortus, or Mariposa tulips, began to reach us from their native California and Mexico. They are bulbous and belong to the *Liliaceae* and some fifty species are known although but a few have taken to outdoor cultivation here. This is a great pity, as they are extremely beautiful, of dwarf habit and with large and richly coloured flowers of infinite grace.

It is understandable that not every plant brought to us from foreign parts will succeed or take kindly to our climate. One in particular which has annoyed me for many years is the pixie moss (*Pyxidanthera barbulata*) from the Pine Barrens of New Jersey. I saw it growing there in abundance a long time ago and was entranced by it. Periodically I have had plants and seeds of it sent to me from America, but it has never thrived. It was in 1806 that the first of these plants came to England and everyone was eager to grow this tiny shrub, never more than an inch in height, its tiny stems clad in wee, box-like leaves. It covers itself with small, tubular, white or more often pink flowers. Should you ever have the chance to battle with it, give it sandy, lime-free soil with plenty of humus and a place in partial shade. In nature it obviously enjoys being closely associated with other dwarf plants, such as, perhaps, a trailing salix. It ought to be perfectly hardy, but I have to admit that the nearest I have ever come to success was when I grew it in a pan of the appropriate compost in an unheated alpine greenhouse.

A popular plant to grow among rhododendrons and other lime-hating plants is the Labrador tea, *Ledum groenlandicum*. It was first introduced in 1763 and is now a well established immigrant. It is a dwarf, evergreen shrub with erect stems, clothed thickly with leaves which are densely covered on the undersides with white tomentum. The white flowers are carried from April until June, in conspicuous terminal clusters. It is widely distributed from Greenland to Washington State. In cold arctic regions a sort of tea was made from its dried leaves by Eskimos and Indians.

The creeping dogwood, *Cornus canadensis*, is a splendid ground cover plant to use beneath lime-hating shrubs. It was introduced in 1774 but, curiously, had to wait until 1937 before being given a well deserved Award of Merit by the Royal Horticultural Society. It makes attractive carpets of foliage, starred in summer with quite large white flowers which are followed by a profusion of holly-red fruits. It is so unlike what we would expect of a cornus that it was once placed in another genus, *Chamaepericlymenum*; happily, it has been returned to the more pronounceable name.

We have reason to be grateful to America for the late summer flowering asters which add their glowing colour to the autumn tints.

Liriodendron tulipifera, the Tulip tree

The first aster introduced was probably *A. tradescantii* in 1633, but others quickly followed. In 1891 the Royal Horticultural Society brought asters into prominence when they arranged a conference on them. *A. tradescantii* survives to this day and is to be seen in many gardens.

The introduction of a fully double form of *Aster novi-belgii*, given the clonal name 'Beauty of Colwall' in 1891, led to increased interest and it was the late Ernest Ballard of Colwall who really took *A. novi-belgii* in hand and was responsible for raising most of the early forms, many of which are still grown. He was an enthusiastic but stern critic and I well remember spending time with him while he selected, from thousands of seedlings flowering for the first time, the few that he felt were worthy of naming and increasing.

All the hybrids and forms of *A. novi-belgii* have suffered during the past several decades from attacks by a wilt disease caused by the fungus *Verticillium vilmorinii*. The fungus lives in the rootstock and, growing in the conducting vessels, produces a poisonous substance which kills the leaves. If the plant is severely affected it should be burnt, but a valued variety can be preserved by taking cuttings of the top two or three inches of young growth. Divisions of the plant should not be retained as the fungus will still exist in the roots.

No collection of alpine plants would be considered complete if it did not contain some members of the genus *Lewisia*, a family of plants confined in its natural distribution to north west America. We owe the initial awareness of the family and its garden value to Captain Meriwether Lewis (1774–1809), after whom the genius is named. He was the leader of the Lewis and Clark expedition (1806–7) across America to advise on the route for the Canadian Pacific Railway.

Compared with the much earlier introduction of plants from the Americas, lewisias are modern, as it was only in the fading years of the nineteenth century that they began to appear in our gardens. We are fortunate that both Lewis and Clark were not only skilled engineers and surveyors, but had a keen interest in plants. It is to Captain William Clark (1770–1838) that we are indebted for the first introduction of the popular annual clarkia, named in his honour.

Among the first species of *Lewisia* of which we became aware were *L. cotyledon*, *L. columbiana*, *L. heckneri* and *L. mariana*. All of these are variable and eager to intermarry with each other, the result being a number of handsome strains which have, in gardens, become so diverse and widely distributed that the original species from which they arose have almost disappeared. Although this may be taxonomically unfortunate, our gardens have scored as the hybrids and variations are on the whole more garden worthy than their parents.

Supreme among lewisias is *L. tweedyi*, from the Wenatchee mountains of the State of Washington, and the Walathian hills of Canada. It is almost the only one of its genus which does not intermarry with others. When I first saw it growing in the wild I was entranced by the beauty of its large flowers, coloured in a suffusion of yellow, pink and apricot. I joyfully collected seeds and grew the resultant plants in rich soil where they made immense rosettes of the wide leaves – and died soon after flowering. Belatedly I remembered that in the Wenatchee mountains they grew in situations which became parched for months during the summer, in thin soil over rock. All lewisias appreciate a drying-off period after flowering. They are averse to lime, but will grow in alkaline soil if given a generous measure of acid compost; drainage must be perfect.

Of the many kinds of aquilegia we grow and enjoy in our gardens, many came to us from North America. A notable example is *Aquilegia caerulea*, the State flower of Colorado, which first reached British gardens in 1864. The type has blue, white and yellow marked flowers,

Aquilegia caerulea

but there are several variants, some probably hybrids, for aquilegias have easy morals and interbreed frequently. A particular treasure which came to us I know not when is *A. jonesii*, from the Rocky Mountains. It is an alpine gem, no more than three or four inches high. From neat tufts of soft, downy leaves rise short stems, each carrying one large blue flower.

Although it is easy to grow, this little charmer has one fault: it is apt to be shy of flowering, and this cannot be due to incorrect cultivation, for I remember walking through an area in the Rockies where it grew in thousands, and only about one in ten of those plants carried flowers. However, even a solitary flower delights me and brings back vivid memories of the majestic surroundings in which it grows in the wild. Also well worth seeking are other American species of aquilegia, such as *A. canadensis*, *A. saximontana*, *A. scopulorum* and *A. laramiensis*.

There have, in the past, been a few rather half-hearted attempts to introduce from the Andes mountains of South America some representatives of the fascinating rosulate violas. Their seeds have been sent home but, although there have been germinations, attempts to grow the resulting plants have met with no success. I believe there is soon to be another botanical expedition to the Andes and I very much hope that there may be new importations of seeds of these desirable plants. Utterly unlike any other known violet in general appearance,

Uvularia grandiflora

these rosulate plants form symmetrical rosettes of fleshy leaves, like those of a sempervivum. From the leaves emerge short stems carrying typical violet flowers. Their impact is yet to be made on our gardens and there will be quite a stir in the alpine gardening world if they arrive and prove to be growable.

The small but delightful genus *Shortia* was named in honour of Dr Charles Short (b. 1794), a botanist in Kentucky, who died in 1863; it was not until 1881 that the American species *S. galacifolia* was introduced to English gardens. It is a plant for shady positions in lime-free woodland soil. Those who can provide such a situation will find much pleasure in this dwarf plant which forms sturdy tufts of leathery, glossy leaves, bright green until the autumn and winter, when they become richly bronzed. On each of the short flower stems appears one funnel-shaped, elegant white flower, its petals flushing to gentle pink as they age.

There are a great many gardeners who willingly accept the challenge offered by plants which are not all that easy to grow. One with which I have struggled for many years, with occasional rewarding successes and some disheartening failures, is *Silene hookeri*, which first ventured onto our shores in 1873 and has been admired, off and on, ever since. I have, very occasionally, seen it flourishing on the open rock garden, but it is really a gem to be accommodated in an alpine house, or unheated greenhouse. The radiating, procumbent stems are clothed with narrow, hairy leaves. The axillary flowers are of great size and the soft pink petals, deeply notched at the tips, have narrow white lines from the throat. Give it lime-free, gritty, but humus-rich soil and you have every chance of success.

It was in 1802, or thereabouts, that someone introduced to British gardens *Uvularia grandiflora*, where it has happily remained ever since. Maybe it has not made a major impact, but it is a plant that pleases those who seek the slightly unusual and appreciate some variation from the common run of garden plants. The curious derivation of its generic name is from the anatomical term *uvula*, the pendant lobe from the back of the palate in man, a reference to the hanging blossoms. It belongs to the lily family and has semi-tuberous roots from which rise the oblong, perfoliate leaves and rather more than foot-high stems carrying attractive, pendant, tubular yellow flowers. A good plant for a semi-shaded position in moisture-retentive soil.

We have to thank North America for the shooting stars, species of *Dodecatheon*, a genus related to primulas and cyclamen. The best known species is *D. meadia*, first introduced in 1744 and now a widely distributed and popular plant for a cool spot. From tufts of narrow, slightly toothed leaves rise foot-high stems carrying umbels of up to twenty rose-coloured flowers with sharply reflexed petals. All the known species, some thirty in number, are American and half a dozen or so are now commonly cultivated in this country, most of them introduced during the century following the coming of *D. meadia*.

Re-reading William Bartram's fascinating description of his travels in America in search of plants I feel that one passage in particular deserves quoting; William, the son of John, was not only a botanist of note, but a poet with a marvellous gift of phrase.

On one of his expeditions he wrote:

> It was now afternoon; I approached a charming vale, amidst sublimely high forests, awful shades! Darkness gathers around; far distant thunder rolls over the trembling hills: the black clouds with august majesty and power, move slowly forward, shading regions of towering hills, and threatening all with the destruction of a thunder storm. All around is now still as death; not a whisper is heard, but a total inactivity and silence seem to pervade the earth; the birds afraid to utter a chirrup, in low, tremulous voices take leave of each other, seeking cover and safety.

Dodecatheon meadia

Every insect is silenced, and nothing heard but the roaring of the approaching hurricane. The mighty cloud now expands its sable wings, extending from north to south, and is driven irresistibly on by the tumultuous winds, speading its livid wings around the gloomy concave, armed with terrors of thunder and fiery shafts of lightning. Now the lofty forests bend low beneath its fury, their limbs and wavy boughs are tossed about and catch hold of each other; the mountains tremble and seem to reel about, and the ancient hills to be shaken to their foundations. The furious storm sweeps along smoking through the vale and over the resounding hills, the face of the earth is obscured by the deluge descending from the firmament, and I am deafened by the din of the thunder. The tempestuous scene damps my spirits, and my horse sinks under me at the tremendous peals.

Leave the Trowel at Home

ANTHONY HUXLEY

Ever since Queen Hatshepsut, ruler of Egypt, sent an expedition to the Land of Punt (Somalia) to collect frankincense trees in 1495 BC – thirty-one out of thirty-two survived to be planted in her gardens at Karnak – people have actively collected plants from other countries for their gardens. Incense trees are perhaps low on the list of introductions, but spices, fruits, vegetables to improve the variety of our diet, and trees, shrubs and flowers to adorn our gardens, have moved across the world in all directions within their climatic ranges – indeed, outside them in certain cases, such as orchids and bromeliads, which can be cultivated under glass or even in dwellings.

This plant 'loot' has followed invasions, such as those of the Spaniards in the Americas and various Europeans in the Crusades, it has followed travellers and trade along main land routes. Britain was probably the first nation to send plant collectors systematically with exploring expeditions, and to despatch collectors on their own specifically to bring back whatever promising plants they could find.

The exploits of these people were often remarkable; they faced unknown territory, fearsome natural obstacles, hostile inhabitants, rulers who thought they were spies. (Some of them actually *were* spies, like Colonel Bailey of blue poppy fame.) Many of them died unpleasantly, far from home. If horticulture has heroes, these collectors are surely the most important.

A lot of plant introduction was in the form of seeds, compact and most likely to succeed, or fleshy roots like bulbs, also fairly enduring. But live plants in one form or another were also transported, like Captain Bligh's famous breadfruit trees, though until the invention of the closed Wardian case in 1829 chances of success were often minimal.

A century ago, there appeared to be so many plants for the taking that collectors could with some justification gather whatever was available without compunction. But even before that some extinctions had occurred: for instance the handsome American tree *Franklinia atamahaca*, discovered in 1765, was extinct in its restricted habitat before 1803, largely due to collection.

Even a notable botanist like Sir Joseph Hooker was an avid collector, though for science rather than profit. He relates how in 1850 he saw the blue orchid *Vanda caerulea* in the Khasia Hills of Assam; it had first been recorded in 1837. He collected 'seven men's loads' of what he described as 'the rarest and most beautiful of Indian orchids' (few survived the journey home). This publicity for this remarkable flower was enough for many nurseries to send collectors to the area, where they cleared the forests of the vanda, often cutting down the trees on which it grew as the simplest method of collecting.

But attitudes were changing. By 1881, Joseph Hooker – who had become Director of Kew in 1866 – was writing, in the Preface of the catalogue of Marianne North's paintings, that so many of the habitats of the plants portrayed 'are already disappearing or are doomed shortly to disappear before the axe and the forest fires, the plough and the flock, of the ever advancing settler or colonist. Such scenes can never be renewed by nature . . .'

This puts plant collecting into perspective compared with the devastation mankind has wrought upon the planet we inhabit, much of it within the last century, in which plants of every kind, often barely known or even not known at all, are being destroyed. But collecting today is aimed almost entirely at making profit. The number of new plants introduced has dwindled to a tiny trickle, and one might as well say that there are surely enough desirable plants of every kind already available to gardeners that wild ones ought to be left well alone.

The lure of a mature plant is however too much of a profit motive, especially when the plants involved are slow to develop from seed, or difficult to grow. This applies especially to certain cacti and succulents, to cycads, those fern-like primeval ancestors of flowers, and to orchids. A giant saguaro cactus from southern North America, and the cycads, take decades to reach good size. Orchids take ten years or more and bulbs, also being plundered, around five, to flower from seed.

Rarity plays an important part in the present pillage of such plants, and pillage it is. One of the rarest cacti in the world, *Pelecyphora aselliformis*, now exists on a single hillside in Mexico; it and other rare species have been scoured off their territory by the lorry load. Cycads are now very rare, and some orchids have already been made extinct, while others are collected without thought for their survival in the wild. Two spectacular new slipper orchids were found quite recently in Yunnan; 36,000 of one have appeared in the US where they are sold at $10,000 or more each.

Horror stories like these could be multiplied *ad nauseam*, though it must be emphasised that the international orchid fraternity is taking active steps to minimise acquisition of wild-collected species.

Two main points need emphasising in connection with this. Orchids and almost all cacti can be grown from seed and, especially with the former, increased with even less trouble by the micropropagation techniques which are among the wonders of modern horticultural science. This cloning from tiny pieces of tissue can result in great numbers of species identical with the parent. In theory the relative cheapness of plants grown in this way should undermine the collecting and poaching markets, but they do take time to mature, and of course they have not the cachet of being 'wild-collected' which is still deep-rooted with some growers.

Secondly, there is now international legislation about plant collecting, under the auspices of the Convention on International Trade in Endangered Species – CITES for short – which invokes prohibition of the collecting of certain species and strongly monitored licensing in many other cases. The entire cactus, orchid, cycad and tree fern families have blanket restrictions on unlicensed collection and trading in them. Plants imported without the appropriate licences can be impounded by Customs authorities and fines imposed on those responsible.

But a Customs officer cannot tell most orchids or cacti apart, and if a licence for *Paphiopedilum* sp. is presented, no one is to know until it flowers that it is *P. armeniacum* from China, whose export is prohibited by the Chinese authorities and a licence for which would not have been granted. Unfortunately too a number of countries have not signed the CITES convention, notably – in terms of desirable ornamental plants – Mexico and Turkey. From the latter come probably most of the flowering bulbs we prize, dug up by the sackful by peasants who do not even know what they are unearthing, whether crocus, tulip, fritillary or cyclamen.

At present there is no CITES restriction on most fleshy-rooted plants, except cyclamen, and the Dutch, who import most of the Turkish bulbs, say that there is no problem that they can see. But we are talking of literally millions of bulbs, and no one can convince me that this is not having a significant effect on large tracts of Turkey.

Also, the import of such bulbs into Britain, 'laundered' by their initial import into Holland, makes a nonsense of our laws against selling wild-collected plants.

To the conservationist it now seems that trade in wild-collected plants which are rare or endangered at any level should be stopped; indeed, there seems no good reason why any plant should be collected in the wild for commercial gain. There are small exceptions to such precepts. New plants need to be collected by botanists to further taxonomy and to be cultivated for reasons I shall expand later; and collecting is justified as a rescue operation, for instance where terrain is threatened by development or where forest is being cut. Specialist horticultural collectors also have a role – to collect plants not in cultivation, and to select unusual forms (which a botanist will probably ignore as non-typical) which are quite likely not to persist in the wild.

Even where plants take a long time to grow from seed or other vegetative ways, this should surely be the main aim. Many fleshy-rooted plants are being raised from seed, notably cyclamens, where it is possible to have saleable tubers within three years. Few cacti cannot be increased readily in this way. As already mentioned, orchids can be raised from seed or by micropropagation, and the latter techniques can be adapted to virtually any plant. Patience is what needs exercising, and it is a pity that a handful of growers, mostly cactus and orchid fanciers, should find themselves lacking in this, continuing to create a demand for plants taken from the wild.

All this applies equally to the amateur gardener faced with novel plants in other countries, which in the general course of things will mainly be alpines, bulbs and their ilk, cacti and succulents. How tempting it is, faced with some gem of a gentian, crocus, cyclamen, houseleek, aeonium or mammillaria, to extract it from the soil and shove it in a poly bag. Yet virtually every plant one might come across in this way is available from a specialist nursery.

The usual counter-comment is that there were so many of the plants around – surely one does not matter. We come back, here, to the well-worn saying that there is little difference between one peasant digging up a thousand tulips and a thousand amateurs digging up one each. Anyone who has been on a 'botanical tour' will know how even a small group can decimate a stand of choice plants.

I would like to see all operators of botanical tours, whether commercial or run by specialist societies, echo the sentiments of Adam Stainton and the late Oleg Polunin in their *Flowers of the Himalaya*, and ask participants to 'bring your camera and leave your trowel behind'. Of course the seed packet can be employed, if seed should be available, and there are ways in which experts can take cuttings of very special subjects and leave the main plant intact, as with the American lewisias, specifically listed under the CITES regulations, where unique colour forms have been propagated in this way. Cuttings of many woody plants can be taken fairly easily; what *did* we do before the invention of polythene!

Collecting of plants, by both amateurs and commercial collectors, results in local inhabitants realising the potential and doing the same thing. In many cities in the tropics one can see poor natives offering large orchid plants in full flower, dragged bodily off trees; in Madagascar this has extended to some of the rare pachypodiums and other highly endangered succulents. The average purchaser will enjoy the plant while it flowers and then very probably throw it away without an attempt at growing it on.

I mentioned scientific collecting earlier. In the first place, new species need to be named and examined for relationships with others to increase botanical knowledge. Equally important is the cultivation of new species, for they may have medicinal, food or other useful potential, apart from ornamental value. If a stock is built up this will constitute a reserve against the plant's destruction in the wild, and if the plant does have useful potential the stock represents a 'gene bank' for breeding experiments. It has become apparent that living plants are often a better safeguard than the much talked about 'seed banks'.

For such reserves of living plant material gardens of every kind, whether botanical, public or private, are increasingly being viewed as vital in the preservation of endangered species, especially in view of the apparently unstoppable destruction of wild habitats. In this country the NCCPG has already organised numerous collections of distinct genera in gardens of all kinds and sizes, and some other countries have similar schemes; or at least there are the collections of influential cultivators in many places, and governments show themselves increasingly aware that such collections are worth maintaining after the owner's death.

It may come to pass that our descendents will only be able to see rare and beautiful plants in cultivation. But while there is some chance, however small, of halting the massive destruction of natural habitats a ban on collecting wild plants for commercial gain or personal pleasure is surely irresistible, especially where these plants are in national parks or reserves, or areas designated as of special natural beauty. While there are still wild places to visit where plants flourish relatively undisturbed, we shall always want to see and enjoy them there.

Gardens in Fiction

Flaubert's Gardens

HERMIA OLIVER

The great French novelist Gustave Flaubert (1821–1880), most famous for his *Madame Bovary*, was in many ways extraordinarily modern for his time. Over a century before the start of the ecological movement, in 1838 in one of his youthful writings he described civilization as 'a lying hypocritical vampire'. In his *Sentimental Education* he created a whole cast of anti-heroes, and in the house of a member of the establishment its chief protagonist defended the Arabs, just when France was 'pacifying' Algeria with the utmost severity.

For most of his life Flaubert lived in the house bought by his doctor father at the then tiny village of Croisset, just outside Rouen, on the banks of the Seine. It had an entrancing garden, rising to the wooded slopes of Canteleu, with its church and Louis XIV château. A terraced walk, planted with magnificent limes, went up the hill. Behind the house were lawns, flower-beds, and a rose hedge. Higher up the slope was a vegetable garden and what George Sand called her 'dear orchard'. She paid three visits to Croisset and advised Flaubert to visit the orchard every day for exercise. Roses, primroses and violets appear in his letters, and his own taste was at the opposite pole from the trim, formal Victorian suburban ideal.

He first came to London in 1851 with his mother when, since they were looking up a former governess of Flaubert's sister, who lived close to it, they visited Highgate cemetery. It was then so clean and tidy that it prompted his comment 'these people seem to have died in white gloves'. He detested the little gardens round the tombs with their raked flower beds and faded flowers, and would infinitely have preferred it as it is today since (as he put it in one of his letters) he loved 'this invasion of nature which suddenly happens to the work of man when his hand is no longer there to defend it'. He returned to England in 1865 and 1866 to see another English governess, this time one employed by his mother to teach his little niece, whose own mother died when she was born. In company with this governess, Juliet Herbert, who lived in Chelsea, he visited Hampton Court (mentioning the pleached alley, which he described as 'covered with elms') and Kew, and they went sight-seeing in London.

The garden in *Madame Bovary* is a very good example of Flaubert's mastery in making their settings reflect the personalities of the characters he was writing about. Emma Bovary's husband Charles was a limited, provincial small-town doctor, a horrendously boring man who was not even a good doctor, as we see in his operation on a club-foot. His garden at Tostes was one of the regimented sub-urban ones, but even more unattractive because it was not so much as brightened by geraniums. It was long and narrow, with daub walls on which a few apricots were espaliered, while a thorn hedge divided it from the fields. Four flower-beds containing a few scraggy dog-roses symmetrically surrounded the more useful 'serious vegetation'. In the middle was a sundial on a stone pedestal, while at the bottom, under a group of spruces, stood a plaster priest reading his breviary. Those 'scraggy dog-roses' sound like un-pruned, totally neglected garden roses which had been taken over by their root stocks. The espaliered apricots on walls which were not even brick and the funereal spruces blocking any view of the fields beyond make it claustrophobic. Poor Emma, who had come from a cheerful farm it will be recalled, was left alone every day and every evening until 10 o'clock or sometimes midnight while Charles did his rounds on horseback. The house stood flush with a dusty road. When she turned from the aggressive yellow wallpaper of the living room, her only outlook was the road or the garden. No wonder when she was given the little Italian greyhound Djali she took it out for walks so that she need no longer see 'the eternal garden and dusty road' before her eyes. No wonder that the day after the Bovarys returned from the ball given by the marquis of the local château seemed endless to Emma. She walked up and down the same paths in the garden, stopping in front of the flower-beds and the plaster priest. Though by then she knew them so well, she looked at them with astonishment. Everything immediately sur-rounding her, which she contrasted with the château and the Paris she was avidly reading about, seemed a special trap in which she was caught.

The Bovarys' garden at that other small country town, Yonville-l'Abbaye, is lightly sketched rather than given a set-piece descrip-tion. Like the Croisset garden, it is at the river's edge, and Rodolphe and Emma exchanged letters in a crack in the terrace there. It is the scene of regular evening meetings between them, including the last one before they were to run away together, though no sooner had he left her than Rodolphe backed out.

In his *Sentimental Education* Flaubert described a garden at Nogent-sur-Seine, a place he knew well because the young Flauberts often stayed with relations who lived there. It was at the end of an island, on a bend in the river with poplars in the meadows beside it.

> The water was smooth as a mirror; large insects skimmed over its un-broken surface. Clumps of reeds and rushes lined it unevenly; all sorts of plants which had taken root there were flaunting golden buds, trailing yellow clusters, pointing spindly purple flowers or darting out random spikes of green. Water-lilies were floating in an inlet; and on this side of the island a row of old willows concealing spring-traps constituted the only defence the garden possessed.

A garden after Flaubert's own heart! Inside was a kitchen. garden enclosed by four walls with slate coping. Squares of newly dug earth made a pattern of brown patches. A gleaming line of cloches over melons in their narrow beds, artichokes, beans, spinach, carrots and tomatoes alternated down to an asparagus bed resembling 'a little forest of feathers'. The whole of this ground had been what was known as a 'folly' under the Directory. Since then the trees had grown enormously. Clematises choked the arbour, the paths were covered with moss, brambles flourished everywhere. Plaster flaked off fragments of statues, lay in the grass with remains of old wire ornaments. Two rooms of a pavilion, with some shreds of blue wallpaper, remained, with an Italian-type pergola which had a wooden trellis supporting a vine.

This is the setting, recalling Impressionist paintings, of a scene between a young man and a girl. He is Frédéric Moreau, just back from Paris where he has lost a lot of money on the stock exchange. His mother, who lives at Nogent, has urged him to make a good marriage. The girl is Louise Roque, illegitimate daughter of his mother's next-door neighbour, a *nouveau riche* son of a former foot-man. He wants his daughter to marry a count and is impressed by Madame Moreau's aristocratic ancestors. Louise had fallen in love with Frédéric while she was still a child, when he became her idol. They walk together under the pergola and he watches the leaf shadows playing on her face. She is a naïve country girl who at every step shows how deeply she loves him, but she won't do – she is wearing a glass imitation emerald in her chignon and straw slippers trimmed with pink satin, although she is in mourning for her mother, and he teases her for using a patois word. In the end she blurts out "Will you be my husband?" Frédéric answers indecisively – "Probably"; he should like nothing better. Yet shortly afterwards he left for Paris saying he would be back soon. He thought of marrying her and was tempted by Roque's fortune, but he felt that a decision to marry would be a weakness, a degradation. This is exactly what Flaubert himself thought when his closest school friend married and shackled himself with the burdens of making a career as a provincial deputy public prosecutor. So the spring-traps in the garden (the French *pièges à loup* earlier on in the Penguin edition translated as man-traps), seem to represent far more than a means of protecting Roque's melons and produce.

As a complete contrast, there is a very funny garden in Flaubert's last book, *Bouvard and Pécuchet*. These are two Parisian copy-clerks who were able to retire from their jobs and set themselves up in the country. Their ignorance is bottomless and their intelligence is small, but they believe they can overcome this by studying the books written by experts. After a disastrous start in farming, they decided to make a garden and found a book by Boitard, *The Garden Architect*. (Larousse 19th century shows that there was a real Pierre Boitard, who was a naturalist and agronomist and wrote, among other works, *The Art of Planning and Decorating Gardens*.) In *The Garden Architect* Boitard had divided gardens into types – the melancholy and romantic, characterized by *immortelles*, ruins, tombs, and an *ex-voto* to the Virgin; the terrible sort composed of hanging rocks, shattered trees and burned-out huts; the exotic, with Peruvian torch-thistles 'to evoke memories in a colonist or traveller'; the solemn, with a temple of philosophy; the majestic, with obelisks and triumphal arches; the mysterious, with moss and caves, and so on.

Faced with the infinite number of types of garden – 'this horizon of marvels' – the two clerks, helped by just one servant and at minimal expense, 'created a residence for themselves without its equal in the whole department'. The existing arbour was opened up to give a view of a copse which was full of winding paths like a maze. They intended to make an archway in a wall which had supported espaliers before these had died of their ill treatment, but as the coping would not stay up and hung in mid-air, the result was a huge gap. They sacrificed an asparagus bed to build an Etruscan tomb, 'that is a black plaster quadrilateral six foot high resembling a dog-kennel'. At its corners they planted four dwarf firs, and it was to be surmounted by an urn with an inscription.

In another part of the kitchen garden they made 'a sort of Rialto straddling a pool', whose edges were decorated with encrusted mussel shells. The earth absorbed the water, but no matter. They believed a clay bottom would form and keep it in. They transformed a hut into a rustic cabin 'with the help of stained glass'. The arbour ended on one side at a vine-clad mound. On top of it they put six squared-off trees to support a tin hat with turned-up points; 'the whole thing represented a Chinese pagoda'. Then the two clerks went down to the banks of the river Orne to select pieces of granite, broke them up, numbered them, brought them back in a cart and 'joined the bits together with cement, piling one on top of the other' – presumably their version of a 'terrible garden'. In the middle of the lawn rose a rock like a gigantic potato. Believing that something further was lacking 'to complete the harmony', they cut down the biggest lime tree in the arbour, 'three-quarters dead in any case', and laid it across the length of the garden 'to convey the impression that it had been brought there by a torrent or struck down by lightning'.

Flaubert is not only making fun of his four 'idiots' but is sending up the styles of gardens suggested by his reading of Boitard.

Changing Fashions with Hellebores

ARTHUR HELLYER

Fashions in flowers can change quite quickly, and sometimes it would seem that it is changes in the flowers themselves that bring this about. Sixty years ago the Christmas rose was the hellebore that everybody wanted. It was liked for the purity of its flowers, the earliness of its season and the freedom and regularity with which it flowered. *Helleborus niger* was not then, nor ever has been since, a notably variable plant, but some forms behaved better than others and there was one, named 'Altifolius', which had much longer stems than the norm, heavily purple-spotted, and bearing rose flushed flowers that could be beginning to open in November. It is perfectly described by William Robinson in *The English Flower Garden*.

All that has changed. Even if *Hellborus niger* 'Altifolius' is still around (and no one seems to offer it), I would not like to be sure that it would flower so early, for it seems difficult to get any Christmas rose today to start flowering much before February. I do not know whether it is the seasons which have altered or whether there has been some change in the plants, but in my own gardens I do not expect to be picking Christmas roses much, if at all, in advance of Lenten roses, which are now the popular favourites.

Some experts regard *Helleborus niger* 'Altifolius' as a synonym for *H. macranthus*, which has also been known as *H. angustifolius* and *H. maximus*, but the description of this in *Flora Europaea* is of a plant with mainly white flowers and glaucescent leaves, with no mention of purple spotting, and is certainly not the plant I knew as 'Altifolius'. My last major encounter with this was in 1925 when my employer, J. C. House of Isaac House and Sons' nursery at Westbury-on-Trym, near Bristol, located a considerable stock of it in a large frame in a cottage garden at Pinhoe just outside Exeter. It was some time before a purchase could be arranged but eventually I was despatched with a van to dig up half the roots (the other half went to Robert Veitch and Sons of Exeter). The plants had been growing in that frame for a great many years, and were huge. I got them safely back to Westbury-on-Trym, the old van groaning under the load, and they were all duly established in the nursery; not long after that I left the firm, and then a few years later the nursery itself was sold for building.

What happened to the plants after that, or to the share which went to Veitch, I do not know, but some surely must be around, for hellebores are long-lived perennials.

The rise in the popularity of the Lenten rose, under which heading I shall include not only *Helleborus orientalis* but also its many hybrids, is due to the comparative ease with which they can be grown, and to the range of colours which has become available, especially during the last twenty years or so. Lenten roses seem less sensitive to root disturbance than Christmas roses, establish themselves more rapidly and are better able to display their flowers, though not if one is comparing them with *H. niger* 'Altifolius'. On top of all this, the colour range is being steadily widened and the poise of the flowers is being improved so that they tend to look up rather than hang down.

Unlike the Christmas rose, which is rather reluctant to produce seedlings, the Lenten roses can be embarrassingly free with them. Give them a place they like, a little shaded but open to the sky, in soil that is rich in humus and rather moist, and seedlings will soon start springing up all around the plants without any effort on the gardener's part. If the parent plants have been chosen well all the seedlings will be satisfactory and a few may be very good. That is more or less the way Mrs Helen Ballard started some twenty years ago at her home, Old Country, Mathon, near Malvern in Worcestershire, except that I think she hand-pollinated the plants from the outset to make certain she got the crosses she wanted. She started with only about eight plants, very carefully chosen for different qualities, but later brought in *H. cyclophyllus*, a Grecian species with yellow-green flowers, to improve the yellow end of the colour range. This species is deciduous and some of the Ballard yellows still have a tendency to shed their leaves in winter; no doubt this legacy will eventually be eliminated by selection.

I think that Mrs Ballard has also used *Helleborus torquatus* to diversify the purples available in Lenten roses, and in particular to give them that dusted look that makes one think of well grown black grapes. However, the two hellebores that seem to have started improvements in this colour area are *H. atrorubens* and *H. purpurascens*. As is usual with hellebores, there is some mystery and confusion about both. What we grow as *H. atrorubens* does not seem to be what botanists call by that name: indeed, they no longer call any species *atrorubens* but use it as a subspecific name for a form of *H. dumetorum*.

Helleborus niger 'Altifolius'

The garden plant has very dark purple flowers which are already opening in my cold garden in January, and do not very much like what they encounter. There is nothing to indicate that *H. atrorubens* flowers so early, but at least botanists and gardeners agree in saying that their plants lose their leaves in winter. This is also true of *H. purpurascens*, although having read numerous descriptions of this I am by no means sure that I have ever seen it.

There is even confusion about *Helleborus torquatus*. There is no doubt at all that a plant identified as this was introduced to Britain from Yugoslavia many years ago by W. E. Th. Ingwersen and that it had rather small dove-grey flowers. This was believed at the time to be a true species, but is now said to be a hybrid, though of what parentage is not clear. To add to the confusion there are two distinct forms of *H. torquatus* around, one with small flowers and the other with larger ones. Both have much divided leaves, and this has led to the suggestion that both may be forms of *H. multifidus seribicus*.

All this confusion, and the ease with which hellebores seem to cross-fertilise one another, suggest to me that this is a genus still in flux which has not yet settled down into tightly enclosed species. Even *H. corsicus*, which grows wild only in Corsica and Sardinia and so must have been on its own for a very long time, will cross with the Christmas rose, and the result, *H. × nigericors* (or should it be *nigricors* as the Royal Horticultural Society's *Dictionary of Gardening* has it?) is a much admired plant, though I personally find it less attractive than *H. corsicus*, which seems to me the handsomest of all the genus. I delight in its glossy, three-parted, spiny leaves, erect habit, and apple green flowers so well displayed on stems that can be a good two feet high. By contrast *H.* × *nigericors* is rather dumpy and tends to huddle its flowers together – but there are a lot of them and it is undoubtedly an eyecatcher.

Helleborus lividus, which seems to be confined to the Balearic islands, has also been brought into this *mélange*, first by crossing it with *H. corsicus* to produce *H.* × *sternii* and then by crossing this with *H. nigericors* to produce 'Nigristern' and 'Alabaster'. This is all good fun, but plain unadulterated *H. lividus* probably outclasses them all in beauty: a rather strange plant with pallid purple flowers and a dislike of cold which makes it unreliable out of doors in all but the mildest parts of Britain.

One's fancy for plants undoubtedly changes with age. When I was young *Helleborus foetidus* was just an interesting plant to be found growing wild in a few places if one searched diligently. It would not have occurred to me then to bring it into the garden but now it is very near the top of my hellebore list. Its leaves are as near perfect as those of *H. corsicus* though very different, much darker in colour and far more complex in pattern, and its little bell shaped flowers are in a constant state of change, all green at first but acquiring a rim of purple as they mature. It seeds prodigiously and not all the seedlings are of equal quality, some lacking the purple edge which puts the final touch of perfection on the flowers. Leaf and stem colour also vary, and there is a particularly beautiful form named 'Wester Flisk' which has reddish stems and glaucous leaves. Unfortunately I lost this through the black stem rot which occasionally attacks hellebores and particularly, it would seem, *H. corsicus* and *H. foetidus*. Sometimes the plants grow up again and seem none the worse for it, but more often they die completely. I do not know what causes the disease, nor have I seen it mentioned in any of the literature on hellebores. Fortunately there are usually so many seedlings that one can afford the loss of a few plants, but not those as good as 'Wester Flisk'. The specific name *foetidus* is a libel, for the plant does not stink and one must crush the leaves to produce an odour no more unpleasant than that of cherry laurel.

It would appear that all hellebores grow wild in limestone areas, and certainly all are happy in an alkaline soil though this is not essential. I have two gardens, both without any free lime, and hellebores grow well in both. However, the soil is not very acid, around pH 6.5, and I do not know how hellebores fare in strongly acid soils. It is a point that never seems to be mentioned.

The Gardens of the Villa La Foce

PENELOPE HOBHOUSE

Many of the great Renaissance villas of Tuscany have been lovingly restored by foreign owners; sometimes, as at La Pietra outside Florence, restoration has in fact been an act of creation, and the garden we see today, a poetic essay in the manipulation of space and architectural symmetry, is entirely twentieth century in execution. The garden of La Foce, south of Siena, is less well known but here again classical proportions and tenets rule. Owned by the Marchesa Origo and her Italian husband Antonio, this garden has evolved since the nineteen twenties. In its firm layout and subtle planting schemes it reveals the dual influences of 16th century Italian architecture and an English-style love of flowers which stems from the Marchesa's own background.

The Villa of La Foce lies on the west slopes of the ridge of hills which forms the watershed between the Val d'Orcia and the Val di Chiana. Today the quickest approach to La Foce from Rome or Florence is the arterial *autostrada del sole*. A turn off at the spa town of Chianciano Terme and a side road over the hills to the west leads in four or five kilometres to the villa which lies protected from the north and east by wood-covered hills. The house itself is framed and almost encircled by tall cypresses and high walls. Beyond the garden, which lies west and south, the land falls steeply to the valley of the Orcia which is dominated by distant Monte Amiato, whose chestnut covered slopes sweep down to meet the barren landscape where centuries of erosion have laid bare grooves of rock and clay creating the moon landscape – the *crete senesi* – typical of this southern part of the province of Siena. To the south the formidable square church tower of Radicofani marks the pass to Rome. Not far away, its roofs just visible from the hill above La Foce, lies the Renaissance town of Pienza where Aeneas Silvius Piccolomini, Pope Pius II, was born in the year 1405. The Pope, famous for his *Commentaries* in which he extols the beauty of landscape, loved his native countryside and his own palace at Pienza looks out over the Val d'Orcia and the chestnut woods of Monte Amiato where he used to confer with his Cardinals. Influenced by his friend Leon Battista Alberti, the author of *De Re Aeedificatoria,* a treatise on architecture based on classical sources, Pope Pious threw out a small terraced garden from which the spectacular view is framed. Alberti recommended that a site should overlook a city or plain 'bounded by familiar mountains' and that in the foreground there should be the 'delicacy of gardens'. Pienza and La Foce seem perfectly to express Alberti's teaching. The gardens at La Foce, almost completed in the fifteen years before the War of 1939–45, have been planned to provide just such an effect as Alberti sought; in fact the contrast between the immaculate levelled lawns and terraces, the delicate foreground view, and the bleakness of the terrain beyond has a dramatic quality almost beyond Alberti's original meaning.

The property of La Foce was acquired by Marchesa Origo (best known as the author Iris Origo) and her husband when they were married in 1924. The 3,500 acres had been long neglected; the ridges of bare clay ran down all the sides of the valley and the river bed was almost dry; little natural vegetation remained except for some tufts of broom. The house, hardly a villa but a dilapidated farmhouse with ancillary *fattoria* for the estate, was uninhabitable. In 1924 the greatest obstacle to making a garden at La Foce was the lack of water and restoring fertility to neglected farms and re-afforestation of the hillsides and ravines were the first priorities. Fortunately a gift from the Marchesa's American grandmother enabled a pipe-line to be laid bringing water from a distance of six miles; within a few years the garden could be started. The house was restored by Cecil Pinsent (1884–1964) who had become a friend during Marchesa Origo's childhood at the Villa Medici at Fiesole then owned by her mother Lady Sybil Cutting, and he designed the first small enclosed garden and pool next to the house in the next few years. The villa is of simple design, its stuccoed façade with a ground floor loggia arched with red brick, its windows framed in similar material. The walls are ornamented with the various *stemma* of previous owners dating back to the 16th century when it was owned by the Sienese hospital of Santa Maria della Scala. Its north-facing forecourt is filled with a pattern of cypress trees; two large evergreen oaks clipped to the shape of mushrooms flank the front door almost hiding the main building.

Perhaps in order to fully understand the combination of talents which have given La Foce its particular atmosphere and charm it is important to consider all the influences in Marchesa Origo's own

La Foce: Simple shapes of clipped box enclose small areas of grass

childhood and family background. Her mother, Lady Sybil Cutting
was Anglo-Irish, daughter of Lord Desart, her husband William
Bayard Cutting, who had died young, an American diplomat from
a wealthy Long Island family. They were married in 1901 and their
daughter Iris was born a year later. Lady Sybil acquired the Villa
Medici in 1910, a year after her husband's death, and this was her
daughter's home until her marriage in 1924. Lady Sybil used Pinsent,
who worked with the architect Geoffrey Scott (who later became
Lady Sybil's second husband), for the restoration of the formal
Renaissance gardens on the terraces overlooking the valley of the
Arno and the city of Florence. The villa, built by Michelozzo between
1458 and 1461, was hewn from the steep rocks with vast cost and
became the centre for Humanist conversation and music during the
succeeding thirty years. Lorenzo de' Medici, Il Magnifico, and his
friends, the poet Poliziano, Ficino and Pico della Mirandola, dined
on the terrace with its incomparable view. Of all the Medici villas

surrounding Florence perhaps that at Fiesole, built earlier than Pious II's palace at Pienza, most perfectly expresses Alberti's maxim on choosing a site. By the early 1900s the villa had been much altered, both inside and out, but for Iris Cutting to live there during her most formative years was a fine preparation and inspiration for the making of La Foce later. At that time Arthur Acton, Sir Harold's father, was laying out the gardens at La Pietra in Renaissance style and Princess Ghyka was restoring the Capponi Villa Gamberaia at Settignano nearby. Edith Wharton's *Italian Villas and Their Gardens* came out in 1904; Sir George Sitwell in 1909 had published his masterpiece *On the Making of Gardens*. In 1910 Cecil Pinsent started the gardens at I Tatti for Bernard Berenson. At the Villa Medici he replanted box-edged beds and repaired the stonework. A *viale* of cypresses under shady ilex trees led to the villa, and the Marchesa Origo recalls two large paulownias which in her childhood framed the view over the city of Florence. Above the villa dark ilex woods were more mysterious; below on descending terraces plots of wheat, beans and thickets of pink roses flourished between silvery olives.

Iris Cutting also spent periods of her childhood with her grandparents at Westbrook on the south shore of Long Island. In her own words 'It was here out of doors that the real charm of Westbrook began, with the tall English oaks . . . the shrubs and ferns bordering the mossy paths that led into the woods, and the three ponds edged with tall trees and shrubs which reflected, in the autumn, the brilliant reds and pinks of swamp maple and dogwood, and in the spring, massed banks of azaleas and hybrid rhododendrons.' The pinetum, mainly planted by her grandparents, still remains as an interesting collection of rare specimens, which thrive in the hot damp climate and the sandy soil. Today Westbrook, made over to the State of New York and endowed by Marchesa Origo's grandmother, is open to the public as a botanical garden and park with the specification that it should remain 'an oasis of beauty and quiet for those who delight in outdoor beauty'. The other grandparents lived in Ireland, at Desart Court in Kilkenny, where the 18th century house of grey limestone (later burnt in 'the Troubles' in 1922) looked out over a formal Italian garden and rolling parkland to misty mountains. The garden was neglected; different indeed from the manicured Westbrook: 'the shrubbery so thick and dark,

La Foce: The box enclosures, emphasising the shape of the pool,
are clipped at two levels

the park so green, the woods so deep in bluebells'. Overgrown groves
of laurel, laburnum and lilac and old fruit trees in a brick-walled
kitchen garden reflected the easy-going and almost impoverished
life style of the Desarts.

The gardens at La Foce are now sixty years old and upkeep is
immaculate. Their design and conception seem to have been shared
by the Origos and by Cecil Pinsent. The latter provided the strong
framework but the Marchesa must have provided the planting
inspiration which differs from the more conventional and typical
'historicizing' style used by Pinsent for most of his villa gardens in
the hills round Florence. In the previous hundred years many old
Italian gardens had been swept away to make space for the *giardini
inglese*, inspired by the 18th century English landscape movement.
As in England fashions changed again and by 1900 there was a

renewed interest in the original garden layouts of the fifteenth and
sixteenth centuries. These layouts, sometimes restorations on old
sites and sometimes completely new designs, were completed by
Pinsent and others and were mostly for English and American clients.
They reflected the 'Italianate' fashions of the late Victorians in
England, when delicate boxwood edging, topiary hedges and
sculptured shapes of the Renaissance period, were interpreted on a
gigantic scale. Pinsent clearly followed the fashion but with far
greater sensitivity. His box hedges, as at La Foce, were wide and
high; tall cypress and bay were used to make secret private enclosures and high stone ramparts supported hanging terraces. Yet
Pinsent avoided the garish flowerbed layouts of his contemporaries
and, in the main, often working in quite small gardens, resisted the
monumental effects of towering and elaborate stonework; his box
hedges surrounded panels of simple green grass, his terraces framed
distant landscapes and merged gently into the wider countryside.

Pinsent made the house at La Foce habitable for the Origos after
their marriage. According to records he designed the small inner
garden and central fountain in 1927. In 1930 the garden was extended
to include box hedged compartments where vast lemon trees in
traditional terracotta vases sit on stone plinths throughout the
summer months. In the flowerbeds at the base of each high wall, the
Marchesa planted tender climbers, honeysuckles, tree peonies and
columbines. In 1938 he designed the upper rose garden above a
wisteria-covered pergola which stretches west from the house then
curves round the shoulder of the hill to the south. At the same time
he designed a new lemon house and garden. In 1939 he made the
final dramatic extension. On the western limit, a balustraded terrace,
constructed in earlier years and supported by tall stone walls, hung
above the valley. The ground below was levelled and a curving line
of tall clipped cypresses, backed by evergreen oaks, were planted to
conceal a new garden which juts out over the valley below. This
elliptic space holds eight symmetrically placed wedge-shaped beds
each edged with double hedges of box, cut at different heights.
These double hedges surround panels of lawn and are copies of
original Renaissance flowerbed design, similar to those in the recently
restored gardens of the vanished Chigi villa in Monte San Quirico a
dozen kilometres distant, and to those of the Palazzo Piccolomini at
Pienza. In the four largest of the beds stand shapely evergreen

La Foce: A pergola offers shade. The stone path is planted with pinks.
Photos: Penelope Hobhouse

magnolias (*Magnolia grandiflora*), their shining green foliage a glowing contrast to feathery cypress and dense box. A double staircase of travertine stone leads down and conceals a grotto with three-layered *tazza*, a copy of a 16th century design. At the far end a stone-edged pond is dominated by a statue of a bowed figure.

These are Pinsent's recorded designs for La Foce. His partnership with Marchesa Origo in making this great modern garden is undisputed. Nevertheless La Foce is in no sense only a garden designer's creation but is almost dominated by the imaginative and charming detail of the planting. In the layout itself straight lines of formal geometry and clipped evergreens give way to gently curving paths which follow the natural contours of the hillside. Near the house hedges and topiary are firmly controlled; further away the garden paths lead into the half-wild woodland where native and exotic plants thrive in neighbouring clumps. A wide pergola of wisteria, underplanted with pinks, aubrietia and thyme leads away round the shoulder of the hill to the south; above it Pinsent's formal rose beds are edged with spreading mats of snow-in-summer (*Cerastium tomentosum*), making a froth of white in May, and lavender hedges mark the edge of terraces. A *viale* of tall cypresses, where white lilies grow in shade, leads up the steep hill side, an extension of the axis of a stone path which crosses the garden to its lowest point, a wall carrying ornaments of fluted urns. At the top of the cypress walk a second bowed stone figure, representing the Autumn Harvest, gazes down another angled vista between an avenue of alternating stone pines and cypresses carrying the eye along the descending shoulder of the hill. Mounded earth ramparts are lavender edged and paths invite further exploration to a seat on a lower level shaded by two tall cypresses. There the path rejoins the curving pergola walk which, now vine-covered, stretches another two hundred metres into the wood. On the open terraces, looking down on agricultural land reclaimed before the war, olives and fruit trees grow in rough grass, with native broom and cistus grouped between Judas trees and philadelphus. There are pink roses – perhaps the same Tuscan monthly rose of the Marchesa's recollection at Fiesole – and scented rosemary and lavender bushes are brushed in passing.

Thus the gardens at La Foce are Italian in style but reflect a plantsman's eye and essentially 'English' interest in flowers and the natural landscape. Inside a strong architectural framework dividing the garden into separate compartments and dominated by straight lines and symmetry, the textured green foliage gives shade and coolness in the hot summers. But even in the enclosed areas near the house plants sprawl and tumble in profusion softening hard lines and giving an almost cottage-garden atmosphere. Wisterias and vines clothe pergolas, walls are curtained with roses, fragrant trachelospermum, pomegranates and myrtle. Tall hedges of bay and cypress are cut to form shady arbours, and another wisteria pergola running round two sides of the house keeps the rooms cool in hottest summer. Gradually the garden was extended to the western terraces and to the hill above and to its curving hillsides. A lemon garden, its outer edge hemmed with bay, lies under the house walls. Beyond and below, where a high wall cuts off the garden from the road, stone paths are flanked with Pinsent's topiary box, today grown to more than four feet wide and high and clipped in three dimensional blocks. These cross the terraces, the changing levels accentuating their architectural form. On a higher level more box hedges make a cross axis running along parallel to the terrace to reach the high western rampart which conceals Pinsent's last garden extension. Here the box is elaborately shaped and topped with hemispherical domes.

A path through the wood beyond the pergola or a track outside the garden walls leads south to the chapel and cemetery at the bottom of the wooded slope. Here in a walled enclosure sheltered by a great oak, where the Marchesa's son Gianni, who died aged eight and her husband Antonio lie buried, the graves are simply edged with box, the centre space carpeted with flowering peri- winkle. Round the walls pittosporum and more trachelospermum fill the air with fragrance in summer.

Marchesa Origo should have the final word (taken from *Images and Shadows*, 1970): 'Gradually, by experiment and failure, I learned what would or would not stand the cold winters and the hot, dry summer winds. I gave up any attempt, in my borders, at growing delphin- iums, lupins or phlox . . . and I learned too to put our lemon trees, plumbago and jasmine under shelter before the winter. But roses flourish in the heavy clay soil, and so do peonies and lilies, while the dry hillside is where lavender thrives – a blue sea in June, buzzing with the bees whose honey is flavoured with its pungent taste, which also, in the winter, not only scents our linen but kindles our fires. Every year the garden grows more beautiful . . . The woods were already carpeted . . . with wild violets, crocuses, cyclamen, *Anemone alpina* and autumn colchicum, and among these I . . . naturalise other kinds of anemones, daffodils and a few scillas.'

Gentian Blue?

STEPHEN G. HAW

Gentians are commonly thought of as blue, and it is true that the purity and intensity of the blues found in this genus is almost unrivalled in the plant kingdom. But although many gentians produce flowers of some shade of this colour, there are also many that do not. The genus *Gentiana* is very large and varied. Flower colour ranges from purest blue to purple, white, yellow and even red, and while many gentians are small tufted or trailing plants, some send up erect stalks to as much as five or six feet in height.

There are more than five hundred species of gentian distributed across the world, from northern areas of Europe, Asia and North America to southerly parts of New Zealand and Chile. They are most abundant on the high meadows of the eastern Himalaya and south-west China. The great majority are plants of alpine or sub-alpine regions, with a few reaching extreme elevations. *Gentiana urnula* has been found growing at over twenty thousand feet in the Nepal Himalaya, close to the altitude record for a flowering plant. Other species descend to just above sea level, especially on exposed rocky or sandy shores, or in boggy areas inland. In Britain, our native Marsh gentian, *Gentiana pneumonanthe* flowers from July to September in wet heathland. The tallest gentian is *Gentiana lutea*, with bright golden-yellow flowers. It is something of an oddity in the genus, for its corolla is of an open star-shape, the segments being joined together only at the base to form a very short tube. The Great Yellow gentian also lacks the small lobes or fringes called 'plicae', which are found between the main segments of the corollas of most species of the genus. It is quite common in alpine meadows up to about eight thousand feet altitude in most of the mountain ranges of Europe, from the Pyrenees eastwards into western Asia. It is a stately, large-leaved and imposing plant, with a long tap-root thrust deep into the soil. This is the gentian-root which has for centuries been used in Europe as medicine and for flavouring liqueurs. This gentian has been in cultivation in Britain since as long ago as 1596. Unfortunately, it is not often seen in gardens today, probably because it is not easy to propagate.

In addition to this species, there are several other erect, broad-

Gentiana pneumonanthe

leaved gentians found in European alpine meadows. Their flowers range in colour from the pale yellow of the Pyrenean *Gentiana burseri* to the spotted brownish-purple of *Gentiana pannonica* from the eastern Alps. None of these is as tall as *Gentiana lutea*, and their flowers are of a more usual gentian shape. They are generally not plants of outstanding beauty, and are only occasionally cultivated.

The remaining European gentian species have blue flowers, and are mostly dwarf plants of the upper Alps. The two major groups of species are the Trumpet gentians typified by *Gentiana acaulis*, and the Spring gentian, *Gentiana verna*, and its relatives. Both groups generally flower quite soon after the snow has melted from their mountain habitats, usually at some time between May and July. They are among the loveliest of mountain flowers. It is their perfect blueness which underlies the association of gentians with blue, though they vary considerably in shade. White varieties of several species are known, some of which are in cultivation.

Many gentians have flowers which are normally white. This is especially common with the New Zealand species, almost all of which have predominantly white flowers. A high proportion of all New Zealand flowers are white, a phenomenon probably linked to the distinctive composition of the insect population of these isolated islands. Gentians from this region generally have rather shallowly cupular flowers, with long, rounded corolla lobes, and grow either on alpine screes or among rocks and sand near the coast. *Gentiana saxosa* is the most frequently-seen New Zealand gentian in British gardens.

Considerably more than two hundred species, of a great diversity of sizes, forms and flower-colour, occur in western China and the eastern Himalaya. Some are tiny annuals only a couple of inches high, others are erect perennials growing to three or four feet tall. Many have blue flowers. It is the blue gentians that are the glory of the high meadows of the Himalaya in late summer, flowering just as the monsoon rains abate and allow the sun to coax their buds into bloom. The gentians of the Ornata group are the most widespread and common, occurring from east-central Nepal eastwards along the Himalaya into western China, and then northwards along the mountain ranges of Yunnan and Sichuan into Qinghai and possibly Mongolia. *Gentiana sino-ornata* must be the best-known of this group, as it is common in gardens, where it has settled better than any of

Gentiana acaulis

its near relatives. It usually has deep blue flowers with greenish-yellow stripes on the outside and, like all the Ornata gentians, flowers in late summer or autumn. Others of this group have sky-blue flowers. *Gentiana ornata* makes a superb show in September and October on the yak pastures of the Nepal Himalaya, rivalling the brilliant azure of the rain-washed skies.

Other gentians of this area are white or yellow, or of various shades of purple. The Nepalese *Gentiana depressa* is one of several species with complex coloration. It has flowers which are basically white and pale blue, with green and mauve tinging. There are also some whose flowers are pink. I have encountered two of these in central Yunnan province in south-west China. *Gentiana rhodantha* is common on rocky hills, making a fine display on sunny days in January and February. Its stems are long and thin, and do not stand erect unless supported by other herbage. Also found in the same area, though less common, is *Gentiana duclouxii*, which has pale rose-pink flowers. It is a delightful tufted, trumpet-flowered species, usually found at the edge of woodland or among open scrub on mountain slopes.

In South America are found the gentians of most vivid coloration. Here the moderate pinks of some of the Asian gentians have developed into brilliant scarlets, crimsons and oranges. But many of the species of this area are rather poorly known. Limited experience seems to suggest that they are difficult plants to cultivate outside their native habitats.

It is unfortunately true that most gentians are not particularly easy to grow in gardens. There are a few exceptions, such as *Gentiana septemfida*, which will grow and flower well in almost any sunny position in the rock garden or border. But most are at best fickle. *Gentiana acaulis*, for example, is notorious for its propensity to bloom well in one situation yet produce scarcely any flowers in apparently identical conditions elsewhere. Many others simply fail to flourish despite the greatest of care lavished upon them. It can also be difficult to obtain gentians. Many species are not in cultivation at all, and only a few are regularly available from commercial sources. But despite all this, it should be possible to find at least two or three that will thrive in any garden.

Because their demands vary so much, it is hard to generalize about how to grow gentians. The great majority prefer an acid soil, and species such as *Gentiana sino-ornata* will not thrive where there is too much lime. A few, however, are lime-lovers. Almost all like plenty of moisture, but this does not mean that they are bog plants! A few enjoy boggy conditions, but most of the alpine species will quickly rot unless drainage is good. They must be given soil that will retain moisture, yet allow excess water to drain away rapidly. A gritty rock garden soil, with plenty of peat or leaf-mould added, will suit many of the smaller gentians. The taller species will usually grow in any good border soil that does not dry out too much, though some are easier to manage than others. Most species enjoy plenty of sun, but in very warm areas where they might desiccate in full sunshine, partial shade is advisable.

Gentians may be propagated by several methods, the most usual being seed-sowing, cuttings and division. Gentian seed should for preference be sown as soon as it is ripe, and left where it will be frosted during the winter. There should then be good germination in the following spring. Seed kept too long will germinate more slowly and much less evenly, some seedlings not appearing for a year or more. It is best to sow very thinly, so that the young plants can be left to grow on undisturbed until they can be planted out. Gentians strongly resent root disturbance, and should always be handled carefully during transplanting.

The smaller, tuft-forming species can often be divided successfully. Spring-flowering species should be split in autumn, and autumn-flowering species in spring. *Gentiana sino-ornata* is one of the easiest species to propagate by division. Some species rarely produce rooted offsets, but put out many shoots suitable for use as cuttings. These shoots may be cut off with a sharp knife in spring and potted into a rooting medium of sharp sand. They should then be watered well, and kept in a frame or glass house with shade from full sun until they send out roots. Provided the rooting medium is well-drained but never allowed to dry out, this method is usually successful.

The growing of most gentians is definitely a challenge, but can be extremely rewarding. This is a genus of distinction. Whether the flowers are brilliant blue, glistening yellow, dazzling scarlet or gleaming white, they are commonly very beautiful, and often spectacular. Seen flowering in quantity in the wild, gentians are quite unforgettable – among the great beauties of the natural world.

Drawings by Lionel Bacon

A Gentle Plea for Chaos

MIRABEL OSLER

Looking round gardens, how many of them lack that quality which adds an extra sensory dimension for the sake of orderliness? There is an antiseptic tidiness which characterizes a well-controlled gardener. And I'd go further and say that usually the gardener is male. Men seem more obsessed with order in the garden than women. They are pre-occupied with flower bed edges cut with the precision of a pre-war hair cut. Using a lethal curved blade, they chop along the grass to make it conform to their schoolboy set squares, and with a dustpan and brush they collect 1 cm. of wanton grass. Or, once they hold a hedge-trimmer, within seconds they have guillotined

all those tender little growths on hawthorn or honeysuckle hedges
that add to the blurring and enchantment of a garden in early June.

The very soul of a garden is shrivelled by zealous regimentation.
Off with their heads go the ferns, ladies' mantles or crane's bill. A
mania for neatness, a lust for conformity and away goes atmosphere
and sensuality. What is left? Earth between plants; the dreaded
tedium of clumps of colour with earth between. So the garden is
reduced to merely a place of plants. Step – one, two. Stop – one, two;
look down (no need ever to look up for there is no mystery ahead to
draw you on), look down at each plant. Individually each is sublime
undoubtedly. For a plantsman this is heaven. But where is lure?
And where, alas, is seduction and gooseflesh on the arms?

There is a place for precision, naturally. Architectural lines such
as those from hedges, walls, paths or topiary are the bones of a
garden. But it is the artist who then allows for dishelvelment and
abandonment to evolve. People say gardening is the one occupation
over which they have control. Fine. But why over-indulge? Control
is vital for the original design and form; and a ruthless strength of
mind is essential when you have planted some hideous thing you
lack the courage to demolish. But there is a point when your steady-
ing hand should be lifted and a bit of native vitality can be allowed
to take over.

One of the small delights of gardening, undramatic but recurring,
is when phlox or columbines seed themselves in unplanned places.
When trickles of creeping jenny soften stony outlines or Welsh
poppies cram a corner with their brilliant cadmium yellow alongside
the deep blue spires of Jacob's ladder all arbitrarily seeding themselves like coloured smells about the place.

Cottage gardens used to have this quality. By their naturally
evolved planting, brought about by the necessity of growing herbs
and fruit trees, cabbages and gooseberries, amongst them there
would be hollyhocks and honesty, campanulas and pinks. How rare
now to see a real cottage garden. It is far more difficult to achieve
than a contrived garden. It requires intuition, a genius for letting
things have their heads.

In the Mediterranean areas this can still be seen. Discarded cans
once used for fetta cheese, olives or salt fish, are painted blue or
white and stuffed to overflowing with geraniums placed with
unaffected artlessness on steps or walls, under trees or on a window

sill. Old tins are planted with basil, they stand on the threshold of a house, not for culinary use because basil is a sacred plant, but for the aromatic pleasure when a sprig is picked for a departing traveller. Under a vine shading the well, are aubergines, melons, courgettes and a scatter of gaudy zinnias. An uncatalogued rose is grown for its scent near a seat where a fig tree provides shade and fruit. Common sense and unselfconsciousness have brought this about. A

natural instinct inspired by practical necessity. We are too clever
by half. We read too many books, we make too many notes. We lie
too long in the bath planning gardens. Have we lost our impulsive
faculties? Have we lost that intuitive feel for the flow and rightness
of things; our awareness of the dynamics of a garden where things
scatter where they please?

And this brings me to another observation which I think goes
with my original longing for a little shambles here and there. For it
seems that proper gardeners never sit in their gardens. Dedicated
and single-minded the garden draws them into its embrace where
their passions are never assuaged unless they are on their knees.
But for us, the unserious, the improper people, who plant and drift,
who prune and amble, we fritter away little dollops of time in sitting
about our gardens. Benches for sunrise, seats for contemplation,
resting perches for the pure sublimity of smelling the evening air
or merely ruminating about a distant shrub. We are the unorthodox
gardeners who don't feel compulsion to pull out campion among the
delphiniums; we can idle away vacantly small chunks of time
without fretting about an outcrop of buttercups groping at the
pulsatillas. Freedom to loll goes with random gardening, it goes
with the modicum of chaos which I long to see here and there in
more gardens.

Not all gardens fail, of course. There are two for instance which
have this enchantment from the moment you enter. One belongs to
people I know who live on the Welsh borders, where all the cottage
garden attributes such as mulberry, quince and damson trees grow
amongst a profusion of valerian and chives, marjoram and sedums.
The whole lush effect is immediate and soothing; it gives you a
feeling of coming home, it reminds you of what life ought to be like.

In complete contrast is Rosemary Verey's garden at Barnsley
House, near Cirencester in Gloucestershire. Here amongst the
strong lines of design, parterres and walks, classical temple and knot
garden, it is as if the owner had washed over the whole layout with
soft, diffused colours so that hard lines are blurred. Sweet rocket and
violas, rock roses and species tulips beguile, flow and confuse. It
may not be chaos, it certainly isn't, but it is as if this truly cohesive
effect happened while the owner had turned away her head. She
hasn't, we know, for a garden like this has been painstakingly
achieved from the brilliance of deliberation. Knowing when not to

do things as vitally as knowing when to. There isn't a dandelion unaccounted for.

So when I make a plea for havoc, what would be lost? Merely the pristine appearance of a garden kept highly manicured which could be squandered for amiable disorder. Just in some places. Just to give a pull at our primeval senses. A mild desire for amorphous confusion which will gently infiltrate and, given time, one day will set the garden singing.

Wood engravings by Yvonne Skargon

Gardens in Fiction

Firbank's Flowering Tributes

JOHN FRANCIS

When Ronald Firbank was living in Piccadilly with his palm tree he
arranged for a gardener to be sent from Sloane Square to tend and
water his palm twice daily. The gardener should wear a green baize
apron and carry a green watering can and, unless it was raining, he
should make the journey on foot.

Sir Osbert Sitwell noted that unlike most palms far from their
native climes, Firbank's flourished. Firbank loved to travel. The
palm was to him what that little lamb was to Mary. But had his
circumstances been otherwise and had he been forced to earn his
living like two of the characters in his novels, Mrs Shamefoot in
Vainglory or The Duchess of Varna in *The Flower Beneath the Foot*, he
might well have run a flower shop. Mrs Shamefoot is the wife of a
politician. They are not the ideal couple the reader may infer. She
says of him, ' "My dear, he never looks. In the spring he goes striding
past the first violet; and it's always the same." ' A brute, clearly. Mrs
Shamefoot does not need the money but rather sells her flowers 'in
order to slap delicately at monotony'. When feeling downcast she
signals her moods via her window displays to passing friends. The
reason the Duchess of Varna opened her shop is less interesting and
more mundane; she's hard up and needs the cash. When feeling
extra put-upon Mrs Shamefoot is apt to construct a large floral
tribute even if none has been ordered. The Duchess skims into her
shop merely to chide the staff and to take what's going from the till.

Anyone who loves flowers and gardens is likely to enjoy Firbank.
Almost every page contains references to them. A lot of the action
takes place in gardens and his characters are sometimes described
in terms of flowers. In *The Flower Beneath the Foot* there is a nun,
Sister Irene, glimpsed 'while professing her rosary, [she] appraised
her surroundings with furtive eyes, crossing herself frequently with
a speed and facility due to practise, whenever her glance chanced to
alight on some nude shape in stone. Keen, meagre, and perhaps
slightly malicious, hers was a curiously pinched face – like a cold
violet.' What a masterly description! Sister Irene, a minor character,

the merest meteorite, is fixed for all time. Certain women *do* look exactly like cold violets.

Having embarked on this piece I was suddenly seized by the thought that my memory might be playing tricks. Was the work of Firbank so liberally studded with references to flowers as I have so confidently stated? A simple test would settle the matter. I took up my copy of *The New Rhythum and Other Pieces* and let it fall open. The sentence I read was, 'They had been invited to pick strawberries,' 'Tea to pick strawberries' at the house of Bertie Waldorf on Upper Park Avenue, and were comparing baskets. One of a pleasant series of *teas*, 'Tea to hammer Jewellery', 'Tea to talk Scandal', 'Tea to gather Gardenias', these five-o'clocks of Bertie Waldorf were often notable affairs.' So that was all right. Perhaps from some heavenly winter garden Firbank himself had directed my fingers, if so, it was good of him. Also what a bonus to be reminded of another more ominous strawberry gathering on that hot day in *Emma*.

I chose my copy of *The New Rythum* because of the three books by Firbank that I own (the others are *Five Novels* and *Three Novels*) *The New Rythum* was the least well known to me, not that it is without interest. There are several photographs including two views of Firbank's rooms at Trinity Hall, Cambridge. Flowers in vases are extremely evident and something, a fern probably, renders the splendid looking glass over the hearth difficult of access unless you are prepared to snip your way to it with shears.

It is not that Firbank, though, sees all things with promiscuous enthusiasm just because they are growing. (It would be interesting to know what he thought about, say, French marigolds. They always remind me of those boiled eggs which, disgustingly, contain a blob of blood. Nor can I imagine him being enthusiastic about some of the day-glo modern roses but, never mind.) It would be very interesting to know what sort of tree he was thinking about when, in *Vainglory*, he wrote '. . . a short path with a twist like a lizard's tail led up to the entrance, where an unremarkable tree with a long Latin name did its best to keep out the light'. The home so described is the residence of the widow Wookie, a discontented lady, fretful about almost everything. Her daughter is unmarried, "curates are such triflers", she complains. "I can get no grapes", and she doesn't expect to survive 'the fall of the leaf'. Perhaps because of the light which struggles through the branches of the unremarkable tree,

Mrs Wookie is prey to nervous fancies amounting to persecution mania. 'Driven out with her Family Rose, and followed by her servant Quirker, and by Kate, she saw herself stumbling at sunset . . . And night would find them (who knew?) where the cornflowers passed through the fields in a firm blue bar.' It is typical that even when things come to such a pretty pass the pass is pretty with cornflowers.

One of Firbank's most telling scenes is the death of the archduchess in *The Flower Beneath the Foot*. The archduchess has contracted a chill brought on by her passion for paddling in the ornamental ponds in the palace gardens. She is wandering in her mind, sometimes imagining she is wading and seeing a minnow, 'a whale!' and then she recalls hearing the first time she heard *The Blue Danube*. ' "It was at Schönbrunn – *schönes* Schönbrunn – my cousin Ludwig of Bavaria came, I wore . . ." ' By her bed a priest is praying. His prayers, in Latin, are like the tolling of a bell. Her Dreaminess the Queen is composing telegrams preparing distant relatives to expect bad news and she rebukes the dying archduchess for breaking in upon her concentration. The queen goes and looks out of the window. The scent of oleander flowers oppresses. The queen's eye is caught by the sight of a gardener 'with long ivory arms' at work.

' "*Judica me, Deus*" ', breaks in the priest 'in imperious tones'. A look of wondrous happiness comes over the archduchess. At this point we enter the dying woman's mind, 'she is wading – wading again among the irises and rushes'. A peacock's cry, that most hideous lamentation, all the worse for being impersonal adds its power to oppress to that of the oleanders. The queen resents the archduchess getting all the attention so she complains to the doctor about her nerves. The couturiers arrive – they've come about the queen's mourning – but Her Dreaminess is too tired for fittings. She goes to the glass, "I don't know why but this glass refuses to flatter me!"

"*Benedicamus Domino!*" The queen relents a little about the courturiers, "Well, just a toque". The archduchess expires but not before remarking that she wants mauve sweet peas. The queen, back at the window, is once again watching the gardner's ivory arms. 'The Angel of Death (who had sat unmoved throughout the day) arose.'

This, boiled down by me, I fear somewhat crudely, is the sixth chapter of *The Flower Beneath the Foot*. I quote it at some length because it seems to encapsulate Firbank. The numerous mentions of flowers. Note the colour of the sweet peas, mauve, the colour of mourning. The faint whiff of lust, like incense, seems to hover over all his work – the queen troubled by the sight of the gardener's arms. The vanity of the queen and of the court; the almost brutal presence of the couturiers to measure the queen for her mourning *before* the archduchess has died – this is life going on with a sort of pitiless precision.

Firbank is an author too often admired by one sort of reader for his 'campness' – an element he isolated tellingly when he wrote, 'a young man with a voice like cheap scent', and who so enjoyed the crass vulgarisation of the musical version of *Valmouth*. He is a more serious writer than is, by some, supposed. Perhaps I tub-thump. I shall return to this point armed with more examples of his ability to express real feelings. The last lines of *The Flower Beneath the Foot* are not in the least comic.

Because Firbank had an enviable inability to write lines which do not flicker with wit has meant that too many have only seen the jokes and have quite missed the real anguish that his characters often experience. Thetis Tooke, preparing to drown herself, removes her hat, "It would be a sin indeed to spoil such expensive plumes . . . It's not a headpiece that would become everyone; – and I can't say I'm sorry!" Poor Thetis loves but her love is not returned. Sad evidence in coroner's courts testifies to human beings going on with the routine of life in the most normal seeming way until they do the supremely abnormal thing and end their life. The late Kenneth Clark in his autobiography *Another Part of the Wood* writing about the death of Philip Heseltine (the composer Peter Warlock) puts it perfectly. 'On Christmas Eve, 1930, having put out the cat, Phil Heseltine put his head in the gas oven.' Just before Thetis Tooke attempts to end her life she had met Carry, a minor character who is carrying 'a huge bright bouquet of Chinese asters, sunflowers, chrysanthemums and dahlias, which she inhaled, or twisted with fabulous nonchalance in the air as she read . . . She appeared very much amused.' Thetis is not so far gone in gloom as not to be stung by curiosity. She asks her why she is laughing. The reply is that she knows *at last* 'about the gentlemen'. Thetis gives a little advice: "Pick up your flowers, Carry Smith, and don't be a dilly". She removes her hat and prepares to die. Luckily, Sister Ecclesia . . . well, you may not have read *Valmouth* so I won't say anymore.

There are surprises in Firbank but little suspense and what little there is should be conserved.

If Firbank had not been of independent means he might well have got by like Mrs Shamefoot, running a flower shop. He understood the tricks of the trade. 'Each time a basket of Arums and Orchids (eked out with Gypsophila) that the Station Master at Montreux had presented her with, rolled to the ground, Mamma screamed and said she was certain that she would be assassinated within the year, which naturally reminded her of the fatal gala performance given to poor Aunt Caroline – *requiescat in pace.*' It seems to me that there is an authentic glimpse of the canny florist revealed by the phrase 'eked out with Gypsophila'. It is unlikely that Firbank knew his onions but he knew the going rate for arums and orchids.

Firbank's personality was, it seems probable, constructed as carefully as his novels. Reading about him he appears to have been a typical *Yellow Book* young man of the nineties. But he was the very last rose of that sometimes sickly summer. Like the would-be Salome character in *The Artificial Princess* he perhaps 'enjoyed colouring his retrospect'. He chose to live in a period where he felt at home. Far too ill to serve in the army and, rather bravely in the circumstances, observing that he had always found the Germans 'most polite' he retreated into an out of date Edwardian world, (George V being on the throne), and wrote his novels.

While civilisation was being pulverised Firbank was creating a new, albeit small civilisation for himself and for us. It is difficult to imagine how anyone could have written *Vainglory* in 1915 or *Valmouth* in 1918 until you remember that Jane Austin never so much as mentions Napoleon.

Firbank died too young (in 1926) to make a garden for himself. But in his writing he creates gardens which can delight us and which never need weeding. We can be sure that any garden he had made would have contained statues. Chapter 4 of *Cardinal Pirelli* is set in the gardens of the Vatican: 'At the season when the oleanders are in their full perfection, their choicest bloom, it was the Pontiff's innovation to install his American type-writing apparatus in the long Loggie of the Apostolic Palace that had been in disuse since the demise of Innocent XVI. Out-of-doorish as Neopolitans usually are, Pope Tertius II was no exception to the rule, preferring blue skies to golden ceilings – a taste for which many were inclined to blame him.'

All the gardens of Firbank, it seems to me are littered with statues and, of course, statues imply fig leaves and these bring out the never far away snigger in R.F.'s nature. Pope Tertius has a pet white squirrel called Slyboots, 'the gift of the Archbishop of Trebizond'. Slyboots enjoys statues too 'with what playful zest she would spring from statue to statue; and it would have amused the Vicar of Christ to watch her slip and slide, had it not suggested many a profound moral metaphor applicable to the church. "Gently, gently", he enjoined; for once, in her struggles she had robbed a fig-leaf off a *Moses*. *Pirelli* was completed in 1925, the year before Firbank died. He had used the same joke in *Valmouth* in 1919. The scene is Hare-Hatch House. Mrs Hurstpierpoint asks her maid, "Is the worst of the storm over, Fowler, do you consider?" Now that the wind has deprived the statues of their fig leaves, " 'm", she replied, "I can hardly bear to look out".

' "Oh? *Has* it? What? Again?" '

'All around the courtyard and in the drive you'd think it was October from the way they lie.'

More statuary in *The Artificial Princess*: 'The statues in the dusk looked terribly emotional as they clung to each other in immortal love. How fervant they seemed. Quite candidly, it was absurd to be alive and yet more cold than they.'

Firbank is perfect reading for those without a garden. 'There were Roses in the Rose Garden, which was remarkable where all was paradox, and from every Rose bush hung a Chinese lantern; between these, the Maids of Honour tripped about, looking like Easter Lilies, they were enjoying themselves immensely and giggled a great deal . . .' 'In the chiaroscuro of a shrubbery, a Society Crystal gazer, swathed in many shades of violet, was predicting misfortunes by the light of the Stars.'

' "People won't come to one in a peach-charmeuse trimmed with Point", she had often lamented. "One requires Moonstones, Veils, and a ghoulish cut to one's skirt . . ." '

Part of the charm of Firbank is the clever illusion he gives his readers who may find themselves more often in municipal parks rather than palace gardens, that they are in a charmed circle where private jokes are as a password to spies. What is a *ghoulish* cut to one's skirt? The devoted reader of Firbank infers a great deal. You have the feeling you have caught the eye of an old and dear friend.

The ideal author, in some ways, to take to the late Mr Plomley's desert island. He is like a stock cube of concentrated flavour dropped into the hot water of your imagination. You catch references to the magnificent image of the god Ptah who was Mrs Shamefoot's travelling companion – 'the terrific immobility of Egyptian things enchanted her' – or a character will request someone not 'to look down my neck like an archer of Carpaccio', a puzzling request until, years later, you find yourself in a church or gallery and you suddenly see exactly what he meant. He flicks drops of erudition at you with the hyssop of his wit.

But above all Firbank traps you in a fragrant garden. He describes even clouds in terms of roses. 'Above the Pietà on the porter's gate, slow speeding clouds, like knots of pink roses, came blowing across the sky, sailing away in titanic bouquets towards the clear horizon.' The sky itself when quite free of clouds still suggests flowers. 'Through the triple windows of the chancel the sky was clear and blue – a blue like the blue of lupins.' And where people are not like flowers they are seen as pearls. ' "People look like pearls, dear, beneath your marvellous trees." ' Firbank celebrates the beauty of the moment because he knows better than most the moment passes.

We value authors for different qualities. His is quite a separate intensity to, say, Emily Brontë's. You can imagine Firbank doing many things but never, for a moment, *wuthering*. Yet, which cry of anguish is more affecting in the end? the 'Cathy! – Heathcliff!' as they thud across the moors or the 'Yousef, Yousef, Yousef . . .' of poor Laura in *The Flower Beneath the Foot* as she unknowingly, in the last extremity of pain beats her hands on the glassed topped walls of the nunnery? She is watching the man she loves ride by after marrying another. 'Oblivious of what she did, she began to beat her hands, until they streamed with blood, against the broken glass upon the wall.' Only a little while before she had watched the clouds, the 'knots of pink roses', the 'titanic bouquets'.

One unusual difficulty which Firbank suffered from were those sudden upwellings of laughter when the delightful absurdity of what he was composing caused him to give up writing that day. We can be grateful that his laughter and the fact that he did not live to see forty still afforded him sufficient time to write as much as he did. He really cannot have been a butterfly, more like the passing character in *The Flower Beneath the Foot*, 'Traversing the flower plat now, with the air of a black-beetle with a purpose, was the Countess Yvorra.' The king in the same novel is much given to employing the royal plural and like so many Firbankian characters suffers dreadfully from fatigue – ' "We'd give perfect worlds," the king went on, "to go, by Ourselves, to bed." '

To go to bed with a novel by Ronald Firbank is to go on a primrose path of laughter to a world of absurd enchantment. Not that he is not in the least strenuous sense an outdoor novelist too. Beautiful light reading while seated under a lime tree and on almost every page you will find gardens, fountains and other endless pleasures.

Chasing Shadows
Plants with black and brown flowers
STEPHEN LACEY

In August 1979 I went on safari to Lake Turkana in northern Kenya. For the first few days we drove through an arid landscape of thorn trees and dry river beds and spent our time spotting reticulated giraffe, Grevy's zebra, secretary birds and flocks of vulturine guinea-fowl. Then, as we approached the lake, the scenery abruptly changed. We entered a lunar terrain of rocks and craters, a grey volcanic desert in which all living things (apart from mad dogs and English-men, of course) seemed to be sensibly nocturnal.

Periodically we had to stop to engage in a bit of road building or tyre changing, and it was during one of these interludes that I noticed something strange a few yards away. It turned out to be a plant in flower. In shape it was like a sea urchin, tight, wrinkled and loosely oval; in colour it was the darkest, most velvety black imaginable. It was a haunting sight, this solitary creature under the roasting sun of Africa. I have no idea what species it was but I shall carry its portrait in my mind forever. What is more, I shall never be able to look at another black flower without thinking of it.

Most of the garden plants that we call black would not bear comparison in blackness to my Kenyan enigma. They are just very dark shades of red, maroon, crimson or purple, which, in a certain light, seem to have all colour drained from them. But there is a handful of plants which can justly claim to be true blackamoors and these are the varieties upon which I shall concentrate here.

To open the year there are two really black hellebores, 'Ballard's Black' and the plant known to gardeners as *H. torquatus*. Neither of these has any trace of the plum purple that one detects in ordinary dark forms of oriental hellebore; instead, the cups are the steely black of obsidian, the metallic sheen serving to intensify the under-lying inkiness of the sepals. Their semi-shaded site in the garden can be shared with the whites and yellows of early daffodils like 'Jenny', 'February Gold' and 'February Silver'.

The gold-laced polyanthus may have its petals edged in yellow but the centres can be as black as pitch. To obtain good forms you must begin with seed and carry out a selection the following year. The offspring will vary greatly in colour. Some will be ruby red, some dusky crimson and some a proper jet. As companions I favour the simple pale yellows of wild primroses, for the flowers of gold-laced polyanthas are small and could not compete with the showy blooms of the modern polyantha strains.

Another spring performer is the snake's head iris, *Hermodactylus tuberosus*. Again it is not completely black – its claw-like 'standards' are a murky lime green – but the falls end in a good smudge of sooty velvet, and a clump of flowers looks decidedly funereal. Bulbs can be obtained from most specialist suppliers and should be planted in a sunny position on well-drained, preferably limy soil. You might try them against the orange of berberis or early tulips.

Fritillaria camschatcensis is the darkest of a generally sober genus. Indeed it is often called the black lily. It is a plant for semi-shaded peat beds where, in late May, it sends up a 12 inch stem topped with a cluster of black bells lit by yellow anthers. It is well displayed among short white dicentras and non-rampant lamiums like the silver-leafed 'White Nancy' or the new marbled yellow archangel 'Silver Carpet'.

The diminutive faces of *Viola* 'Bowles's Black' peer out through the foreground vegetation of many plantsmen's borders. Seedlings pop up in all sorts of odd corners and are particularly welcome among the 'difficult' flower colours, the mauves and magentas, the carmines and lilacs. I weed out all the purple shades and the ones with too bold an eye, and this keeps the population under control. But even the truly dark offspring cannot compare with the black satin of the viola 'Molly Sanderson'. I have it in front of the dwarf, clump-forming, golden grass *Hakonechloa macra* 'Aureola', and it never fails to attract comment for it is seldom without flowers. Richard Cawthorne (Lower Dalton's Nursery, Swanley Village, Swanley, Kent) sells it and you see it in many other lists under the name 'Penny Black'. (Or is this something else?)

Similar but altogether larger blooms are exhibited by the pansy, 'King of the Blacks'. A spring bedding scheme that I have had in mind for ages but never got around to realising would comprise this variety (or Thompson & Morgan's improved form, 'T & M's Black') in partnership with a white, black-eyed pansy (try 'T & M's Jumbo White') as a ground cover for a drift of black and white tulips,

'Queen of the Night' and 'Duke of Wellington'. In fact, as you know, black tulips are really a dark plum colour but I still think the effect would be good, and refreshingly ascetic.

One of my best black finds is *Iris chrysographes*. Jack Drake (Inshriach Nursery, Aviemore, Inverness-shire, Scotland) sells a superior variety called 'Black Form' which comes more or less true from seed. I sowed a batch several years ago and had a fascinating crop, 80 per cent of which were velvet black and the remainder crimson, wine and imperial purple. The flowers appear in June and scarcely last a week but the leaves are rushy and plants do not occupy much space. They have a preference for acid soil I have been told, but plants I have given to owners of limy gardens seem to be thriving. Sun or part shade suits them and they grow to a height of two feet. Among bearded irises, 'Sable Knight' is probably the blackest, but has a definite purple cast.

I wouldn't have thought of including *Cosmos atrosanguineus* in this list were it not for the fact that it is growing just below my study window as I write. The dahlia flowers really are black until the petals are properly expanded and sunlight reveals the dark blood red pigment within. Three other borderline blackamoors are *Veratrum nigrum, Salvia discolor* and *Geranium sinense*. The veratrum's candelabra is maroonish, the salvia's hoods are indigo-ish and the geranium's cones are purplish. See what your friends think.

Thompson & Morgan (London Road, Ipswich, Suffolk) have certainly come up trumps with their black hollyhock, 'Nigra'. The catalogue photograph does not do justice to their new introduction which, in my garden at least, turned out to be as black as pitch. I grow it with a lemon yellow variety but it would be equally successful with the pastel pinks and apricots of cottage garden forms or just standing alone against a whitewashed wall.

You will deduce from my suggested companions for these various plants that I think it is possible to combine black attractively with all other colours, whether they are from the warm or cool side of the spectrum. The same is not true of brown. Brown is nothing more than very dark orange, and many of its variants, notably the tans, have a marked orange flavour about them. This makes them eminently suitable for hot schemes of yellows, creams, flame reds and lime greens but distinctly uncomfortable among the cooler blues, pinks and violets.

It is a pity that there is such a dearth of brown flowers available to the gardener. I heard recently of someone who was planning a brown border and I would love to know how many different plants she accumulated. You may think the idea sounds depressing but I imagine she would admit some orange proper into the composition to relieve the monotony with items like brown-knobbed heleniums and *Euphorbia griffithii*. I would also include apricot-flowered *Crocosmia* 'Solfatare' which, like the euphorbia, has tan-flushed leaves, the soft orange daylily, 'Bonanza', which has a pronounced brown zone, the yellow osteospermum 'Buttermilk' whose petals have a brown reverse, hardy chrysanthemums like 'Mei Kyo' which have a bronze patina, and the buff, brown-centred verbascum, 'Cotswold Queen'. She would have no difficulty in assembling foliage, of course – copper beech, bronze fennel, brown clover, *Carex buchanani* and the dwarf *C. comans* 'Bronze Form', *Acaena* 'Copper Carpet', and the tiny chocolate geranium *G. sessiliflorum* 'Nigricans', for example. But what about genuine brown flowers?

I can only come up with a handful. The first is one of Barnhaven's polyantha seed strains, sold under the name 'Spice shades'. This provides a range of tans and reddish browns with which to cover the ground in March and April. They are perfect around the young unfurling foliage of *Paeonia mlokosewitschii*, which has similar tones, and the early cream tulip, *T. fosteriana* 'Purissima'.

A number of iris species have brown in their make-up, often in the form of veining or netting. *I. innominata* is a good example and in its biscuit colour forms would almost pass for a brown-flowered plant. It is worth scouring the *spuria* clan too. But among the ranks of the bearded iris you can find the most exciting shades, and these provide you with the only opportunity of orchestrating an extensive summer scheme. Kelways Nurseries (Langport, Somerset) have the longest list of named hybrids. I would single out 'Gay Trip', a warm mahogany; 'Rocket', a golden tan; 'Bronze Bird', a pale coffee, and 'Red Rum', a reddish brown. The best dwarf brown irises Kelways do not seem to stock. They are 'Jasper Gem', a reddish chestnut, and 'Nancy's Khaki'; these can be obtained from V. H. Humphrey (8 Howbeck Road, Arnold, Nottingham) and Four Seasons (Hillhouse Farm, Cheney's Lane, Forncett St Mary, Norwich) respectively.

Three foxgloves produce brown flowers. Those of *Digitalis parviflora* are, as you would expect, extremely small and despite being densely carried, do not make sufficient impact for inclusion anywhere but the wild garden. *D. ferruginea* has larger blooms, which are rounded and generally amber-coloured, with chestnut netting within. But the pick of the trio is undoubtedly *D. laevigata*, whose rich mid-tan bells hang beautifully on their spikes and have a protruding pointed white lip. In my hands it has always been biennial, but it may last an extra year or so in yours.

I don't know what you will think of my last plant. It is a floribunda rose called 'Cafe' and I came across it in a cottage garden in North Wales last year. Now that I live with it (I got it from David Austin Roses, Bowling Green Lane, Albrighton, Wolverhampton) my enthusiasm for it has waned. Its blooms are large, flat and very double, a lovely mocha at their peak but, and here's the rub, a decandent milky Nescafé later. It is a plant that will either intrigue you or turn your stomach.

Flowers for a Flagship

AUDREY LE LIÈVRE

A tanker takes how far – 2 miles? – to come to a halt. The gardening press took a comparable length of time to recognise the outbreak of World War One: once it did so, however, all was grist to the patriotic mill, and in *The Garden* for 11th March, 1916, there appeared a short piece which recently caught my attention:

Hyacinth grown on HMS IRQN DUKE
It may come as a pleasant surprise to many readers to learn that spring-flowering bulbs like Hyacinths, Crocuses and Daffodils are grown by our gallant defenders at sea on board some of our warships. A vase of white Narcissi grown in moss fibre actually bloomed on board HMS KENT during the battle of the Falkland Islands, while the Hyacinth shown in the accompanying illustration was grown and recently flowered on board HMS IRON DUKE ... The photograph was first sent to Robert Syden-ham Ltd, Birmingham, accompanied by the following letter: 'I enclose a photograph which, although it is not a very good one, may have some slight interest in the fact that it shows a white Hyacinth grown in your moss fibre [Robert Sydenham Ltd were Nurserymen] under wartime conditions. As you may imagine, the conditions obtaining in a ship of war at the present time are by no means ideal. The result, however, is not entirely unsatisfactory. The height of the flower above the moss fibre was $11\frac{1}{2}$ inches" '. [The photograph which is too poor to reproduce clearly shows a well-grown flower spike.]

Does this happen nowadays, I wonder? Perhaps it wasn't too popular even in 1916 aboard the Flagship of the Grand Fleet, as the naval gardener's name is never revealed. But two things are certain: quarters must then have provided more space for such activities and, as Jellicoe's Flagship knew about indoor gardening in other ships of the Grand Fleet, the grapevine must indeed have been both swift and effective.

Can anyone emulate the correspondent in IRON DUKE? The 1982 Falklands campaign did not take place at hyacinth time, and Sydenhams ceased trading in 1967, but perhaps there was someone, somewhere in the Task Force who was busy in odd moments with bulb bowl, some other firm's moss fibre – and perhaps autumn crocus in mind?

Christmas in a New Zealand Garden

KERRY CARMAN

To those who live in the Antipodes a European Christmas is synonymous with snow and skating parties, perky robins and roaring log fires, roasted chestnuts, mulled wines and all that goes with icy mid-winter in the northern hemisphere.

December in the southern hemisphere is totally different. My brief is to tell you of my personal pleasure ground, to weave you a chaplet of sweet summer buds and steep you in the essence of my mid-summer Christmas at a time when activity in the northern garden is at its lowest ebb.

As you sit in your firelit rooms enjoying the rarified scents from a nearby glass of winter flowers (have you noticed how the fragrance released from winter aconites, *Eranthis hyemalis*, in a warm room exactly approximates that of sweet peas?) I am drowning my senses in the sights and sounds, niffs and whiffs, colours and textures of the mid-summer pomps of my December garden.

While you contemplate a favourite book or turn the pages of an old botanical tome, or perhaps watch for the slow unfurling of your stylosa iris buds, I am sampling the parallel pleasure of the more rapid unfolding of my moonflowers, the parasol buds of which tremble into bloom with the suddeness of time-lapse photography.

Like all winter-bound gardeners you are no doubt scheming and dreaming for the seasons to come and building horticultural castles in the air. Here in your dream the sweet succession of the seasons will lay ever more delights and floral treasures at your feet. While you so dream, let me whisk you south in imagination to the land of the long white cloud, Ao-tea-roa, a land where gardening dreams often do come true.

Right now it is summer, three days past the summer solstice, Christmas Day. Our shores are wreathed with the crimson garland of pohutukawa, the New Zealand Christmas tree, (*Metrosideros excelsa*), flaunting its nectar-laden puffs of bloom at every passing bee. Our hillsides are white-mantled with the snow of manuka (*Leptospermum scoparium*) in bloom.

The gardens are full of bright flowers and the scents of summer. The French have an apt word for this tide of petals that drowns the garden, this flood of warm roses and spicy-throated pinks. They call it *floraison*, the blooming season. In many of our gardens this efflorescence is sub-tropical in nature and these plots boast many tender beauties not possible in more temperate regions. Extravagantly scented stephanotis, frangipani and creamy gardenias, celestial blue jacarandas, the legendary lotus, bright hibiscus, sparkling tropical impatiens, banana palms and many other tenderfoots grace many of these gardens. Also becoming very popular are the Vireya rhododendrons from south east Asia. These tender species flower for eight months of the year, their dazzling blends of colour and variety of flower forms, many of which are fragrant, ensure their place in many gardens where protection from frost may be provided.

Most of the above plants may be container grown and kept under cover for the winter in cooler areas, for most New Zealand gardens are like mine; temperate climate gardens with four defined seasons, though a shorter and less severe winter in most areas extends the range of plants we may grow.

Christmas is an especially busy time for the southern hemisphere gardener. Not only must the traditional rites be observed but it is also the season of summer holidays and one of the most demanding periods in the garden. In particular must the garden's constant cry for water be met; not an easy task in many towns where summer hosing restrictions have to be rigorously enforced. Many have their own artesian wells, a happy solution where such water is available. Watering container plants twice a day is not too much in hot summers. Beverley Nichols once remarked when visiting our country that the amount of summer watering necessary was the only factor deterring him from wanting to live here, in what was otherwise a gardener's paradise. Nowadays automatic sprinkler systems take much of the pain out of this problem.

As every gardener knows, you can never get up too early when you own a garden. Christmas Day is no exception. Tiny, new potatoes, peas and strawberries must be harvested for the festive meal and lavender gathered to make wands for gift-giving. Deadheads must be clipped, stakes placed where sudden giraffe-like aspirations have appeared and wayward tendrils must be gently tweaked and tied into place. The sprinklers must be set and cans of water carried to the ever-thirsty potted lilies and moonflowers.

I am up and about at five o'clock on Christmas morning. In

neighbouring houses the sound of tin whistles and excited childish voices heralds the special nature of the day. As we step into the courtyard and the freshness of the morning, our senses are assailed by cool fragrance;

"Odours of orange flowers and spice . . .
Like airs that breathe from Paradise."

The odours that reach us, of lily, jasmine and moonflower, seem almost tangible, culminating in the icy tumble of dew-drenched Paul's Lemon Pillar roses in the courtyard corner. A lone blackbird carols his greeting from the top of the ancient kowhai tree, relic of the bush days, green now with ferny leaves.

A garden is a personal place. While many New Zealand gardens are filled with the mid-summer gauds of scarlet hibiscus, pink oleanders, orange and gold canna lilies and sparkling impatiens and Livingstone daisies, my delight consists in arranging sensitive colour schemes and plant harmonies, in pleasuring the senses and in grow-ing old-fashioned and scented 'domesticall flowers'. In my garden, the bright colours which our hot summer skies demand are isolated. I feel their intensity gains in impact. It is said a garden reflects its owner. I am principally a lover of flowers and the natural world, ever intrigued by my patch of ground and the life it contains. I spend many happy hours recording that life with pen and brush. My garden, though small, also reflects my passion for collecting plants, therefore making it a varied place with much of interest. As I have not yet been blessed with that gardener's dream, 'a back with a hinge in it', this small garden of Eden is also, all too often, my garden of Weeden.

Old cottage flowers like pinks, wallflowers, violas, hollyhocks and sweet-williams and especially those from the primrose, violet, snowdrop and rose families are a favourite field of research. Another time I must tell you of my magic violet, the double green auricula, the tiny mountain flowers and rare hebes, of my Primavera garden, the double galtonia and the host of scented winter treasures but this is not the season. Now it is mid-summer: mid-summer of the lily and the rose and we must wend our way through my patch where the plants, both invited guests and gatecrashers bring much pleasure all year round.

First let us visit the lilies. We cross the paving and tiny courtyard

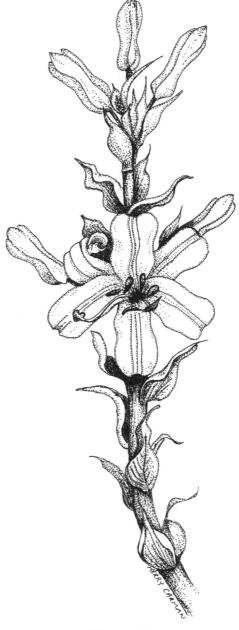

Lilium candidum

lawn to where these graceful maidens 'folded in hoods of silver lawn' stand with bowed heads, for all the world like a reverent group of novice nuns at morning prayer. Quicksilver droplets roll out upon my hand when I tuck a finger under the chin of one pendulous beauty to lift her face to mine, spilling dewdrops and fragrance in equal measure. Dew also lingers on the lawn and the upturned cups of campanula and nierembergia nearby. The lilies are doing exceptionally well this year, many being over six feet tall. One of my favourites, an 'Emerald' hybrid, is not yet out but has many fat buds. The *Lilium auratum* are full of eastern promise. There are plenty of *Lilium regale* and 'Dutch Glory' hybrids for Christmas picking and still a few of my favourite Christmas lily, *Lilium candidum* which for me is forever associated with Christmas in my grandmother's South Island garden, where my infant nose was always pollen-stained in December from standing on tiptoe to sniff the waxen-petalled blooms.

Then there are the moonflowers. Usually they have folded their little tents by dawn but there are still a few unspoiled ones where the sun's rays have not reached their tender petals. There are many plants with the common name of moonflower. What they all share is their superb fragrance, white colour, large blooms and dramatic method of unfolding in the dark. There is something almost mystical about them. In Edwardian times, people used to make up parties to go with lights and view the opening of these moonflowers. I cannot think of a finer excuse for a party than to invite friends around on a fine mid-summer evening for the same purpose. I grow two varieties. The shrubby *Datura meteloides* (syn. *wrightii*) which has a light, tropical fragrance with fresh lemon overtones, and the tropical vine, *Calonyction aculeatum* (syn. *Ipomoea bona-nox*) which makes a splendid container plant in a large pot if trained on a tripod of bamboo. The long spiralled buds of this tender twiner open in a few seconds to a broad, shimmering disc that seems to absorb and reflect moonlight in its pearly petals. The fragrance is cool and a little astringent.

Leaving these pallid flowers of the dawn, let us cross the courtyard and turn the corner to something brighter. Red is the colour of Christmas and it is not lacking in our southern celebration. I do not grow pohutukawa in my inland garden, but here in a sunny sheltered corner I have my own floral flaunt in honour of the season, the one place in the garden where bright scarlet is allowed full rein. Lightened

Unfolding moonflower – *Datura meteloides*

by flowers of dazzling white this scheme reaches its peak at Christmas, a truly festive corner.

The fragrant white stars of Chilean jasmine, *Mandevilla suaveolens*, form the background where they clamber to the roof. Crisp red and white geraniums are the main display – the cheerful, scarlet heart of the scheme. They, too, scramble up to the roof, inspired perhaps by the waywardness of their South American companions. An old, black-red cottage hollyhock provides depth and a glistening stand of scented 'Dutch Glory' lilies nearby fills in the bottom storey. In the foreground, creeping white *Campanula isophylla* and red nasturtiums spill over the rocky edge. This Christmas vignette is a treat for both nose and eye. I am tempted to add that bright little shout of a floribunda rose 'Satchmo', *Lobelia cardinalis*, flagrant oriental poppies or deliciously-scented white bouvardia but as always in a small garden, space is at a premium and I suspect that the success of this scheme lies in its simplicity. Less is more after all.

As we push past the fragrant branches of the lemon verbena, (*Lippia citriodora* syn. *Aloysia triphylla*) which is allowed to trespass over the path for the sudden scent shock it provides, my fingers automatically reach out to fondle its leaves. Cut back hard each year, it unfailingly breaks forth in tender green shoots each spring, soon expanding to a fair-sized bush providing a harvest of lemon leaves for winter pot-pourri. Just now it is crowned with the lacy panicles of bloom that also contain the sweet lemon aroma. I find them useful in tussie-mussies where they add a light effect to more 'solid' flowers.

We have many plants endemic to New Zealand and Australia with their own sweetness or spiciness, thereby extending the range of

Mandevilla suaveolens, the Chilean jasmine

scented plants we may grow. Fragrant, old-world favourites thrive for us too. The southern sun is as good as sugar for bringing out the essential essence in the heart of a plant. Our generous summer sun releases the aromatic spiciness from sweeping bushes of the wax-flower (eriostomen), acacia, thryptomene, boronia, native myrtles, lemonwood, orange jasmine (*Murraya exotica*), and smaller delights like lemon-grass or the more traditional pungencies of moss roses, lemon verbena, pineapple sage or lavender. December is drenched in perfume: perfumes that are intoxicating in their sweetness, matching the mood of the long, drowsy summer days.

Our native myrtle, (*Lophomyrtus bullata*) is a very dainty and useful small evergreen shrub. It forms a neat spire of attractively textured leaves which release a pleasantly aromatic scent when torn. There are many hybrids available. Lophomyrtus is a botanical cousin of the common European myrtle, (*Myrtus communis*) though it does not grow so large. It is also related to the tree from which cloves are obtained (*Szygium aromaticum*); the clove as we know it being the flower bud, picked before it opens. Another of the group yields allspice. *Lophomyrtus bullata* 'Krinkly' produces the distinct odour of nutmeg when the leaf is crushed. I like to use the attractive bronze sprays of crinkled leaves as a backing for a buttonhole or posy of the little apricot rose, 'Perle d'Or.'

Among other native plants I grow are the tiny creeping lobelias, (*Pratia macrodon* and *Pratia angulata*) with their violet-like flyaway petalled flowers; sweet-scented Maori jasmine, (*Parsonsia heterophylla*); the little mountain harebells (wahlenbergia species); a rare

Pratia puberula, one of the 'creeping lobelias'

pink form of the renga-renga lily from the Kermadec Islands in the Pacific Ocean, north of New Zealand, and native orchids such as the epiphytic Easter orchid, (*Earina autumnalis*) which has a piercing scent that perfumes large areas of forest from mid to late summer. I make my own 'Bush Blend' pot-pourri from many of these sweet scented leaves and flowers, limiting the mixture strictly to those plants from New Zealand or Australia. With the addition of lemon-scented gums, boronia, mimosa, wax-flowers, fragrant fern, lemon-scented tea tree (*Leptospermum petersonii*) and moss fragments, a very pleasant, long-lasting combination results. It has a uniquely sweet fragrance that seems to capture all the freshness and tang of the native bush.

Baronia magastigma used in 'Bush Blend' pot-pourri

Chief joys in the tiny rock garden right now are the tri-petalled *Weldenia candicans*, the powered lilac hats of *Primula capitata* and the summer gentians. D. H. Lawrence's smoking blue torches have long had a place in my heart and among the incomparable blues now in bloom are *Gentiana septemfida* and *G. freyniana*; *G. siphonantha* has been giving sprays of bloom for picking since before Christmas and *G. sundermanni* is well set with shining black buds. These unfold to an open-vase shaped flower of bright blue with neatly fringed plicae between the petals.

Leptospermum petersonii, the lemon-scented tea tree

The dwarf bearded iris 'Gingerbread Man' still has some of its curious ginger-brown blooms topped by the startling blue beard that always reminds me of some crested tropical bird. Here, too, are Bowles' Golden grass, *Millium effusum* 'Aureum' and the cheeky little 'Bowles' Black' viola with its yellow Cyclopian eye in the middle of its dusky face. This is the flower of which the dear man once said, "I'm not so black as I was painted on that label", when a Chelsea shown form was mislabelled as 'Black Bowles'. Another

Viola 'Bowles' Black'

reminder of the great plantsman is thriving under the lemon tree in the form of the sweetest and tastiest mint we have ever grown. Known affectionately as 'Bowles' Rubbish Heap Mint', it was a gift from a friend who was one of E. A. Bowles' honorary nieces.

There have been plenty of lemons this year from which we make our own fresh lemonade, and still the blossoms come, heavy with fruity scent and such a delightful addition to pot-pourris and fragrant bath waters. Here, too, are the tiny wild strawberries, so sweet in the morning sun, columbines, lavender and other herbal delights like rosemary, melissa and clipped myrtle in terracotta pots.

The most glowing jewels that summer strews at our feet, the old roses, are distilling their heady fragrance nearby. Blended with catnip, pinks, alyssum, violas and sweet peas they form a rich-smelling bouquet of all the summer sunshine. These antique roses with their swathed and tucked blooms, some streaked or stippled, have sumptuous colours and textures reminiscent of old silks, taffetas and velvets. 'Mme. Isaac Pereire' is one of my favourites for scent, though her complexion is a little hectic for some tastes. Two other madames, 'Mme. Hardy' and 'Mme. Legras de St Germaine' bear neat white, flat-topped blooms, but the latter is apt to swoon and drop her petals prematurely. The muslin rose, 'Blanc Double de Coubert' is another virginal beauty whose delicate white petalled blooms were once in demand as coronets for young brides. Not so virginal is 'Cuisse de Nymphe Emue', the Maiden's Blush rose. And well might she blush with those old continental warriors 'General Schablikine' and 'General Jacqueminot' tucked up in the next bed twirling their military moustachios in her direction. 'Mme. Pierre Oger' is suffused in rosy blushes though the hot summer sun has also been known to have this effect on her delicate complexion. 'La Reine Victoria' is not at all amused, while the only ecclesiastic in the bunch, 'Cardinal Richilieu' trails his purple robes dis-approvingly in the background.

The buds of the old pink moss rose, (*R.* x *centifolia muscosa*) are worth a closer look. The outer petals of this rich pink rose project well beyond the inner ones which are neatly tucked down within, like chickens in a nest. The raspberry and white striped 'York and Lancaster' rose is another favourite and is one I like to include in a mixed bunch with other pinks and purples like 'Reine des Violettes' and striped and splashed dianthus, some as rich as boysenberries and cream, some as clear as the frosty white green-eyed 'Charles Musgrave'. White forget-me-nots make a dainty edging to this delightful posy.

Past the roses, under the old apple tree we have a piece of waste, shady ground which I have planted with violets, primroses, ferns and foxgloves. White herb Robert is starring the ground along with the white forget-me-nots that made such a beautiful display among the white Roman hyacinths when the apple tree was in bloom. Furry leaved *Meconopsis grandis* is also growing well in this situation. There is a mossy stone bench under the old apple tree where we may enjoy the scent of the variegated apple mint and the double Roman chamomile that pops up between the paving stones, its leaves and flowers as sweet as sugar drops. From here we may view the shaded border at the foot of the high back fence. The huge lily-like blooms on *Rhododendron nuttallii* are an especial joy, with a cool spicy sweetness emanating from their green throats. A tall gatecrasher of elegant proportions has appeared here, one I am not familiar with. Its attractively textured leaves and curiously swingboat-like blossoms turn out to be the Himalayan balsam, (*Impatiens balsamifera*). Now where did that come from? It is not known locally.

Nearby, grow some more Himalayans. Elephant-eared cardiocrinums are thriving, but there are no flowers yet. A week before Christmas I visited some of these tall lilies in bloom at Highden, a large old country garden nearby. The cardiocrinums have been naturalising here in woodland conditions for many years, the tallest stems being four to five metres high. Vita Sackville-West once said that to succeed with these elegant creatures it was necessary to bury a dead horse or its equivalent under each bulb. I wish she could have seen these giants, thriving on nothing but leafmould. The creamy, burgundy-striped flowers have a spicy scent exactly like that of winter-flowering *Michelia doltsopa,* another Himalayan.

Digitalis lutea still waves some waxen green wands; the hostas are now bearing their lily-like spires of pendulous bloom and the goats-beard, (*Aruncus sylvester*) is crowned with creamy plumes.

Lilium hansonii has reflexed yellow melon-rind flowers that are as much at home here as *Lilium martagon,* whose brightness lights up the shadows. Another small native plant known as blueberry (though it is not an edible fruit) is *Dianella nigra*, smothered at this season with sprays of porcelain-like berries of a particularly pretty shade of blue. The berries form the perfect complement to a nearby clump of *Anemone rivularis*; these snow-white windflowers of summer erupt like some floral firework from the top of foot-high stems, each blue-backed enamel-like bloom having anthers and stamens of bright navy blue. A native lacebark, (*Hoheria populnea*) spreads its delicate canopy above this scene. The lacebarks, which also come in variegated and purple leaved forms, make very attractive small garden trees, most of which bloom in autumn. There is also a summer flowering species *H. lyallii* which covers itself with lacy white blossoms in December and January. The lacebarks are so called because of the multitudinous layers of fine lacy fibre that form a network under the outer bark of the tree. This strong but delicate looking webbing was much used by the early Maoris for making baskets and for shawls for carrying babies. The English pioneer women used it to make ribbons; lacebark bonnets were once all the rage in nineteenth century Nelson.

We cross the lawn past a lilac and lemon display centred on the creamy floribunda roses 'Dimples' and 'Moonraker'. These are surrounded by dainty Swan River daisies, cornflowers, thalictrum and larkspurs in lavender-blue shades, the pale lemon *Potentilla* 'Moonlight', starry *Thalictrum dipterocarpum* and the ferny-leaved misty plumes of *Thalictrum aquilegifolium*. Purple and lemon alpine linaria creeps around at ground level while another favourite old rose, *R. spinosissima* 'Frülingsgold' is still bearing sprays of its single gold blooms on the fence behind. I have heard the unique scent of this rose compared to many things; to us it has an oily, tarry quality very similar to Lapsang Souchong tea.

Under my bedroom window grow more old roses in shades of pink that form the rosy heart of a sweet-scented pink and blue planting. The swathed silken blooms of 'Fantin Latour' rose have a luxurious quality as do the deeper-toned tucked and quartered blossoms of 'Queen of Denmark'. This full petalled, richly fragrant rose has such cunningly shaped buds with ferny sepals that I often pluck them for posies long before they open.

Chief treasure among the blue flowers is the herbaceous clematis, *C. heraclifolia*. This generous plant provides its hyaline bells for three months. The sweetly scented spikes of bloom are very reminiscent of blue hyacinths. Powder-blue hounds-tongues, *Cynoglossom nervosum*, violet cupped *Nierembergia violacea* and larkspurs act efficiently as filling-in plants while the miniature roses 'Pink Cherub' and 'Stars and Stripes' sit obediently in front of the border like neatly-mannered schoolgirls. 'Pink Cherub' is a fat pink darling and 'Stars and Stripes' has a neat raspberry striped dress topped with a fresh white pinafore. Harebells, white arabis, candytuft and low-growing campanulas froth around their feet.

On the house corner, among a misty, dustily-fragrant patch of old-fashioned mignonette (the Frenchman's 'little darling') is a thriving patch of *Osteospermum ecklonis*. This is the hybrid known as 'Starry Eyes' which has curiously twisted and spoon-shaped petals. This attractive daisy was the source of much amusement to a friend when her neighbour, who knew only the plain petalled form, quite

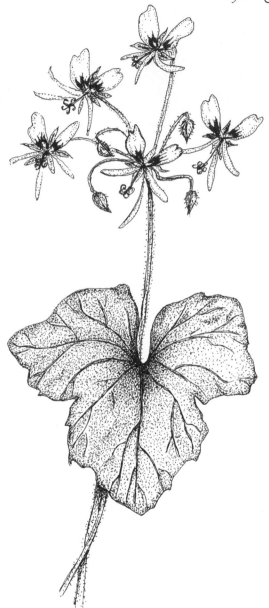

Pelargonium tomentosum. Their peppermint-scented leaves
are used in peppermint jelly

seriously asked how she achieved the quilled petal effect. Never one to miss the chance of a practical joke my friend explained that she wound tight rubber bands around each flower before it opened. Imagine her contrition next morning when she observed her neighbour laboriously winding elastic bands around each of her daisy buds!

I also grow *Centaurea nervosa,* one of the knapweeds. This flower, now resembling a purple blue cornflower or full-petalled thistle, has a very unusual bud and a most intriguing manner of opening. Initially the flowering stem is surmounted by a delicate filigree of golden filaments that are clustered to give a golden cage effect, within which the first blue flower petals resemble a captive bird.

There are so many more things I could show you in the garden today, but time will not allow. We must return indoors with our basket of flowers and arrange our main Christmas flower-piece of the gold and white lilies in the antique metal urn with clouds of gypsophila, small yellow and green kniphofias, feverfew and trails of star jasmine, *Trachelospermum jasminoides,* the tiny white windmills of which exhude a delicious tropical scent.

As I pile the velvet-dressed pomanders and ribboned lavender wands into festive bowls and baskets for Christmas gift giving, I reflect on this midsummer Christmas. Our Christmas garden bestows so many timely gifts of summer tastes and fragrances. They are distilled and captured in freshly made pot-pourris, sweet bags and sleep pillows; tiny pots of peppermint or rosemary jelly; sweet orange pomanders spiced with cloves; delicate lavender wands; damson cheeses; twig baskets of wild strawberries lined with cool green leaves accompanied by jars of fresh gooseberry and elder-flower-flavoured muscat syrup. And, of course, there are baskets of my own 'Bush Blend' pot-pourri, all green and gold with touches of black and redolent of lemon-scented leaves, fragrant gums and mossy bush.

Sunlight spills over the windowsills. The evocatively resinous pine stands in the corner, sunbeams dance around the gleaming baubles and catch in the tinselled robe of the old waxen angel on the top branch. It is going to be a lovely day; a day with the bead of summer in its eye; Christmas Day in New Zealand.

Drawings by the author

Oh My!

JOHN FRANCIS

at Cranborne Manor, Dorset

I know where there is a bungalow built of brick and in the front garden there is a flowering cherry. So what? I'll tell you what: the bricks are the red of meat about to go off, they have a purple bloom. When the cherry comes into foam, each flower being double or even triple, the colour is the same as the veining in a raspberry-ripple ice cream. It is a truly dreadful sight. Rounding a corner, thus coming on it unprepared, a sensitive cyclist might well topple to his doom under the wheels of an articulated lorry.

I conjured this dreadful vision in order to set your mind at rest. Nothing terrible like this will affright the eye of the visitor to the gardens of Cranborne Manor in Dorset.

The first thing that struck me about the grass as we approached the archway which gracefully connects the two gatehouses was that it was a-wave with weeds – or, shall we say, wildflowers? Letting things happen by chance is part of the art of gardening. Lichen on old walls is a favour, so is that lovely green film that forms on old tombstones.

The gatehouses are built of mellow old brick. They would not hold back or even inconvenience an army. But at the time the house was built the fortifications had become a formality only. The time was gone when anyone approaching was regarded narrowly through slits of windows and just as likely greeted with a cauldron of boiling oil. Cranborne Manor greets you trustingly, smilingly embowered in great trees and basking in its beautiful gardens which were laid out by Mounten Jennings and the illustrious John Tradescant in the seventeenth century.

In the courtyard a fountain spurts a wavering thread of water which genuflects when the wind blows and totters upright when there is a lull.

The house is not open to the public and it is difficult not to steal an illicit glance as you turn left to the knot garden. This was my first knot garden. Indeed the first time I even heard the term was when Sir Michael Tippett wrote his opera. I had no idea what to expect.

Leaving the knot garden for other visitors who understand the finer points we made for the mount – I should say, the Jacobean Mount.

About twelve years ago I had a bare dull rectangle of a garden – the American term 'yard' suited it better. What it lacked was mystery as well as shade. It had a path like a concrete runway and, a legacy from previous owners, more beetroot than you might think justified. I sowed lawns, planted shrubs in the wrong positions and the more I stared at what I had done the more I knew it was no good. So I announced that I would have a mountain. Perhaps some old memory had worked its way, like a tooth, to the surface. Anyway, in my folly having decreed a mountain, I got myself a pimple, a grassed-over bonfire. Deaf to reason I planted miniature trees on it which got lost when the grass grew. The mower refused it like a nervous horse and gnawed at its own electric lead in fury. The shears snipped but it never looked tidy and I forgot where the trees were and snipped them too. A disaster.

But lo, what had shimmered in my imagination was, at Cranborne, a felicitous reality. What had been ludicrous in a small suburban garden was an adornment in the right place. How important is proportion. Gardeners should keep repeating 'Proportion', at all times. My mountain was a silly mistake, like hanging a chandelier designed for a ballroom in a kitchen-diner. But confession is good for the soul and I'm happy to have got the mountain off my chest.

I imagine the Jacobeans built their mounts not just to give them that I'm-king-of-the-castle feeling, but with the more serious aim of providing the person who had just trotted through the garden a flying-low bird's view of the path of their tranced progress. In an age before the camera perhaps they felt the need of a fresh angle.

Do not imagine this Mount at Cranborne is a bald grassy knoll. I'm writing this a year after my visit and memory selects and distorts, but I retain the impression that the Mount was graced with broken circles of hedge. And were there clumps of pampas? Seems unlikely.

Leaving the Mount we wandered among some beds full of good things which had closed down for the season. No garden can be at its best in all areas at any one moment. Feeling keenly the loss of what we might have enjoyed if only we'd come earlier, we moved on until green leaves met over our heads and we were in what seemed like a small wood on a path that ran along side a silky stream. Again regret, how fine the daffodils must have been! But there was plenty to see:

a lilac-like shrub that was not lilac eluding identification, and much else besides.

But it was the artful way the stream had been deployed that intrigued me. At some time someone had, looking at the stream, felt that it went too fast, for its bed was naturally tilted. So they had arranged barriers at regular intervals over which the water now demurely slid, reminding us of Marvell,

> Here at the fountain's sliding foot,
> Or at some fruit tree's mossy root,
> Casting the body's vest aside,
> My soul into the boughs does glide.

When you reached the end of the stream and turned to look back the way you had come, there was a water staircase, a magical conceit. Each step, I should guess, no more than a few inches high.

Walking up a gentle slope we were struck all of a heap by the sight of amazingly tall roses, covered with flowers the colour of the top of gold-top milk, climbing into trees as high as houses. And not those great big crude things, but roses that had not forgotten their ancestry. Roses, in short, that you dream about and sometimes see in old pictures. I'm pretty sure that there is a label naming the variety, and who knows? perhaps you can buy one for yourself in the nursery by the car park.

And so to the walled garden. Now, it is important to have an idea of the scale. Walled gardens can come in any size, so perhaps it will help if I say that the walled garden in question could easily accommodate a small block of flats (sheltered accommodation for the elderly), but luckily it didn't: but it did contain a long central flower bed thickly planted with white single pinks. They were flowering and flourishing under the shelter of a line of severely pruned, so not tall, apple trees. What a sight they must be in blossom, but at the time of this visit they were scarcely less decorative full of green apples, bright green apples of the sort which would have made old Cézanne whinny with pleasure and reach for his brush. Something I had never thought of before: the leaves of the pinks were quite distinctly blue.

Let us now consider the walls. These are of grey stone, no doubt as old as the house; and at the risk of sounding precious, the adjective 'grey' does not do full justice to them, for the greyness was of a quality that contained within it the potential of becoming yellow. It was as if the walls had the ability to act as containers for old sunshine.

Lady Salisbury, whose garden this is (and she has Hatfield House to think about, too) must be like a wise editor. She knows when to give nature a nudge and when to let her have her head. For example, here and there a glossy fern had lodged. The keen do-it-yourselfers would have been worried at once about the pointing and plucked out the fern in a trice. That same tolerant eye that had wisely seen that the weeds waving by the gatehouses were better left, has spared the fern and not spoiled the walls.

Between the lawn and the walls there are deep borders with white Canterbury bells, white delphiniums and white lupins. White flowering shrubs and white roses too. But you cannot be watching every bird and bee. Sometimes lawless nature had mutinied, and a blue delphinium had been suffered to flourish.

From the walled garden the house looked taller than ever. Immense. You felt you were approaching a cliff; it loomed, but being lacy with mullioned windows and fragile-seeming, it did not threaten. As you climbed the steps, roses, roses all the way, some of them a lovely apricot. The kindly scrutiny of the house tempted one to peer in but, nun-like, we kept custody of our eyes. To have been glimpsed looking in would have been to be caught out. It was a relief to veer away from the house: besides, we were only half-way round.

Of course we were not the only visitors that day. There is no prescribed route. Our paths criss-crossed so we kept encountering the same people over and over. Mostly they spoke quietly, as if in a church. Several of the women seemed to be related to the late Joyce Grenfell: 'Daphne, come over here and adore these dear little black pansies.'

Then there was a scholarly-looking gent who might have been Alistair Sim's brother. He was like Mr Mole in that he kept saying 'Oh my! Oh my!' An alabaster rose: 'Oh my!' Evidently the water staircase had pleased him to a dangerous pitch. His heavy tweed trousers were extra heavy, the skirts of his raincoat streaked with gravel and waterweed, his shoes made sucking noises with every step and the tip of his nose was yellow with pollen. As he bent down to read a label ('Oh my!') his dear old knees made sharp cracks of protest, but I've never seen a happier man. No wonder.

Who's Who

RONALD BLYTHE is a critic, poet and author of short stories, *Akenfield*, *The View in Winter* and *Divine Landscapes*.

KERRY CARMAN lives in New Zealand where she worked as a teacher. She has written *The Creative Gardener* and *Portrait of a Garden*.

BETH CHATTO is a nurserywoman and gardener whose books include *The Dry Garden*, *The Damp Garden* and *Beth Chatto's Garden Notebook*.

DAME SYLVIA CROWE has worked both as a landscape architect and town planner. Her books include *Tomorrow's Landscape*, *Garden Design*, *The Landscape of Power* and *The Landscape of Roads*.

ROBERT DASH is a painter whose studios and garden lie at the far end of Long Island, New York.

JOHN FRANCIS is an essayist whose work features regularly in HORTUS. He has written about gardens in Giuseppe di Lampedusa's *The Leopard* and the novels of Elizabeth Bowen, Alice Thomas Ellis, Barbara Pym and Molly Keane.

NANCY-MARY GOODALL is a garden writer, photographer and lecturer. Her pieces for HORTUS have been about arbours in literature, gardens in children's books, Milton's *Paradise Lost* and Painshill Park.

STEPHEN G. HAW has been both a student and a teacher in a Chinese university. His first book, *The Lilies of China*, was published in 1986.

ARTHUR HELLYER MBE is the author of many books and is the gardening correspondent of the *Financial Times*. He holds the Royal Horticultural Society's Victoria Medal of Honour.

PENELOPE HOBHOUSE is the National Trust tenant of Tintinhull House in Somerset. She travels widely to lecture on many aspects of gardening and at home works as an author, editor and gardener.

ANTHONY HUXLEY is a member of the Council of the Royal Horticultural Society and holder of its Victoria Medal of Honour. He has written many books dealing with both the scientific and the practical issues of gardening.

WILL INGWERSEN was a nurseryman who specialised in alpine plants. He wrote several books and contributed articles to a variety of journals. He died in June 1990 at the age of 86.

STEPHEN LACEY is the author of *The Startling Jungle*. He has lectured on plants, and is currently completing a manuscript concerned with fragrance in the garden.

ALVILDE LEES-MILNE is the co-editor of *The Englishwoman's Garden*, *The Englishman's Garden* and *The New Englishwoman's Garden*.

AUDREY LE LIÈVRE is the author of *Miss Willmott of Warley Place*. She is a garden historian with a wide interest in plants. She has written important articles for HORTUS on the life of Max Leichtlin and about violas and tulips.

HAZEL LE ROUGETEL is the author of *A Heritage of Roses* and *The Chelsea Gardener*, a life of Philip Miller, 1691–1771.

HERMIA OLIVER is the author of *Flaubert and an English Governess*. For HORTUS she has written about the haunted gardens of M. R. James, and the gardens in novels by Jane Austen and Colette.

MIRABEL OSLER has written a book also called *A Gentle Plea for Chaos*, and she was the Essayist in the Garden for HORTUS in 1990, a year in which she spent time in France for her book about French gardens.

ALLEN PATERSON is a former Curator of the Chelsea Physic Garden and currently Director of the Royal Botanic Gardens, Hamilton, Ontario. His book, *Herbs in the Garden*, was published in 1985.

KAY N. SANECKI writes and lectures on a wide variety of garden and garden-related topics.

DAVID SAYERS runs his own travel tours specialising in botanical interests throughout the world. He has written for HORTUS about several countries and their flora.

PAMELA SCHWERDT began working for Vita Sackville-West and Harold Nicolson at Sissinghurst Castle in 1959. In 1990 she retired, with Sybille Kreutzberger, as joint head gardener.

ROSEMARY VEREY is a garden lecturer, author of many books and co-editor of *The Englishwoman's Garden*, *The Englishman's Garden* and *The New Englishwoman's Garden*. She contributed to HORTUS a series of four major articles about the making of her Gloucestershire garden, Barnsley House.

DENIS WOOD has worked in gardens including Royal Lodge at Windsor, the Kennedy Memorial at Runnymede, and the Festival Gardens in London's Battersea Park. He is the author of several books.

Index

Page numbers in *italic* refer to the illustrations

HORTUS Subscription Information

HORTUS is available by post and can be sent to an address
anywhere in the world.

Full subscription details available from

HORTUS
The Neuadd
Rhayader
Powys LD6 5HH, Wales

Telephone: Rhayader (0597) 810227; Facsimile: Rhayader (0597) 811386